Uncovering the Drivers
of Utility Performance

DIRECTIONS IN DEVELOPMENT
Infrastructure

Uncovering the Drivers of Utility Performance

Lessons from Latin America and the Caribbean on the Role of the Private Sector, Regulation, and Governance in the Power, Water, and Telecommunication Sectors

Luis A. Andrés
Jordan Schwartz
J. Luis Guasch

THE WORLD BANK
Washington, D.C.

ISBN (paper): 978-0-8213-9660-5
ISBN (electronic): 978-0-8213-9700-8
DOI: 10.1596/978-0-8213-9660-5

Cover drawing: Emily Cash Wilmoth; *Cover design*: Naylor Design

Library of Congress Cataloging-in-Publication Data

Andrés, Luis Alberto.
Uncovering the drivers of utility performance : lessons from Latin America and the Caribbean on the role of the private sector, regulation, and governance in the power, water, and telecommunication sectors. / Luis A. Andrés, Jordan Schwartz, J. Luis Guasch.
    p. cm.
  Includes bibliographical references.
ISBN 978-0-8213-9660-5 — ISBN 978-0-8213-9700-8
  1. Public utilities—Latin America. 2. Public utilities—Government policy—Latin America. 3. Privatization—Latin America. 4. Infrastructure (Economics)—Latin America. 5. Public utilities—Caribbean Area. 6. Public utilities—Government policy—Caribbean Area. 7. Privatization—Caribbean Area. 8. Infrastructure (Economics)—Caribbean Area. I. Schwartz, Jordan. II. Guasch, J. Luis. III. Title.
    HD2768.L294A53 2013
    363.6098—dc23   2012030889

Contents

Box

Figures

Tables

Acknowledgments

Uncovering the Drivers of Utility Performance: Lessons from Latin America and the Caribbean on the Role of the Private Sector, Regulation, and Governance in the Power, Water, and Telecommunication Sectors is the product of a team effort by the Economics Unit of the Sustainable Development Department in the Latin America and the Caribbean Region of the World Bank, co-led by Luis A. Andrés, Jordan Schwartz, and J. Luis Guasch. The team gratefully acknowledges the support of Diana Cubas, Barbara Cunha, Jose Guillermo Diaz, Georgeta Dragoiu, Raquel Fernandez, Julio Gonzalez, Alejandro Guerrero, and Maria Claudia Pachon. They also thank Sebastian Lopez Azumendi, who coauthored the background papers to chapters 4 and 5.

The team received valuable feedback through a rich consultation and peer review process. It received ongoing support and technical inputs from the regional chief economist, Augusto de la Torre, and his team, including Tito Cordella, Pablo Fajnzylber, and William Maloney. The team also gratefully acknowledges early inputs from the Sustainable Development Department team of Latin America and the Caribbean (LCSSD), which contributed ideas and suggestions at several meetings and workshops, through comments on earlier versions of the chapters, and at a seminar on the main findings and messages of the report. The team appreciated early inputs from Daniel Benitez, Philippe Benoit, Susan Bogach, Juan Miguel Cayo, Makhtar Diop, Joshua Gallo, Manuel Mariño, Martin Rossi, Tomas Serebrisky, Tova Solo, Maria Angelica Sotomayor, and Carlos Velez. Insightful and constructive comments were also received from peer reviewers, Marianne Fay, Antonio Estache, Maximo Torero, and Maria Vagliasindi.

For their generous financial support, the team is grateful to the Latin America and the Caribbean Chief Economist Office for the overall preparation of this report, to the Energy Sector Management Assistance Program (ESMAP) for funding the collection of the performance data in the electricity distribution sector, to the Public-Private Infrastructure Advisory Facility (PPIAF) for its support of the background material for chapter 3, and to the U.K. Department for International Development (DFID) for its support of the background material on corporate governance of state-owned enterprises.

⊡PPIAF
PUBLIC-PRIVATE INFRASTRUCTURE ADVISORY FACILITY

About the Authors

Luis A. Andrés is Lead Economist in the Sustainable Development Department for the South Asia Region of the World Bank. His work involves both analytical and advisory services and economic inputs, with a focus on infrastructure (mainly in the water and energy sectors), impact evaluations, private sector participation, regulation, and empirical microeconomics. Before joining the World Bank, he was the Chief of Staff for the Secretary of Fiscal and Social Equity and held other top positions in the Chief of the Cabinet of Ministries and the Ministry of Economy for the Government of Argentina. He holds a Ph.D. in Economics from the University of Chicago and has authored more than 30 publications on development policy issues.

Jordan Schwartz is the World Bank's Manager for Infrastructure Policy. He has worked in the field of infrastructure and economic development for over 20 years, focusing on investment design and strategies, PPPs, logistics, regulation, and regional integration. At the World Bank, Jordan has led analytical work and operations covering every sector of infrastructure. Before joining the World Bank in 1998, Jordan worked in management consulting, first in Booz Allen Hamilton's Transport Strategy Consulting Group, and later, as the Senior Manager for Utility and Infrastructure Consulting at Deloitte Emerging Markets.

J. Luis Guasch is the former Senior Regional Advisor in the Latin America and Caribbean Region in the World Bank, responsible for regulation, competitiveness, infrastructure and public-private partnerships (PPPs), innovation and technology issues, and investment climate. He was the Head of the World Bank Global Expert Team on PPP. He has also been a Professor of Economics at the University of California, San Diego, since 1980. He has assisted and advised governments in more than 50 countries on a variety of issues, among them competitiveness and infrastructure and PPPs. He holds a Ph.D. in Economics from Stanford University and an Industrial Engineering degree from the Polytechnic University of Barcelona. He has written extensively in leading economic and finance journals, and has written several books.

Abbreviations

GDP	gross domestic product
GWh	gigawatt hours
IRA	independent regulatory agency
IRGI	Infrastructure Regulatory Governance Index
ITU	International Telecommunication Union
kWh	kilowatt hours
LAC	Latin America and the Caribbean Region
MDG	Millennium Development Goals
MWh	megawatt hours
OECD	Organisation for Economic Co-operation and Development
PCA	principal component approach
PPP	Public-Private Partnership
SOE	state-owned enterprise
Twh	terawatt hours
UNICEF	United Nations Children's Fund
WHO	World Health Organization

All dollar amounts are U.S. dollars unless otherwise indicated.

Overview

For the past three decades, infrastructure economics has been preoccupied with answering the question "How?" When it appeared as if public ownership of utilities was the sole cause of massive utility debt and poor service throughout the developing world, economists were rolled out to figure out how to privatize state-owned enterprises (SOEs). When the capture of utility operators became a concern, the question evolved into "How should public services be regulated?" And when, in recent years, the public's patience with private operators began to wear thin, the questions became "How do we rebalance risks? How do we best design public-private partnerships (PPPs)? How do we take account of the rise in populism, the volatility in financial markets, and the flight of capital to safety?"

The primary purpose of this study is to step back from the question of "how" and to answer the underlying question of "why." Why do some utilities perform well and others perform poorly?

This book provides insight into infrastructure sector performance by focusing on the links between key indicators for private and public utilities and changes in ownership, regulatory agency governance, and corporate governance, among other dimensions. By linking inputs and outputs over a 15-year period of reform, the analysis uncovers key determinants that have affected sector performance in infrastructure sectors in the region. The book explains why the effects of such variables result in significant changes in the performance of infrastructure service provision.

Lack of adequate infrastructure is hampering the region's ability to grow, compete, and reduce poverty (Fay and Morrison 2006). This book proposes a framework of analysis that addresses key elements in the design of mechanisms that can reduce the region's infrastructure gap.

The book focuses on the distribution segment of three types of basic infrastructure services: electricity, water and sanitation, and fixed telecommunications. It uses original data on the performance of utility companies, including data on private providers and survey data from regulatory agencies and SOEs throughout the region.[1] The databases are rich not only in the number and types of utilities surveyed but also in the diversity and comprehensiveness of the indicators collected (for electricity and water alone, more than 20 indicators for each sector were collected). The analysis shows how performance indicators—on output, coverage, labor productivity, inputs, operating performance, service quality, and prices—have shaped the three sectors over the past decade.

Until now, data constraints have forced researchers to use small samples of companies, small samples of countries, and limited indicators. By collecting information from more than 250 electricity distribution companies and more than 1,700 water and sanitation companies, this study analyzes sector performance more comprehensively. It focuses on the relationship between sector performance and ownership structure, regulatory agencies, and corporate governance. It tackles sensitive relationships and issues—such as the role of the private sector—without the bias of case studies or the margins of error of partial datasets. It also provides enough observations to consider the effects of related elements, such as contract design and market structure.

The methodology identifies the determinants of sector performance. It facilitates the analysis of trends over time as well as a comparison of features common to all three sectors. This book does not describe all possible factors and conditions that may affect performance. It does not, for example, focus on the external environment or analyze factors that cannot be standardized. It does do the following:

- analyzes sector performance against a broad set of indicators that describe the current situation as well its evolution over the past 15 years
- proposes an analytical framework for issues that have not been well developed in the literature on infrastructure economics, such as regulatory governance and corporate governance for SOEs
- benchmarks the institutional designs of regulatory agencies in the water and electricity sectors
- analyzes the relationship between sector performance and regulation, private sector participation, and corporate governance.

The book's main messages can be summarized as follows:

1. Even in regions such as Latin America and the Caribbean (LAC), where reform has led to sector performance improvements in electricity distribution, water and sanitation, and fixed telecommunications, there is still much room for improvement.
2. Both the government (as regulator and service provider) and the private sector (as service provider) can play active roles in enhancing sector performance. The analysis reveals three important corollaries to this finding:
   - When carefully designed and implemented, private sector participation in service provision has a positive effect on sector performance.

- When independent regulatory agencies (IRAs) are transparent, accountable, and free of political interference, they contribute positively to sector performance.
- A strong accountability mechanism that prevents discriminatory management is fundamental for improving SOE performance.

3. One size does not fit all. Improving performance requires a comprehensive approach that integrates a variety of mechanisms to address different aspects of sector performance.

Message 1: Even in regions such as LAC, where reform has led to sector performance improvements in electricity distribution, water and sanitation, and fixed telecommunications, there is still much room for improvement

Between 1990 and 2005, the LAC region witnessed significant improvements in coverage, service quality, and labor productivity in all three sectors. Coverage increased to 95 percent for electricity distribution, 97 percent for the water utilities within the sample,[2] and 62 percent for fixed telecommunications. For households with access to these services, regional coverage reached about 92 percent in electricity, 80 percent in water, and 62 percent in fixed telecommunications.

A similar pattern of improvement is evident for labor productivity. For electricity distribution, labor productivity doubled between 1995 and 2006. For water, labor productivity almost doubled, rising from 252 to 425 connections per employee. In the telecommunications sector, labor productivity increased by a factor of seven between 1995 and 2007.

Quality of service also improved. For electricity distribution, the frequency of interruptions fell 42 percent and the duration of interruptions fell 40 percent. The water sector experienced an 8 percent increase in the continuity of service during this period. The telecommunications sector saw a gradual but significant increase in the percentage of digital main lines and the number of telephone faults cleared by the next working day. The share of main lines that are digital increased from 63 percent in 1995 to 100 percent in 2007. The number of telephone faults per 100 main fixed lines a year dropped from 23 in 1995 to 8 by the end of 2007. Such improvements in quality have been accompanied by a reduction in the waiting list for main fixed lines, which averaged zero by 2007.

The region hosts a wide range of strong and weak performers. In water and sanitation, the top 10 percent of utilities average 100 percent water and sanitation coverage. In contrast, the bottom 10 percent of water utilities average 66 percent coverage, and the worst sewerage utilities average just 15 percent coverage. In electricity distribution, utilities in the top 10 percentile were 10 times more productive than and sold 6 times as much energy (per connection) as utilities in the bottom 10 percent in 2005.

On average, private utilities outperform public utilities—although there are good public and private utilities and underperforming private and public utilities. For several indicators, the top 10 percent of public utilities performed better than the average private utilities; for other indicators, the bottom 10 percent of private utilities performed worse than the average public utility. The benchmarking exercise and data allow utilities to target improvements toward areas in which they lag most. Even top performers can improve their performance by analyzing selected indicators.

LAC is performing well relative to other developing regions. In 2007, the weighted average for phone penetration (mobile and fixed-line telephone subscribers) was 85 percent in LAC, 71 percent for the world as a whole, 64 percent for middle-income countries, and 67 percent in East Asia and Pacific (authors' calculations using data from the International Telecommunication Union dataset). In 2004, household water coverage was 80 percent in LAC, 70 percent in East Asia and Pacific, 54 percent for the world as a whole, 26 percent in Africa, and 20 percent in South Asia (authors' calculations using data from JMP).

These achievements notwithstanding, millions of people in LAC still lack access to basic services. Although electricity coverage increased from 85 in 1996 to 95 percent in 2005 in the sample studied, many people, almost all of them poor and in rural areas, still lack electricity.[3] Twenty-nine million households do not have a water connection. These figures indicate the importance of expanding electrification and water and sanitation services in rural areas in LAC, which lag urban areas.

Differences in the performance of utilities raise a number of questions about its determinants. Has private sector participation in service provision changed the dynamics of the sector? Does the type of regulation—and in particular the way it is governed—affect utility performance? Do corporate governance frameworks that provide SOEs and private providers with similar incentives improve performance? Previous research yields few answers to these important questions. The analysis presented in this book shows that differences in ownership, regulatory governance, and corporate governance of SOEs explain some of the dispersion in utilities' performance.

Message 2: Both the government (as regulator and service provider) and the private sector (as service provider) can play active roles in improving sector performance

- *When carefully designed and implemented, private sector participation in service provision improves sector performance.*

This book presents a comprehensive and systemic assessment of the impact of private sector participation in LAC. It considers what happened before, during, and after the change in ownership in the electricity, water and sanitation, and telecommunications sectors because often the most dramatic effects of private sector participation are found in the transition period, when the enterprise is overhauled as part of the transaction process.

Private sector participation has had a significantly positive effect on labor productivity, efficiency, and the quality of the service. In telecommunications, it has also increased output and coverage. After controlling for firm-specific time trends, there do not appear to be significant impacts on output and coverage. Although the picture is highly variable across sectors, prices tended to increase slightly. For electricity, labor productivity in private utilities is twice that of public utilities. Distribution losses declined 12 percent in private utilities over the period studied, while public utilities saw their performance deteriorate by 5 percent. Annual service interruptions fell from 24 to 12 compared for private utilities and from 24 to 19 for public utilities. The average duration of outages also fell by more at private utilities.

Examination of private sector participation contracts and process variables reveals how various design variables affect performance. Depending on a country's priorities, certain contract characteristics may be more important than others. One element of a contract, for example, could positively affect one variable while having a negative or insignificant impact on another.

- *When independent regulatory agencies (IRAs) are transparent, accountable, and free of political interference, they contribute positively to sector performance.*

The existence of a regulatory agency has significant impact on sector performance, raising labor productivity, residential tariffs, and the cost-recovery ratio and reducing operational expenses and distribution losses. Different elements of the regulatory governance design affect performance indicators differently. Changes to the formal component or regulatory governance increase labor productivity, reduce the frequency of interruptions, and raise residential tariffs. Increases in formal autonomy and flexibility with respect to tariff setting are associated with higher labor productivity and shorter service interruptions. IRAs that promote transparency, autonomy, independence, and accountability thus improve sector performance.

- *A strong accountability mechanism that prevents discriminatory management is fundamental for improving the performance of SOEs.*

Corporate governance arrangements in SOEs in water and electricity vary widely. Private enterprises tend to adopt standard corporate strategies. Standards at SOEs depend on countries' institutional systems and the characteristics of the service. Performance at SOEs is directly and indirectly related to overall governance within the country or province.

A best practice corporate governance design for SOEs with a corporatized framework includes an independent performance-driven board of directors, a professional staff, transparency and clear disclosure policies, and a clear mechanism for evaluating performance. A corporate structure that prevents political intervention, rewards performance, and is subject to public scrutiny serves as a benchmark for design comparison.

State enterprises face conflicting goals that affect the establishment of a business strategy. Several departments usually compete to have their agenda prioritized, often at the expense of service. Interference in the companies' business is often done informally, making it difficult for management to identify ways to improve efficiency. Because government subsidies can replace low revenues, efforts to increase efficiency are often muted. Poor accountability systems (at the regulatory or management levels) prevent development of an ownership structure that triggers efficient behavior by senior management.

In utilities with high levels of corruption and inefficiency, accountability systems should be created that prevent discretional management (from both management and political authorities) and create incentives for good performance. Regulation and performance-based management can be considered complementary ways of achieving these goals. A system of checks and balances, such as parliamentary oversight and state auditing, should be built into the governance design.

Good corporate governance is associated with high levels of performance. Performance orientation and professional management seem to be the most important contributors to performance, although all of the factors cited above are associated with some performance indicators.

Message 3: Improving sector performance requires a holistic approach that is tailored to specific circumstances

The analysis in this book is based on a number of key dimensions; however, there are certainly other elements that can influence and explain sector performance. While the purpose of this book is to focus on particular utility level variables as determinants of sector performance, the book briefly summarizes a number of additional factors and the interaction of some of these factors, as they may impact sector performance. Researchers have modeled and empirically tested the influence of such issues as corruption, market structure, economies of scope and density, renegotiation, and reputation. Other factors—such as subsidy mechanisms, lack of cost recovery, the political economy of different sectors, and social accountability—also affect sector performance. Although these issues are widely discussed, few econometric studies have been conducted; most analyses rely on comprehensive analytical case studies.

By proposing a new framework of analysis and building a comprehensive data set, this book builds a foundation for innovative research that can explain links and variables for which theoretical models and case-based evidence but little empirical analysis exists. By identifying differences in performance among utilities, decision makers and utility managers can find ways to improve service provision.

The heterogeneity across utilities warrants a holistic approach to solving shortcomings in performance. Improving sector performance demands that key determinants—such as ownership structure, regulatory governance and corporate governance—be addressed strategically, not in isolation.

Moving Forward

Improving sector performance goes beyond conducting a comprehensive assessment of a key determinant and proposing specific designs; it entails an approach that integrates policies that address a wide range of issues, some of which are discussed in detail in this book. The region can afford universal coverage of water, sanitation, and electricity if appropriate technologies and standards are used. Scarce resources imply that investments need to focus on bottlenecks in existing systems rather than overall expansion (Fay and Morrison 2006). Understanding differences in service providers and the environments in which they operate can help policy makers design comprehensive solutions to complex problems in infrastructure service provision.

Policy makers considering sector reforms should first prioritize their performance objectives, in order to determine which solutions seem most appropriate. For instance, if a utility prioritizes quality and efficiency over retention of employees, private sector participation is likely to be an attractive option. If reducing distributional losses by an SOE is a key objective, governance changes in favor of corporate performance-oriented rules could be considered.

The results presented in this book highlight pitfalls in sector reform programs. Poor design and faulty implementation explain many of the shortcomings of reform. Identifying the potential for problems in advance can help policy makers design countermeasures. This book can help policy makers make informed decisions and craft well-designed change strategies for achieving technical and political objectives.

Policy makers need to heed lessons from the past. Concession laws and contracts should focus on securing long-term sector efficiency, assigning and mitigating risk, and discouraging opportunistic bidding and renegotiation. They should be embedded in regulations that foster transparency and predictability, support incentives for efficient behavior, impede opportunistic renegotiation, and force contract compliance; address social concerns and focus on poverty; and promote accountability.

Governments remain at the heart of infrastructure service delivery; even in the presence of private sector participation, public involvement is necessary. SOEs that have a corporate governance structure that reduces political interference, rewards performance, and opens decisions to public scrutiny perform better than SOEs whose structure allows politics to influence decision making. Governments need to regulate infrastructure provision, contribute a substantial share of the investment, leverage their resources to attract complementary financing, set distributional objectives, and ensure that resources and policies increase access for the poor.

To make reforms sustainable, policy makers need to address not only the technical and financial aspects but also the social aspects most responsible for backlash. To do so, they need to support people in need who are adversely affected by reform (through lay-offs and higher tariffs) and improve communication. It is essential to publicize initiatives, promote program improvements, explain the (unsustainable) impact of maintaining the status quo, and make the case for cost-benefit tradeoffs represented by reforms. The communication strategy must not only justify programs but also periodically inform on progress, changes, or problems. Reforms must not only be successful, their success must be communicated, in order to safeguard against corruption and build and maintain popular support.

Notes

1. The exceptions are the databases for telecommunications and contract design (Guasch 2004).
2. The database includes 59 percent of the water connections in LAC.
3. These regional estimates correspond to the weighted average across the 250 utilities in the sample, which represent 89 percent of the total number of electricity connections.

References

Fay, M., and M. Morrison. 2006. *Infrastructure in Latin America and the Caribbean: Recent Developments and Key Challenges.* Washington, DC: World Bank.

Guasch, J. L. 2004. *Granting and Renegotiating Infrastructure Concessions. Doing it Right.* Washington, DC: World Bank.

CHAPTER 1

Introduction

This book conducts a micro-level analysis of various determinants of infrastructure sector performance that affect development. Analyzing infrastructure sector performance is about measuring, understanding, and improving conditions at the micro level in order to understand how utilities, and regulatory agents, contribute to the broader development agenda. Ultimately, sector performance is about the delivery of efficient, affordable, and sustainable infrastructure services. By correlating inputs and outcomes over the past 15 years, this book aims to understand the various determinants of sector performance in infrastructure sectors in Latin America and the Caribbean (LAC). It is about understanding how, and to what extent, several potential factors (including private sector participation, regulation, corporate governance) have resulted in significant changes in the performance of infrastructure services.

A large body of empirical literature shows that infrastructure development promotes economic growth and poverty reduction. By facilitating access to basic services for the poor, infrastructure fosters development along all levels of the results chain. Different players are involved at each level of sector performance: consumers, communities, service providers, regulators, investors, governments, and nongovernmental organizations. A holistic understanding of infrastructure sector performance creates and strengthens a positive dynamic among key stakeholders.

During the 1990s, most LAC countries implemented substantial reforms in the infrastructure sector to increase private sector participation and economic regulation and, when possible, promote competition as the main instruments for improving the quality, accessibility, and efficiency of services. Although some reforms successfully achieved these objectives, overall the reforms encountered difficulties, and most countries in the region now face new challenges. By the late 1990s and early 2000s, the region faced a series of financial and economic crises, corporate scandals, and market failures, within LAC and around the world. These challenges led to a significant decline in the rate of private investment, an increase in political opposition, and some dissatisfaction with privatization and liberalization policies.

LAC's infrastructure history, including the sectors in which LAC has performed relatively well, leaves no room for complacency: 112 million people in the region lack access to household water connections, and 47 million have no access to electricity (World Bank 2010). Although time trends point to improved coverage and performance in LAC, they also shed light on the gap in infrastructure services for many people. LAC increased coverage of piped potable water in premises from 73 percent of the population in 1990 to 86 percent in 2010 (WHO–UNICEF 2008). However, there are significant differences across countries. Similarly, although electricity coverage in the region as a whole increased from 82 percent in 1990 to 92 percent by 2007, many households, most of them rural, have been left behind. An integral component of the findings presented in this book is the data collected for each chapter. The conclusions of the research are based entirely on these data. The wealth of information produced also lends itself to further analysis. The data are available upon request for repurposing, allowing readers to pose ad hoc queries and regression analyses. The benchmarking efforts provide a regional and utility-level frame of reference for strong and weak sector performance in LAC.

Understanding the various interventions and conditions that explain sector performance is indispensable to reducing the region's infrastructure gap. To do so, the analysis draws on six sources of data (all except the ITU/ICT database are World Bank databases):

- The LAC Electricity Distribution Database contains detailed annual information on 250 public and private utilities in 26 countries that cover 89 percent of the connections in the region.[1] It contains data on more than 20 variables, on output, input, operating performance, quality and customer services, and prices. Data as early as 1990 are available, but the focus is 1995–2005.

- The LAC Water and Sanitation Database contains detailed annual information on more than 1,700 public and private utilities in 16 countries that cover 59 percent of the water connections in the region.[2] Like the Electricity Distribution Database, it contains data on more than 20 variables, on output, input, operating performance, quality and customer services, and prices. Data as early as 1990 are available, but the focus is 1995–2008.

- The ITU World Telecommunication/ICT Indicators Database contains annual time series for 1975–2007 for about 100 telecommunication statistics, covering telephone network size and dimension, mobile services, quality of service, traffic, staff, tariffs, revenue, and investment.[3]

- The Comprehensive Database on Impact of Private Sector Participation in LAC covers what happened before, during, and after private sector participation in three sectors—electricity distribution, water and sewerage, and telecommunications—by focusing on a range of performance variables (Andrés and others 2008).

- Additional data explore the governance of independent regulatory agencies (IRAs) in the water and electricity distribution sectors of LAC and the link between the governance of IRAs and the performance of both sectors (Andrés and others 2007).

- Data on corporate governance of state-owned enterprises (SOEs) were collected through surveys sent to utilities in the region in the electricity distribution and water sectors. These data cover 45 SOEs, including both public companies with full state ownership and companies in which the state owns at least 51 percent of all shares (only a few utilities fell into this category) (Andrés, Guasch, and Azumendi 2011). This book focuses on the distribution segment of three basic infrastructure services: electricity, water and sanitation, and fixed telecommunications. Some of the features are similar across sectors, allowing lessons to be drawn through comparison.[4]

This books aims to answer four main sets of questions:

- *What are the main performance trends in the region, and how heterogeneous are they?*

- *How does the performance of state-owned and private utilities differ?* What correlations can be made between performance and regulation and between performance and specific characteristics of market reforms (such as the introduction of wholesale markets and third-party access)? What impact did private sector participation have on performance? Does regulatory quality matter? Does competition (when possible) matter? What can be done to increase the efficiency of SOEs? What are the conditions for success? Are firms recovering costs?

- *How does the institutional design of regulatory agencies affect sector performance?* To what extent does regulatory quality matter? Does regulation have any effect on sector performance? Is the independent regulatory agency model still valid for the region? Are there better alternatives? Who are the leaders in the region? Are procedures aimed at improving the governance of regulatory agencies being implemented?

- *What management mechanisms create incentives for improved performance?* What have boards and managers of the most competitive and efficient utilities done to improve their governance? What have the governments that own utilities done? Why have they focused on corporate governance? What are the main legal difficulties and other obstacles they face in this work? How important is it to enjoy a good reputation and solid social support in carrying out governance reforms? Under what circumstances does social support make reform easier? How does operating in regions facing challenging social problems affect the chances of introducing reforms? What are the main lessons so far? Are there any differences across sectors?

Analytical Framework and Scope

This book begins by describing the main elements that characterize sector performance, defined as the delivery of reliable, affordable service that complies with certain quality standards. (Although any number of variables can be used to define performance, the set of indicators analyzed provides an overall assessment of the utilities; a different selection of indicators would not significantly change the key messages of this analysis.) It also analyzes some intermediate outcomes. For instance, distributional losses and labor productivity, as a proxy of efficiency, may be highly correlated with the quality of the service provided. Figure 1.1 depicts the framework of this analysis.

Access to reliable infrastructure in the region as a whole improved significantly since the 1990s. However, the results are far from homogeneous at the utility level. This book aims to understand the drivers of these differences. It analyzes the effects of changes in policies on changes in performance. It focuses on the relationship between sector performance and the following determinants: private sector participation, regulatory agencies, and corporate governance. It also examines related aspects, such as contract design, market structure, and, for telecommunications, market competition.

This book argues that these determinants significantly changed the landscape of the sectors studied. Other elements that are not examined may also affect sector performance (figure 1.2 depicts some of them). Even when exploring the specified determinants of sector performance, the book does not describe all possible links or spheres of influence between each variable and sector performance. Figure 1.2 displays different environments of impact.

This book first explains the dynamics of utility performance and the interactions between key internal variables and utility performance in each sector. Although it may refer to the components and impact of the external environment,

Figure 1.1 Analytical Framework for Analyzing Sector Performance

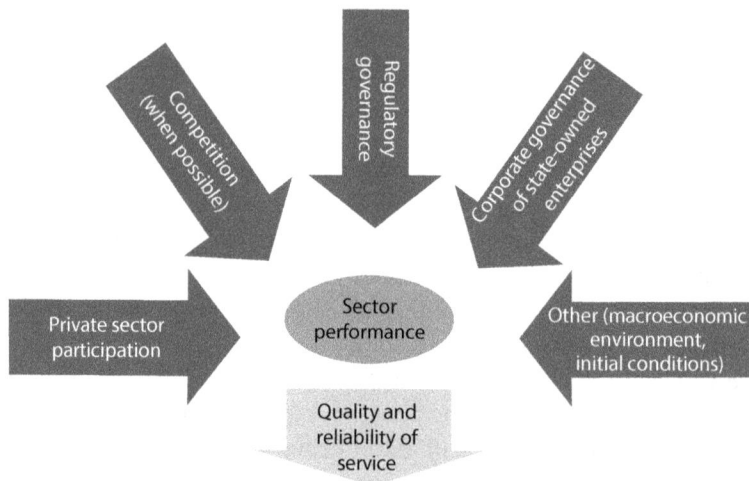

Figure 1.2 Internal, Sectoral, and External Conditions Affecting Utility Performance

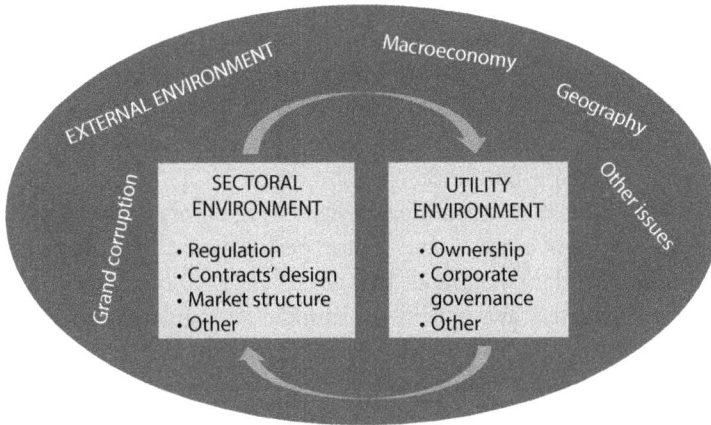

it does not explain these elements, as they relate to sector performance. The impact of factors such as sovereign risk ratings, corruption, or consumer propensity to pay bills is external to sector and utility control and thus external to this analysis. The main objective of this analysis is to provide a factual description of changes and policies that can be empirically tested and analyzed "internally" by people with decision-making authority over sector policy, regulation, governance, and investment.

This book does the following:

- depicts sector performance with a broad set of indicators that describe the current situation as well its evolution over the past 15 years
- provides analytical frameworks for themes less developed in the broader literature on utilities, such as regulatory governance and corporate governance for SOEs
- benchmarks the institutional designs of regulatory agencies in the LAC region for the water and electricity distribution sectors
- analyzes the relationship between sector performance and regulation, private sector participation, and corporate governance.

The book is organized as follows. Chapter 2 outlines changes in the electricity distribution, water and sanitation, and fixed telecommunications sectors in the LAC region over the past 15 years. These changes are captured through benchmarking assessments based on the results of performance indicators such as output, coverage, labor productivity, inputs, operating performance, service quality, and prices. This chapter tells multiple stories of the substantial improvement in these sectors and fills in knowledge gaps by benchmarking utility performance at the regional, country, and utility levels.

Chapter 3 synthesizes the impact private sector participation has had on electricity distribution, water and sewerage, and fixed-line telecommunications.

In an attempt to understand the true impacts and determinants of private sector participation, it examines what happened before, during, and after private sector participation in LAC in these sectors by focusing on a range of performance variables. It then examines scenarios with and without private sector participation. This chapter also identifies whether private sector participation characteristics such as the sale method (for example, auction); investor nationality; and award criterion affect performance.

Chapter 4 explores the institutional design of regulatory agencies and the link between regulatory governance and sector performance. The first part of the chapter evaluates and benchmarks the governance of regulatory agencies in the electricity sector. It draws heavily on an index of regulatory governance that ranks all agencies in LAC. The index is an aggregate of four key governance characteristics: autonomy, transparency, accountability, and regulatory tools, including not only formal aspects of regulation but also indicators related to actual implementation. The second part of the chapter builds on the benchmarking analysis. It examines whether there is a correlation between regulatory governance and sector performance.

Chapter 5 assesses the governance of SOEs in infrastructure, based on survey results from 45 SOEs in the water and electricity distribution sector of LAC. It proposes an analytical framework for analyzing corporate governance of these utilities and benchmarks their institutional internal design. The chapter also evaluates the contribution of these dimensions to sector performance.

Chapters 6 examines other potential determinants for sector performance, including corruption, cost recovery, contract arrangements, and competition. Chapter 7 summarizes the book's main results and describes the array of possibilities for moving forward.

Notes

1. These data are publicly available. The complete database can be accessed at http://info.worldbank.org/etools/lacelectricity/home.htm.
2. This database will be publicly available shortly.
3. These data are publicly available. The complete database can be accessed at http://www.itu.int/ITU-D/ict/publications/world/world.html.
4. Good data exist on the electricity distribution and telecommunications sectors. Better data are needed on water in order to compare this sector with the other two.

References

Andrés, L., J.L. Guasch, and S.L. Azumendi. 2011. "Governance in State-Owned Enterprises Revisited: The Cases of Water and Electricity in Latin America and the Caribbean." Policy Research Working Paper, World Bank, Washington, DC.

Andrés, L., J.L. Guasch, M. Diop, and S.L. Azumendi. 2007. "Assessing the Governance of Electricity Regulatory Agencies in the Latin American and the Caribbean Region: Benchmarking Analysis." Policy Research Working Paper 4380, World Bank, Washington, DC.

Andrés, L., J.L. Guasch, T. Haven, and V. Foster. 2008. *The Impact of Private Sector Participation in Infrastructure: Lights, Shadows, and the Road Ahead.* Washington, DC: World Bank.

WHO (World Health Organization)–UNICEF (United Nations Children's Fund). 2008. Joint Monitoring Programme (JMP) for Water Supply and Sanitation Database. http://www.wssinfo.org/data-estimates/table/.

World Bank. 2010. "Understanding Sector Performance: The Case of Utilities in Latin America and the Caribbean." Regional study under the Chief Economist Office for the LAC region.

CHAPTER 2

Benchmarking Utility Performance

This chapter outlines the changes that have occurred in the electricity distribution, water and sanitation, and fixed telecommunications sectors during the main period of utility reform (1995 to 2006) in Latin America and the Caribbean (LAC). The first part analyzes changes that have shaped the performance of these sectors. This analysis is derived from previous benchmarking initiatives for the electricity distribution sector (Andrés, Diop, and Guasch 2008) as well as databases for the water sector (World Bank 2012) and the telecommunications sector (ITU 2009). The chapter documents these changes and accounts for current performance of the sectors at the regional and utility levels.

The findings were captured through benchmarking assessments based on the following performance indicators: output, coverage, labor productivity, inputs, operating performance, service quality, and prices. Considering the changes that have shaped the sectors during the past decade, such benchmarking efforts provide a regional and utility-level frame of reference for strong and weak sector performance in LAC.

There is a sharp divide between rural and urban coverage within countries. For water, electricity, roads, and telecommunications, coverage rates in rural areas tend to be much lower than average. Although more than 90 percent of the urban population of most countries in the region has access to safe water, rural access in Brazil (58 percent) and Chile (59 percent) is lower than in several much poorer African countries, such as Burundi (78 percent) and Zimbabwe (74 percent) (Fay and Morrison 2006). Given that poverty rates are usually much higher in the countryside, lower rural access rates explain much, though by no means all, of the great disparity in coverage between rich and poor in the region. Although this chapter does not make a distinction between urban and rural electricity and water and sanitation, it acknowledges rural-urban differences and intends to provoke further work in order to bridge this gap.

Why Benchmark Infrastructure Sectors?

Benchmarking is a means of providing countries and utilities with a point of reference regarding their performance. Electricity lights homes and powers industries, but in many developing countries, service quality remains unreliable—even for people who can afford to pay high prices. Expanding service to people in the region who live without basic infrastructure and improving the quality and reliability of service delivery are urgent socioeconomic priorities. The lack of good infrastructure services also costs businesses dearly. Against this backdrop, the benchmarking initiatives outlined in this chapter provide regional and utility-level direction and a framework for identifying where LAC utilities stand in relation to others, detecting their strengths and weaknesses, and setting goals for improvement.

A number of empirical studies have used benchmarking methods within the electricity supply industry. These studies have traditionally focused on generation or vertically integrated utilities. Perhaps because of regulators' demand, interest in benchmarking the natural monopoly segments (transmission and distribution) has recently increased. Surveys of the benchmarking literature (Jamasb and others 2005) conclude that because of problems of data standardization and currency conversion, international benchmarking has not been widely used. When international efficiency comparisons have been used, they have traditionally focused on developed countries.

This chapter describes sectoral performance at the regional and utility levels. It does not assume an analytical or explanatory role. The intent is to contribute to a more consistent benchmarking analysis in the distribution segments and serve as a pathbreaker for other regional benchmarking initiatives.

The benchmarking exercise covers the following databases (see appendix C for details):

- The LAC Electricity Distribution Database contains detailed annual information on 250 public and private utilities in 26 countries that cover 89 percent of the connections in the region.[1] It contains data on more than 20 variables, on output, input, operating performance, quality and customer services, and prices. Data as early as 1990 are available, but the focus is 1995–2005.

- The LAC Water and Sanitation Database contains detailed annual information on more than 1,700 public and private utilities in 16 countries that cover 59 percent of the water connections in the region.[2] Like the Electricity Distribution Database, it contains data on more than 20 variables, on output, input, operating performance, quality and customer services, and prices. Data as early as 1990 are available, but the focus is 1995–2006.

- The ITU World Telecommunication/ICT Indicators Database contains annual time series for 1975–2007 for about 100 telecommunication statistics, covering telephone network size and dimension, mobile services, quality of service, traffic, staff, tariffs, revenue, and investment.[3]

Table 2.1 defines the variables used in the analysis.

The following sections describe the benchmarking analyses for the three sectors evaluated. For simplicity, we present in this chapter the summary of the results. The results for each of the indicators can be found in appendix C.

Table 2.1 Variable Definitions, by Sector

Variable	Electricity distribution	Water distribution	Fixed telecommunications
Output	• Total number of subscribers and residential subscribers, as of December of each year • Total energy sold annually (MWh) • Energy sold per connection (MWh)	• Total number of water subscribers and residential water subscribers • Total number of residential water subscribers and residential sewerage subscribers • Total water production per year (millions of cubic meters) • Total water sold per year (millions of cubic meters)	• Total number of active connections, as of December of each year • Total number of local minutes annually • Total minutes per active connection
Labor	• Number of employees	• Number of employees	• Number of employees
Labor productivity	• Number of subscribers per employee • Total energy sold annually per employee	• Number of water connections per employee • Water sold per employee	• Number of active connections per employee • Local minutes per employee
Efficiency	• Energy lost in distribution (because of technical losses and illegal connections)	• Percentage of total water produced that was not charged to the consumers	• Percentage of incomplete calls
Quality	• Average duration of interruptions per consumer (hours/year) • Average frequency of interruptions per consumer (number/year)	• Average number of hours with water service per day • Percentage of samples that passed a potability test	• Percentage of incomplete calls (faults) • Percentage of digital connections in the network
Coverage	• Number of residential subscribers per 100 households	• Number of residential water subscribers per 100 households • Number of residential sewerage subscribers per 100 households	• Number of active connections per 100 inhabitants
Prices	• Average tariff (including fixed and variable costs) for 1 MWh for residential service in December of each year (dollars) • Average tariff (including fixed and variable costs) for 1 MWh for industrial service in December of each year (dollars)	• Average price per cubic meter of supplied water (dollars) • Average price per cubic meter of collected waste (dollars)	• Average cost for a three-minute, nonpeak local call (dollars) • Average monthly cost for residential service (dollars)
Expenses	• Annual operational expenses per connection (dollars) • Annual operational expenses per MWh sold (dollars)	• Annual operational expenses per water connection (dollars) • Annual operational expenses per cubic meter sold (dollars)	

Electricity Distribution[4]

Since the late 1980s, a wave of reform has transformed the institutional framework, organization, and operational environment of infrastructure sectors, particularly the electricity sectors, in most developed and developing countries. Although the structure of the power sectors and the approaches to reform vary across countries, all reforms seek to improve the efficiency of the sector as well as to increase coverage and improve the quality of service. Separation of roles, unbundling, competition, and private participation were used as key instruments to improve efficiency, the government's fiscal position, and access to electricity

Uncovering the Drivers of Utility Performance • http://dx.doi.org/10.1596/978-0-8213-9660-5

service for the poor. In many countries in the region, the combination of private participation, competition, and better regulation was effective in improving productive efficiency and quality of service.

The last decade has witnessed significant progress in the power sector of LAC. Although there are differences across countries, overall supply increased substantially and with it access to electricity. In terms of coverage, the best electricity distribution performer in LAC is Uruguay, with 97 percent coverage, followed by Costa Rica, Brazil, Argentina, Chile, and Mexico, all of which have more than 95 percent coverage. Equally important is the improvement in coverage, as reflected in the growth rate of Peru, Paraguay, Honduras, and El Salvador, all of which increased coverage by an average of 20 percentage points between 1995 and 2005.

Electricity distribution is at the forefront of infrastructure improvement in LAC. By 2005, 95 percent of the region's residents had electricity, a 10 percentage point increase over 1995.[5] Between 1995 and 2005, most countries in the region made considerable progress in expanding access to electricity and improving the quality of their service. Private sector participation in electricity connections increased from 11 percent in 1995 to 60 percent 2005, and labor productivity doubled. Over the same period, the frequency of interruptions decreased 42 percent, and the duration of the interruptions per connection per year declined 40 percent. Meanwhile, operational expenditures increased by 41–44 percent between 1995 and 2005 and tariffs rose 70 percent for residential users and 91 percent for industrial users. There were no significant changes in distributional losses.

Although electricity coverage in LAC increased from 85 percent in 1995 to 95 percent in 2005, the rural poor were not the main beneficiaries. In many countries, industrial consumers and high-income residential consumers were the main beneficiaries of competition and the rebalancing of tariffs, which reduced substantial cross-subsidies of the prereform period (World Bank 2007). However, it is also true that private sector participation and cost-covering tariffs ensured the financial feasibility of efficient electricity providers, which were able to expand access and improve the quality of service to a large number of consumers in urban and peri-urban areas, including poor people.

Regional Benchmarking Assessment
Increased electricity coverage reflects high demand for access to the network by a growing number of residential, nonresidential, and rural users. As demand for electricity increased, so did private participation in electricity distribution throughout the region. Private participation grew substantially between 1990 and 2005, especially between 1995 and 1998. In 1990, there was little significant participation of the private sector in electricity distribution; by 1995, the private sector accounted for 11.1 percent of electricity connections in the region. By 2005, private utilities were providing 60 percent of electrical connections.

Between 1995 and 2005, $102.6 billion was invested in 384 private electricity projects in the region. With important exceptions—most notably Mexico—most

LAC countries introduced private participation in electricity distribution as part of broader reforms attempting to establish a more competitive market structure. Private participation remained stagnant between 1995 and 2005, with low levels of investments. It is worth considering this phenomenon when analyzing the regional performance of electricity distribution in the following sections.

Many people in LAC remain without electricity, almost all of them poor and in rural areas.[6] Large increases in electricity coverage in Argentina, for example, are related to the normalization of illegal connections in urban slums rather than the expansion of electricity service to rural areas. Private investors have been effective in connecting consumers in urban and rural areas near the power grid, but they are reluctant to extend access to rural areas, where electricity service is not financially viable. In Bolivia and Nicaragua, both of which privatized distribution, only 30 percent of the rural population has access to electricity. Further increases in coverage in rural areas usually require substantial investment subsidies and strong government support. The government of Chile, a leader in reform and privatization, provided investment subsidies of about $1,500 per household to increase electricity coverage in rural areas from 62 percent in 1995 to 92 percent in 2005.

Energy sold per connection per year exhibits an increasing trend until 2000 followed by a sudden drop in sales, which continued to decrease until the end of 2005. Between 1995 and 2005, the average energy sold per connection was 5.5 MWh. Although the number of connections rose 45 percent between 1995 and 2005, the total amount of energy sold per connection declined. The fluctuating values of the energy sold per connection may reflect the increase in residential and industrial tariffs and the associated decrease in demand as well as the expansion of service into less wealthy peri-urban communities.[7]

Regional distribution losses experienced sporadic increases and decreases throughout the 10-year period. The lowest distributional loss was observed in 2001, with a 0.9 percentage point decrease from a 14.5 percent distributional loss in 1995. Between 2001 and 2005, distributional losses rose 1 percentage point, reaching 14.7 percent in 2005.

The quality of electricity distribution improved between 1995 and 2005. The frequency of interruptions decreased by almost half, with a 42.4 percent drop in the frequency of the interruptions and a 40.2 percent decrease in the duration of the interruptions per connection per year. The number of interruptions per connection declined steadily over this period, falling from 20.5 times in 1995 to 11.8 times in 2005, a reduction of 5.4 percent a year or 42.4 percent in 10 years.

A second indicator used to measure quality of service is the average number of hours the customer did not have service. This figure fell 40 percent between 1995 and 2005. Brazil and Paraguay were the main contributors to the increase in service disruptions in 1996; the hurricanes that affected the quality of service in Mexico explain the peak in 2002. These two indicators capture two root causes of interruptions: the reduction in the number of outages per connection shows managerial improvement; the duration of the interruption serves as a proxy for natural events or disasters that affect service.

The decrease in the number of employees between 1995 and 2005 is inversely related to the rise in private participation. Between 1995 and 2000, when private sector participation reached its peak, the number of employees declined 23.2 percent. No significant changes in the regional level of the labor force occurred between 2000 and 2005, consistent with decreased private participation levels.

Among the measures used for estimating labor productivity is the number of residential connections per employee. This value doubled between 1995 and 2005, rising from 384 residential connections in 1995 to 701 in 2005. Growth in population (about 1.1 percent a year) accounts for about one-fifth of that gain in labor productivity. A second factor is the substantial increase in electricity coverage. A third factor is the reduction in the labor force in the sector. Energy sold per employee—another measure of labor productivity—increased gradually from 2.2 TWh sold per employee in 1995 to 4.1 TWh in 2005, an increase of 85.1 percent.

Average end-user tariffs for electricity supplied to residential connections increased, except in 1999, when tariffs fell 12 percent, mainly because of the crisis in Brazil. By the end of 2005, the average residential tariff was $104 per MWh, a 70 percent increase over the 1995 average residential tariff of $61 per MWh. Following the same pattern, the average industrial tariff increased 91 percent, rising from $44 in 1995 to $84 in 2005. Industrial tariffs rose steadily over this period, except in 1997–99, when there was a slight decrease in prices.[8] The financial analysis does not consider reductions in state transfers to the power sector, which may have accompanied private participation.

With respect to input indicators, the region witnessed fluctuating values of operational expenditures, with more prominent changes toward the end of the decade. Operational expenditures per connection increased 40.8 percent between 1995 and 2005. Despite irregular activity over this period, with unexpected changes in expenditures between 2000 and 2003, the regional average was $128, with an average annual increase of 3.5 percent. The results for total expenditures per connection express the overall direction of operational and capital expenditures for LAC in the past decade. Total expenditures (defined as total operation and capital expenditures) exhibit a steady increase, except for declines between 1998 and 1999 and between 2001 and 2003. By the end of 2005, total expenditures reached $174 per connection, up from $99 in 1995.

The results for operational expenditures per MWh energy sold show a similar tendency. Operational expenditures per unit of energy sold rose 44 percent, an annual growth rate of 3.7 percent, from a regional average of $26.60 per connection in 1995 to $33 per connection by 2005.

Utility-Level Benchmarking Assessment

Three main features characterize electricity distribution performance in LAC:

- significant differences in performance across utilities
- improvement by underperforming utilities

- significant deterioration in distribution performance by some utilities, as reflected by indicators such as average tariffs and distributional losses.

In order to assess the performance of electricity distributors at the utility level, the authors ranked the 250 utilities studied, placing them in three categories: the top 10 percent, the middle 80 percent, and the bottom 10 percent of distribution performance. Utilities in the top group have 100 percent electrification, an average of 897 residential connections (6,402 MWh of energy sold) per employee, 6.5 percent distributional losses, and residential prices in the range of $591 per MWh consumed.

Between 1995 and 2005, utilities not in the top 10 percent of performers doubled their electricity coverage and labor productivity, reduced the frequency of interruptions per connection by 73 percent and the duration of interruptions by 56 percent, and decreased total expenditures per connection by 26 percent.

Significant progress was made by the majority of the utilities in all categories throughout the past decade. But major differences are evident across utilities. In 2005, for example, utilities in the top 10 percent were 10 times more productive and sold 6 times the energy (per connection) of utilities in the bottom 10 percent. Utilities in the top decile had one fifth the distributional losses of utilities in the bottom 10 percent.

Coverage by utilities in the bottom 10 percent increased from 40 percent in 1995 to 61 percent in 2005—an increase of more than 50 percent. Similar improvements were observed in the frequency and duration of interruptions. Weak performers also improved their labor productivity, which tripled between 1995 and 2005.

Some utilities experienced significant deterioration in performance, with both tariffs and distributional losses increasing. For the middle 80 percent, the average residential tariff increased 256 percent, from $44.40 in 1995 to $114.40 in 2005. In contrast, the top 10 percent increased their residential tariffs 37 percent, from $127 per MWh sold in 1995 to $174 in 2005. With respect to distributional losses, whereas the middle 80 percent did not exhibit a significant change during the decade, the bottom 10 percent showed a 27 percent increase in distribution losses.

Summary

During the study period, the top decile of utilities in LAC achieved universal coverage, the middle 80 percent increased coverage by almost 15 percent, and the bottom 10 percent increased coverage by 26 percent.

Although there are some variations within and among countries, in general, several companies in Brazil display the best performance in terms of labor productivity, distributional losses, operational expenditures, and coverage. Costa Rica benchmarks good performance in coverage, operational expenditures, and tariffs. Several utilities in Chile produced leaders for indicators measuring labor productivity and technical efficiency.

Water and Sanitation

Of the 220 million people living in poverty in LAC, 112 million people lack access to a water connection. These figures attest to the challenge the region faces in meeting the Millennium Development Goals (MDGs) in a sustainable way. It also underscores the need for timely and efficient interventions in the sector.

Detailed information was collected on 16 countries and 1,700 water and sanitation utilities in the region (see appendix B for details). An analytical framework was designed to produce a comprehensive description of the sector as well as a mechanism for ranking countries and utilities. The data collected for this benchmarking project are representative of 59 percent of the water and sanitation connections in the region from 1995 to 2006.

Regional Benchmarking Assessment

The main finding of this chapter is one of overall improvement across the region between 1995 and 2006. Significant achievements include the following:

- a 4 percent increase in water coverage, which reached 97 percent within the coverage area of the utilities in the database[9]
- an almost doubling of labor productivity, from 252 connections per employee to 425
- slight increases in the average tariffs for both water and sanitation (27 percent for water and 35 percent for sewerage)
- an 8 percent increase in the continuity of service.

Water and sanitation coverage for the utilities benchmarked increased from 93 percent to 97 percent between 1999 and 2006. However, this coverage level represents about half of the households in the utilities' area. This 4 percentage point improvement is consistent with the overall improvement in coverage for all the water and sanitation operators in the region, which reached 81 percent in 2006. Sewerage coverage rose 12 percentage points, from 72 percent in 1999 to 84 percent in 2006.[10]

Utility-Level Benchmarking Assessment

Water and sanitation utilities were ranked based on their coverage, labor productivity, output, input, operating performance, service quality, and prices and divided into three groups: the top 10 percent, the middle 80 percent, and the bottom 10 percent. (For certain indicators, such as operation and capital expenditures, ranking in the top or bottom 10 percent is not necessarily a benchmark of good performance.)

Substantive differences are evident between the top and bottom performers. The top 10 percent of utilities have 100 percent water and sanitation coverage, an average of 581 cubic meters of water sold per connection a year, an average of 541 residential connections per employee, 15 percent losses in nonrevenue water, water residential prices of about $0.11 per cubic meters of water, and residential sewerage prices averaging $0.07 per cubic meter.

In contrast, the bottom 10 percent average 66 percent water coverage and 15 percent sewerage coverage. Between 2000 and 2006, the top 10 performers maintained an average of 100 percent coverage in water and sanitation. Whereas the middle 80 percent of performers improved coverage slightly, the bottom 10 percent of water and sanitation utilities increased coverage 23 percent.

This study assesses the efficiency of the water and sanitation sector based on the following indicators: labor productivity, nonrevenue water, collection ratio, and water connections that are micrometered. Significant heterogeneity is evident across utilities.

Compared with utilities in the lowest performance decile, utilities in the top decile are five times more productive, incur one-quarter of the nonrevenue water losses, collect 50 percent more revenue per total water billed, and have five times more micrometered households. In 2006, the best performers provided 24 hours of water service a day—about 1.5 hours more than the middle 80 percent. The bottom 10 percent of performers averaged just eight hours a day during 1997–2006.

Progress in the water and sanitation sector has been made—including by weak performers—but there is still much room for improvement. Challenges include high nonrevenue water levels, low collection ratios (averaging 50 percent for the sample as a whole), and insufficient tariffs.

Fixed Telecommunications

During the 1980s and the 1990s, the state owned the fixed telecommunications company, which operated as monopolies. After Chile privatized its telecommunications companies in the 1980s, most countries in the region followed suit. The new owners generally had to comply with requirements such as network expansion and quality standards. In exchange, they were granted a monopoly period, after which new firms could enter the market.

In most countries, liberalization of the long-distance market took place within a few years after privatization (Andrés, Diop, and Guasch 2008). Hence, it is possible that the perceived impacts of privatization were actually caused by liberalization. Although the indicators used refer to local telephone service, liberalization of the long-distance market could be an indicator that liberalization of the local market was to come.

By 2005, private companies operated almost 85 percent of the fixed lines in LAC. Only Colombia, Costa Rica, Paraguay, and Uruguay still had state-owned main telecommunication operators.

By 2007, LAC had invested an average of $12 billion in telecommunication services—a 40 percentage point increase over the $8 billion invested in 1995. Of the $12 billion invested in 2007, $2.3 billion was allocated to fixed telephone services. By 2007, the share of households with a fixed telephone line reached 62 percent, up from 31 percent in 1995.

Because mobile and fixed-line telephones are substitutes, penetration rates should consider both technologies. The total number of subscribers per 100 inhabitants for both fixed and mobile increased from 10 in 1995 to 83 in 2007. For fixed lines, the number of subscribers per 100 inhabitants doubled, rising from 10 to 20. The number of mobile line subscribers per 100 inhabitants surged, rising from 0.7 in 1995 to 64 in 2007—a 90-fold increase in 12 years.

By 2007, the region served 464 million (fixed and mobile line) telephone subscribers, 9.2 times the number in 1995. The number of main fixed lines in operation (73 percent of which were residential) increased 150 percent. The number of residential main lines increased steadily between 1995 and 2006. Perhaps because of increasing reliance on mobile services, it fell 2 percentage points between 2006 and 2007. Labor productivity, measured as the number of fixed and mobile connections per employee, increased by a factor of more than 11 between 2006 and 2007.

Throughout the study period, service quality gradually improved. The number of telephone faults per 100 main fixed lines a year dropped from 23 in 1995 to 8 by the end of 2007. Such quality improvements were accompanied by a reduction in the waiting list for main fixed lines, which by 2007 averaged zero.

Do Utilities with Private Sector Participation Outperform Public Utilities?

The data allow for various desegregations, including by country, size, ownership, and structure. The data are publicly available and allow users to identify and produce their own benchmarking exercises. All figures for this exercise are available in appendix D.

One of the scenarios selected compares public utilities with utilities that include private sector participation. The following results are based on averages across utilities in the electricity distribution benchmarking database. The utilities are divided into three categories: utilities that were public throughout 1995–2005, utilities that privatized before 1995 and remained private through 2005, and utilities that privatized after 1995 and remained private through 2005. The initial conditions in 1995 as well as the overall trend between 1995 and 2005 were considered. As in the previous sections, the results are shown for the top 10 percent of performers, the middle 80 percent, and the bottom 10 percent.

The findings reveal considerable improvement in the performance of the electricity distribution sector. The main differences in performance between the two types of utilities have to do with labor productivity, distribution losses, the quality of service, and tariffs. Other indicators, such as coverage and operation expenditures, are similar in utilities with and without private participation.

On average, utilities with private participation performed better than public utilities, with clear improvements after the change in ownership.

- In 1995, the number of connections per employee was only 10.7 percent higher at utilities that subsequently privatized than at utilities that would remain public. However, by 2005, utilities that had privatized had tripled their productivity, whereas productivity at public utilities had only doubled.
- In 1995, utilities that would remain public had distributional losses of 17.9 percent, where utilities that subsequently had private sector

participation had losses of 15.3 percent. By 2005, the privatized utilities had reduced distribution losses by 12.6 percent, whereas losses at public utilities had increased 4.9 percent.

- In 1995, utilities that would remain public experienced an average frequency of 22 interruptions per connection, 5 interruptions fewer than utilities that subsequently had private sector participation. By 2005, public utilities had reduced the average frequency of interruptions to 18, whereas utilities that had private sector participation had cut their average frequency of interruptions to 13. In 1995, the difference in the duration of service interruptions was one hour. By 2005, the duration had risen 48.8 percent at public utilities and fallen 28.2 percent at utilities that had private sector participation.

There are good public and private utilities and underperforming private and public utilities. For several indicators, the top 10 percent of public utilities performed better than the average private utilities. In other cases, the bottom 10 percent of private utilities performed worse than the average public utilities. Distribution losses in particular run counter to the overall trend of greater improvement by privatized utilities. Public utilities in the bottom 10 percent have fewer distribution losses than the average private utilities. Utilities that had private sector participation in the top decile have greater distribution losses than the average public utilities.

Conclusions

This chapter analyzes sector performance based on information on more than 250 public and private electricity distribution companies, more than 1,700 water and sanitation companies, and more than 40 telecommunications companies in 32 countries. The database is rich not only in the number and types of utilities surveyed but also in the diversity and representativeness of the collected indicators. As a result, the conclusions are diverse and conditioned by the unique characteristics of each sector and service provider.

A Leap Forward in Sector Performance

Sector performance for electricity distribution, water and sanitation, and fixed telecommunications improved significantly in LAC. Between 1990 and 2005, the region witnessed significant improvements, especially in coverage, service quality, and labor productivity in all three sectors. Coverage in the sample increased to 95 percent for electricity distribution, 97 percent for water utilities, and 62 percent for fixed telecommunications.

A similar pattern of improvement is evident for labor productivity. For electricity distribution, labor productivity doubled between 1995 and 2005; for water, it almost doubled (the number of connections per employee rose from 252 in 1995 to 425 in 2006). The telecommunications sector experienced a seven-fold increase between 1995 and 2007.

Uncovering the Drivers of Utility Performance • http://dx.doi.org/10.1596/978-0-8213-9660-5

The quality of service also improved. For electricity distribution, the frequency of interruptions fell 42 percent, and the duration of interruptions fell 40 percent. The water sector experienced an 8 percent increase in the continuity of service. In fixed telecommunications, gradual but significant increases occurred in the number of digital main lines and the share of telephone faults cleared by the following working day. For example, the share of digital main lines increased from 63 percent in 1995 to 100 percent in 2007. The number of telephone faults per 100 main fixed lines a year declined from 23 in 1995 to 8 in 2007. Such improvements in quality were accompanied by reductions in the waiting list for main fixed lines, which by 2007 averaged zero.

Wide Differences between the Strongest and the Weakest Performers

The region is home to a wide range of strong and weak performers. In water and sanitation, the top 10 percent of performers averaged 100 percent water and sanitation coverage. In contrast, the bottom 10 percent averaged 66 percent coverage, and the bottom 10 percent of sewerage utilities averaged just 15 percent coverage. Electricity distribution utilities in the top 10 percent were 10 times more productive in 2005 and sold 6 times more energy per connection than utilities in the bottom 10 percent. On average, private utilities outperformed public utilities—but there are good public and private utilities and underperforming private and public utilities.

Remaining Challenges

Although sector performance has improved, the region still faces challenges, particularly in expanding services in rural areas, minimizing distributional losses, and increasing cost-recovery levels. Despite the fact that electricity coverage in LAC increased to 95 percent in 2005, millions of people, almost all poor and in rural areas, remain without electricity. In the same vein, 29 million households, mostly in rural areas, do not have a water connection. These figures underscore the need to expand electrification and water and sanitation services in rural areas.

Regional distribution losses display no apparent trend but rather sporadic increases and decreases. For electricity, the lowest distributional loss was observed in 2001, when losses fell to 13.7 percent, down 9 percentage points from 1995; average losses rose to 14.7 percent in 2005. Nonrevenue water increased slightly between 1995 and 2005, from 38 to 39 percent; it remains an obstacle for the region's water utilities.

Lack of cost recovery continues to hamper many utilities in LAC. As outlined in chapter 1, improving cost recovery requires an integrated approach involving tariff adjustments, the control of both operational and capital expenditures, and reliable transfers from government when capital expenditures are viewed as a public good, as may be the case with the expansion of sewerage networks or even rural electrification. The approach will depend on the specific conditions and environment of each sector and utility provider.

Although the findings reported here provide only a glimpse of the three sectors, they yield insights about the region's strengths and weaknesses. One of the goals of this work was to motivate research that builds on this knowledge and examines specific case studies.

Notes

1. These data are publicly available. The complete database can be accessed at http://info.worldbank.org/etools/lacelectricity/home.htm.
2. This database will be publicly available shortly.
3. These data are publicly available. The complete database can be accessed at http://www.itu.int/ITU-D/ict/publications/world/world.html. The water database is available at www.lacbenchmarkingutilities.org.
4. All the numbers in this section are from Andrés and Dragoiu (2008).
5. These coverage figures correspond to the weighted average of the 250 utilities in the LAC benchmarking database. Regional electricity coverage is estimated to have been 92 percent in 2007.
6. These regional estimates correspond to the weighted average across the 250 utilities in the sample, which represents 90 percent of the total number of electricity connections.
7. This reduction in energy sold per connection could also be related to the increase in residential access to poor families, which brings down the average intensity of electricity usage.
8. Tariffs in absolute terms are not an efficiency measure of utilities per se, as retail tariffs are related to generation costs. Ideally, one would need to measure the tariff gap or the value added of distribution (VAD) to isolate the cost for the distribution segment from the rest of the value chain. Data on costs are extremely difficult to collect. The authors attempted to collect these data. However, availability of operational expense indicators is uneven at best.
9. These figures correspond to the coverage area for the concessionaires. Some 146 million LAC residents lack adequate access to water supply; this measure is equivalent to access to potable water in 2004 (WHO–UNICEF 2008). The main difference between these estimates and the estimated by the World Health Organization and UNICEF is that the lack of service estimate is calculated using census and household surveys and thus includes the rural population and the population in areas not covered by the concessionaires in the sample used here. The changes in coverage presented here are based on data on 1,700 water and sanitation utilities, which cover half of the water connections in LAC. Extrapolating these figures to the connections not covered by the sample could be inappropriate, because the utilities not included in the sample may have lower coverage.
10. The percentage point increase in coverage may also depend on other factors, such as demographics. Although this chapter considers possible determinants for such observed changes, explaining the possible link between the results and determinants is beyond its scope.

References

Andrés, L., M. Diop, and J. L. Guasch. 2008. "Achievements and Challenges of Private Participation in Infrastructure in Latin America: Evaluation and Future Prospects." In *Euromoney Infrastructure Financing*, edited by. H. Davis, 182–201. Oxford: Oxford University Press.

Andrés, L., and G. Dragoiu. 2008. *Benchmarking Electricity Distribution Report 1995–2005.* World Bank, Washington, DC.

Fay, M., and M. Morrison. 2006. *Infrastructure in Latin America and the Caribbean: Recent Developments and Key Challenges.* Washington, DC: World Bank.

ITU (International Telecommunication Union). 2009. World Telecommunication/ICT Indicators Database. Geneva.

Jamasb, T., R. Mota, D. Newbery, and M. Pollitt. 2005. "Electricity Sector Reform in Developing Countries: A Survey of Empirical Evidence on Determinants and Performance." Policy Research Working Paper 3549, World Bank, Washington, DC.

WHO (World Health Organization)–UNICEF (United Nations Children Fund). 2008. Joint Monitoring Programme (JMP) for Water Supply and Sanitation. http://www.wssinfo.org/.

World Bank. 2007. *LCR Energy Strategy.* Washington, DC.

———. 2012 *Water and Sewerage Utilities: A Benchmarking Analysis for Latin America and the Caribbean.* LCSSD Economics Team, Washington, DC.

Understanding the Impact of Private Sector Participation on the Performance of Utilities

Massive private investment in infrastructure flowed into Latin America and the Caribbean (LAC) beginning in the 1990s. This chapter focuses on the role private players played in shaping the region's electricity distribution, water and sewerage, and fixed-line telecommunications sectors.[1]

The introduction of private participation in infrastructure was an attempt to compensate for the shortcomings of state-operated utilities and to improve the coverage and quality of infrastructure.[2] Between 1995 and 1998, private participation in LAC rose from roughly $17 billion to a peak of more than $70 billion, before dropping back to $20 billion in 2002 (World Bank 2007).

Until the 1980s, infrastructure services throughout the world were operated and financed exclusively by public entities. Ownership began to change in the 1990s, as a growing number of countries turned to a new approach. The private sector participation phenomenon was based on the coincidence of two distinct but complementary trends. On the one hand, governments began to see the private sector as an attractive and manageable solution to the problems posed by infrastructure services. On the other hand, the private sector began to see the commercial attraction of investing in emerging economies.

As a result, private capital flows to infrastructure projects in developing countries grew sixfold during the mid-1990s (although they declined sharply thereafter). From a baseline of $20 billion in the mid-1990s, global investments swelled to a peak of $131 billion in 1997. The increase was driven primarily by the rapid adoption of the new model in Latin America and East Asia. The countries of Eastern Europe and Central Asia were also partly responsible for the increase, as the transition economies launched massive privatization programs.

From 1997 until recently, private capital flows were in marked decline. Triggered by the financial crises—and resulting currency devaluations—in East Asia and Latin America, the decline coincided with various corporate crises. Some of the major telecommunications companies that invested in emerging economies saw their average share prices fall 90 percent, and the shares of global energy firms fell as much as 70 percent. Private investment fell from $71 billion in 1998 to $16 billion in 2003, and the average contract attracted only two bidders (Fay and Morrison 2006). Rebuilding public and business confidence in private-public partnerships in LAC will not be easy.

Private participation has improved utility performance in the region, as chapter 2 shows. However, since the beginning of this decade, it has become a topic of contention among LAC governments, and the region's ability to attract investors has diminished. In November 2000, 36 percent of Argentines believed that infrastructure services should come back under government control; five years later, 78 percent supported government control (*El Cronista*, April 18, 2005). The change in Argentina reflects a general trend in Latin America.[3] Public resistance has become a major constraint on private participation in infrastructure in some countries, both politically and operationally. The average number of bidders for power distribution privatizations in the region fell from more than four in 1998 to less than two in 2000 and 2001 (Harris 2003).

There is a remarkable contrast between generally positive evaluations of private sector participation and the extreme public disaffection with it. Martimort and Straub (2005) conclude that either important failures have gone unreported (although clearly not unnoticed by the people who suffered) or there has been a major problem with perceptions (and therefore a massive communication failure). Although estimates of impact on service coverage, quality, and redistribution are generally positive, it is possible that some negative aspects were underreported. The quality of service may have deteriorated or failed to improve as much as expected; the redistributional impact of price increases may not have been sufficiently mitigated by subsidies; and the effect on jobs in infrastructure was negative, although sector employment rebounded somewhat in the medium term (Fay and Morrison 2006).

Perceptions may be the main driver for this disaffection. Negative public perception of private sector participation may actually reflect the downturn in the economic cycle (Boix 2005), perceptions may have suffered from a gap between actual and expected performance, and the perceived transparency of the private sector participation process is likely to have been crucial in shaping public perceptions (Fay and Morrison 2006).

Perhaps the gravest misconception during the peak of private participation in infrastructure was that governments could now pass on responsibility for infrastructure financing and management to the private sector. Although private participation held promises of a new flow of finance and technological innovations, it was not intended to substitute or play the role of the public sector but rather to complement it. As Fay and Morrison (2006) emphasize, governments remain at the heart of infrastructure service delivery. They should continue to regulate and oversee infrastructure provision and pay for a large share of investments.

The challenge currently facing the region is the low level of public and private investment in infrastructure. Low levels of investment are a concern because of the widely documented link between infrastructure and growth, productivity, and poverty reduction (see Briceño-Garmendia, Estache, and Shafik 2004; Calderón and Servén 2004; Fay and Morrison 2006). Public investment in infrastructure in LAC dropped from 3 percent of gross domestic product (GDP) in 1980 to less than 1 percent in 2001 (De Ferranti and others 2004. By 2009, it reached 3–4 percent of GDP, including the stimulus packages launched in response to the financial crisis (Schwartz, Andrés, and Dragoiu 2009). In order to revive both public and private investment in the region, it is important to understand their distinct yet complementary roles and the true impacts and determinants of private sector participation in LAC. If governments and private actors are to increase infrastructure investments in feasible ways, it is critical that they learn from experiences, in order to make better investment and maintenance choices.

This chapter contributes to this aim by presenting a comprehensive and systemic analysis of the impact of private sector participation in LAC. It looks at what happened before, during, and after private sector participation in three sectors (electricity distribution, water and sewerage, and telecommunications) by focusing on a range of performance variables. It is necessary to look at all three periods because the most dramatic effects of private sector participation are often found in the transition period, when the enterprise is overhauled as part of the transaction process. These changes constitute a one-time adjustment, however, and present a pace of improvement that is not necessarily sustained in the long run. The chapter focuses on changes and rates of changes in the three periods rather than on absolute numbers, because in many cases, the performance variables exhibit natural changes over time (with or without private sector participation). The analysis controls for such naturally occurring rates of changes.

The changes associated with private sector participation had a significant effect on labor productivity, efficiency, and quality (for fixed-line telecommunications, they also had significant effects on output and coverage) (table 3.1). Prices tended to increase somewhat following the change in ownership, although the picture varies across sectors. Moreover, care should be exercised in interpreting changes in prices, because prices were highly distorted—most did not represent cost recovery—before private sector participation began. There do not appear to have been significant impacts on output or coverage

The differences between publicly and privately operated distribution utilities showed up primarily with regard to labor productivity, distribution losses, quality of service, and tariffs. Other indicators, such as coverage and operational expenditures, were not significantly different in the two groups.[4] The analysis in this chapter addresses the determinants of performance.

Impact of Private Sector Participation on Electricity Distribution

The poor performance of the public model of electricity distribution in the 1990s beckoned for reform in the sector. Reform introduced market principles, in an attempt to improve the quality, reliability, and efficiency of electricity services; strengthen the government's fiscal position; and increase affordable access to energy services for the poor.

Table 3.1 Effects of Private Participation in Electricity Distribution, Water Distribution, and Fixed-Line Telecommunications in Latin America and the Caribbean

	Electricity distribution		Fixed-line telecommunications		Water distribution	
	Transition	Posttransition	Transition	Posttransition	Transition	Posttransition
Number of subscribers[a]	=	↓	↑	↑	=	↓
Output[a]	=	↓	↑	↑	=	↓
Number of employees	↓	↓	↓	↓	↓	↓
Labor productivity[a]	↑	↑	↑	↑	↑	↑
Decline in distributional losses	↑	↑	↑	↑	↑	↑
Quality	↑	↑	↑	↑	↑	↑
Coverage[a]	=	=	↑	↑	=	=
Average prices	↓	↑	↓	=	↑ ?	↑ ?
Monthly residential charges			↑	↑		
Price for a residential installation			↓	↓		

Source: Andrés and others 2008.

Note: Up and down arrows indicate that a positive or negative change occurred in addition to the natural change that would have been expected in the absence of private sector participation. An equal sign indicates that the trend observed during the previous period was sustained. A question mark indicates that insufficient observations were available to reach a conclusion. The size of the arrow represents the magnitude of the change.
a. Net of firm-specific time trend.

Market-oriented reform promoted the separation of policymaking, regulation, and service provision, limiting the role of the state to policymaking and regulation and relying on the private sector as the main investor and provider of electricity service. Wherever possible, reform also introduced competition and economic regulation of natural monopolies to improve economic efficiency. This market model was supposed to improve the government's fiscal position and ensure the financial sustainability of the sector by promoting the participation of private investors and the establishment of competitive prices for generation and cost-covering tariffs for transmission and distribution. It was considered socially and politically acceptable because it would improve access to energy services by the poor, based on a scheme of efficient subsidies.

This section draws on the work of Andrés, Foster, and Guasch (2006), who built an original data set based on information from 116 electricity distribution companies in the region before and after their private sector participation. Their study used two complementary methodologies—a means and medians analysis and an econometric analysis—to examine the effects of changes in ownership. This section synthesizes their results, summarizing the effects on output and coverage, employment and labor productivity, prices, distributional losses, and service quality during three periods: before the private sector participation (pre-transition), the three-year transition period, and after the private sector participation (posttransition).[5] Doing so reveals both the short- and longer-term effects.

The change in ownership did not change the growth trend for number of connections, energy sold, or coverage. Employment fell during both periods, primarily during the transition. Labor productivity accelerated during the transition, followed by a deceleration during the posttransition period. Distributional losses and quality improved during both periods. Average prices in real local currency increased somewhat over both periods (results for dollar price changes were smaller given Brazil's currency devaluation in 1999).

Output and Coverage

The number of connections, quantity of energy sold each year, and coverage levels increased across all three periods—pretransition, transition, and posttransition—but the effects were driven by secular trends. The annual changes in energy sold declined slightly after the private sector participation.

Two measures were used to estimate output: the volume of energy sold each year (in MWhs) and the total number of connections at the end of each year. The amount of energy sold increased in all three periods (figure 3.1).[6] According to the econometric analysis, the average amount of energy sold increased 22.3 percent during the transition; the average amount sold after the transition was 18.4 percent higher than transition levels.[7]

These output indicators exhibit a natural rate of growth that must be controlled for to isolate the impacts of private sector participation. The econometric results show that there was a slight increase in the growth trend during the transition. After the transition (during the period after private sector participation), however, the growth trend in the volume of energy sold slowed slightly.[8]

The number of connections increased significantly during all three periods.[9] According to the econometric analysis, the average level of connection numbers was 16.2 percent higher during the transition than before the transition. The average level after the transition was 19.2 percent higher than during the transition (see appendix table D.3). These increases were statistically significant by both the means and median analysis (see appendix table D.1) and the econometric analysis (see appendix table D.3). Examination of figure 3.1, however, shows that the increases largely followed a trend. The cross-country differences in the evolution of connection numbers could potentially be explained by differences in initial coverage conditions or differences in contract and regulator characteristics.

Increases in coverage occurred during all three periods: the average increase during the transition was 5.4 percent, and the average increase after that (with respect to transition levels) was 8 percent. Like the output increases, the coverage increases were statistically significant. However, after controlling for time trends and growth patterns, the impact of private sector participation becomes negligible or difficult to discern (figure 3.2). Brazil overtook Argentina to have the highest coverage level—more than 95 percent—during the posttransition

Figure 3.1 Energy Distribution before, during, and after Private Sector Participation

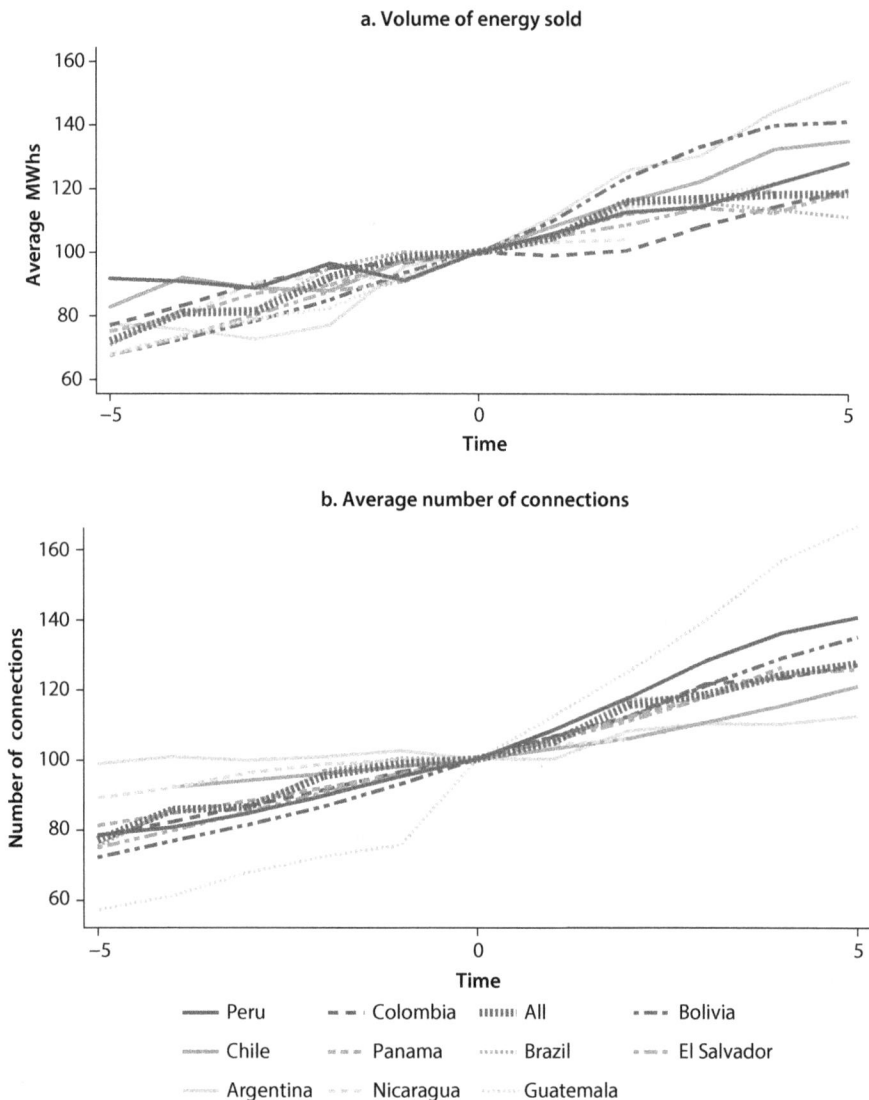

a. Volume of energy sold

b. Average number of connections

—— Peru	– · – Colombia	ⅢⅢⅢⅢ All	– · – Bolivia
—— Chile	– – – Panama	······· Brazil	– · – El Salvador
—— Argentina	– – – Nicaragua	········ Guatemala	

Source: Andrés and others 2008.
Note: $t = 0$ is the base year, the last year in which the utility was publicly owned for at least six months. The y-axis is normalized at 100 when $t = 0$.

period. Guatemala experienced the largest jump between the before and after transition periods.

Employment and Labor Productivity

Employment levels dropped substantially during the transition, not controlling for time trends. They also fell after the transition, but to a lesser extent. Most state-owned enterprises (SOEs) had excess personnel. Hence, as expected, significant reductions in the number of employees were observed across the three

Figure 3.2 Electricity Coverage before and after Private Sector Participation

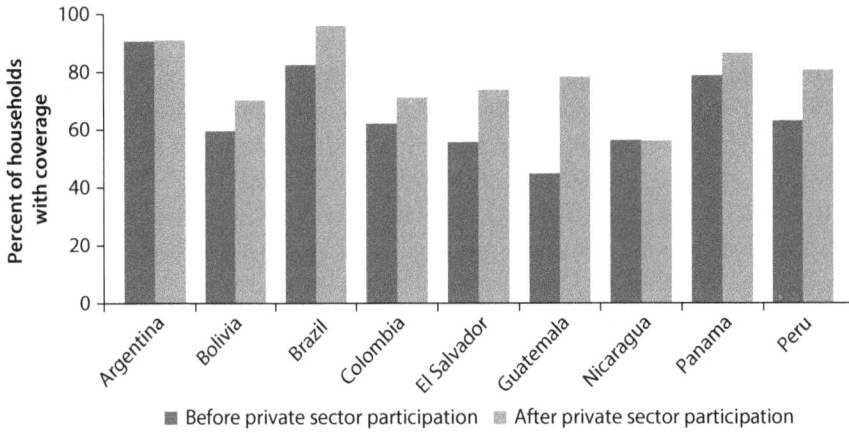

Source: Andrés and others 2008.

Figure 3.3 Employment in the Electricity Distribution Sector before, during, and after Private Sector Participation

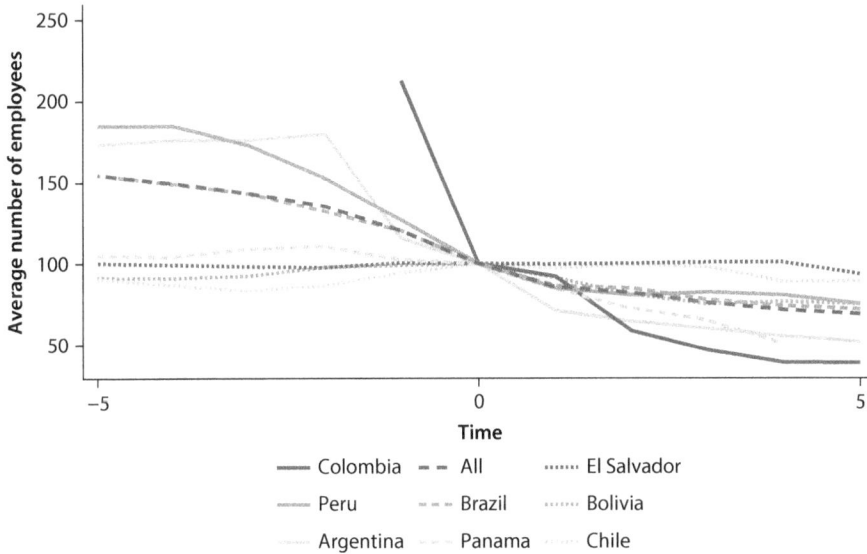

Note: t = 0 is the base year, the last year in which the utility was publicly owned for at least six months. The y-axis is normalized at 100 when t = 0.

periods (figure 3.3).[10] In some cases, the government reduced the number of employees before the change in ownership in order to increase the value of the firms (Chong and López-de-Silanes 2003). The analysis conducted here finds that labor force reductions during the transition were substantially larger than those after. The econometric analysis finds a 26.4 percent drop in the number of employees during the transition; after the transition, there was an additional drop of 17.6 percent.[11] Employment levels dropped substantially during the transition;

they also fell after the transition, but to a lesser extent. Appendix table D.3 shows the changes in employment levels found by the econometric analysis.

Increases in output and reductions in the number of employees increased labor productivity during both the transition and posttransition periods (figure 3.4). Although the greatest gains came during the transition period, both the number of connections per employee and the quantity of energy sold per employee showed significant improvements during the transition and posttransition periods relative to the previous period.[12] According to the econometric analysis, connections per employee were 55.6 percent higher during the transition and another 44.5 percent higher after the transition. Equivalent numbers for energy sold per employee are 60.6 percent and 41.3 percent.

Figure 3.4 Labor Productivity in Electricity Distribution before, during, and after Private Sector Participation

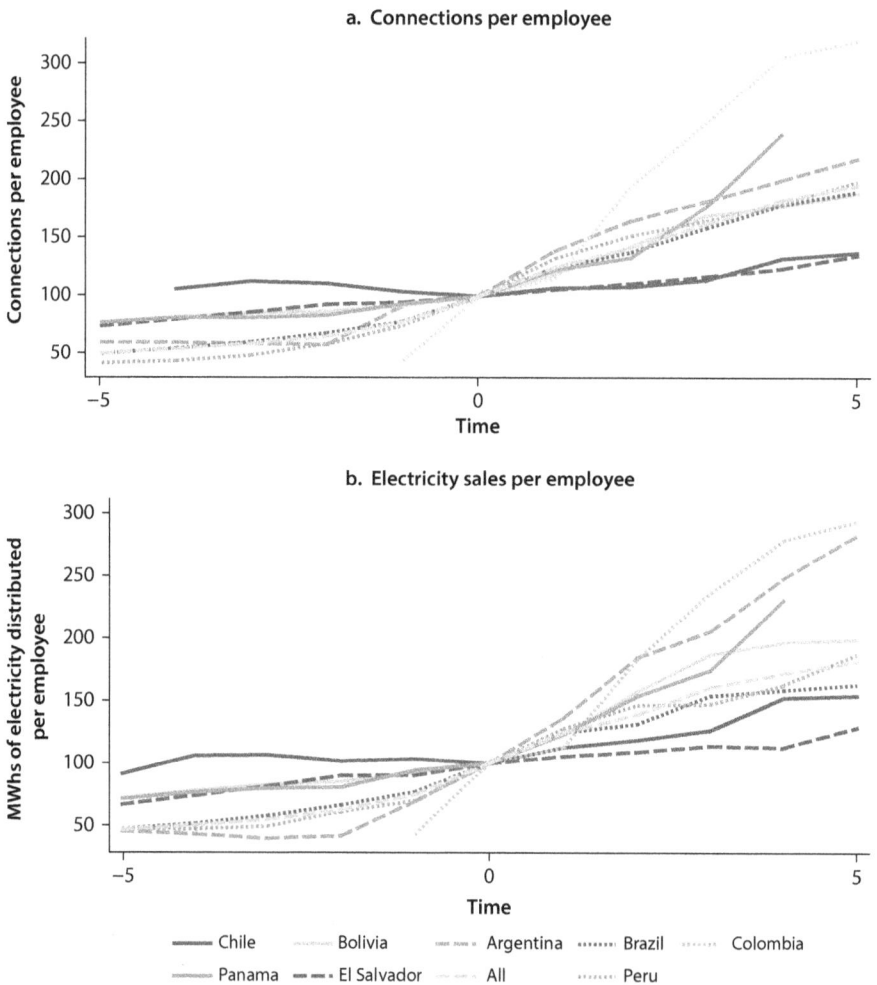

a. Connections per employee

b. Electricity sales per employee

Chile   Bolivia   Argentina   Brazil   Colombia
Panama   El Salvador   All   Peru

Note: $t = 0$ is the base year, the last year in which the utility was publicly owned for at least six months. The y-axis is normalized at 100 when $t = 0$.

As was the case for the output and labor indicators, controlling for trends dramatically reduces the private sector participation impacts. With the effect of time trends removed, the number of connections per employee increased 5 percent and energy per employee increased 9 percent during the transition. Levels after the transition decreased slightly with respect to transition levels (–3.6 percent for connections per employee and –7.7 percent for energy per employee). The econometric growth rate analysis produced similar results: the average annual growth rate for both connections per employee and energy per employee increased during the transition and decreased after the transition.

Connections per employee and energy sold per employee showed large gains during both the transition and posttransition periods. A temporary growth acceleration occurred during the transition, followed by a deceleration after the transition.

Prices

Average prices in real local currency increased somewhat during the transition and posttransition periods. After excluding Brazil (which devalued its currency in 1999), dollar prices increased slightly. Tariffs in real local currency showed a clearly increasing trend, but prices in dollars decreased. The econometric analysis showed statistically significant increases in real local currency prices of 11.1 percent during the transition and 7.4 percent after the transition. In dollars, there was no significant change during the transition period and a –2.8 percent drop during the posttransition period.

A plausible explanation for these trends is the 1999 currency devaluation in Brazil. To test this explanation, the analysis was repeated with Brazil excluded from the sample. With Brazil excluded, both series show increasing prices, but at a much lower rate. As a result of the smaller sample size and relatively small price changes, no significant differences were found between consecutive periods in the means and medians analysis. The same analysis found small but significant price increases in both local currency and dollars when comparing the pretransition and posttransition periods.

Distributional Losses

Distributional losses under public ownership varied, increasing in some countries and decreasing in others before private sector participation (figure 3.5). After the transition, almost all countries reduced their average distributional losses. The reason for the temporary increase in losses in some countries part way through the posttransition period is unclear.

The transition period saw an average drop in distributional losses of 3.1 percent, according to the econometric analysis. In contrast, distributional losses plunged 13.2 percent during the posttransition period.

The means and medians analysis tells a slightly different story. The mean for the transition period was 11.5 percent lower than the mean during the pretransition period; the mean during the posttransition period was about 10 percent lower than during the transition period. Changes in the median are more similar

Figure 3.5 Distributional Losses in the Electricity Sector before, during, and after Private Sector Participation

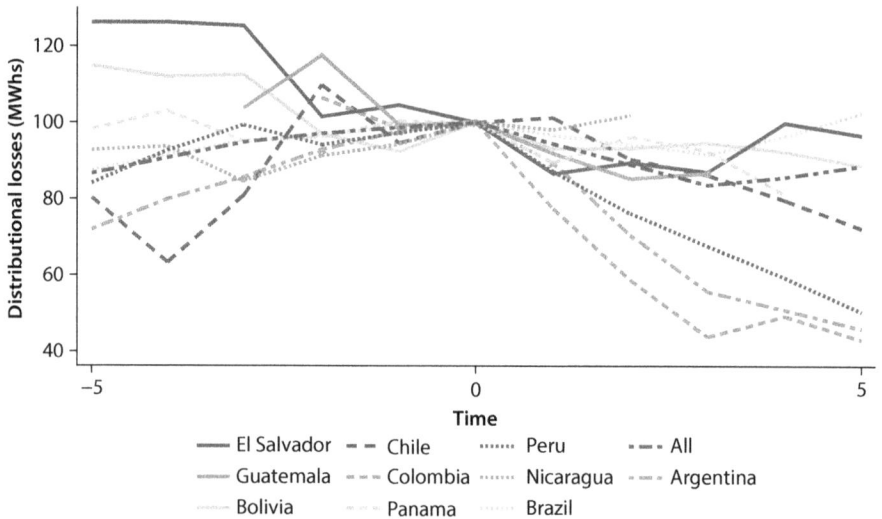

Note: $t = 0$ is the base year, the last year in which the utility was publicly owned for at least six months. The y-axis is normalized at 100 when $t = 0$.

to the econometric analysis. The median distributional loss was 6 percent lower during the transition period and 11 percent lower during the posttransition period with respect to the previous period (see appendix table D.1). (In this case, it makes more sense to analyze changes in loss levels rather than trends, because a natural trend is not expected.)

The mixed results are likely the result of a conflation of technical and commercial distributional losses. To curb technical losses, new investments and upgrades are required that take time to implement. Hence, technical losses would be expected to occur following the transition period. In contrast, commercial losses can often be reduced quickly, by shutting off the connections of nonpaying customers. Declines in distributional losses during the transition period could be attributed to commercial losses.

Quality of Service

The quality of electricity distribution is measured by the frequency and duration of service interruptions per consumer. In general, these measures were defined at the time of reform, along with the creation of regulatory agencies, making it difficult to build long time series.

The good data that exist from the pretransition period indicate that both the average duration of interruptions and the average frequency of interruptions per consumer fell during both the transition and posttransition periods. Combining these two indicators yields an overall quality measure that shows improvement in both periods.

Only Argentina and Brazil had information for the years before the transition. Argentina stands out as having been particularly successful in reducing the average duration and frequency of interruptions per consumer, in both relative and absolute terms (figure 3.6). In countries where quantitative quality data before private sector participation are not available, strong anecdotal evidence suggests that quality was poor.

Both methodologies found improvements in average frequency and duration of interruptions. According to the econometric analysis, the duration of interruptions fell 13.4 percent during the transition and an additional 29.1 percent after the transition. The frequency of interruptions fell 10.1 percent during the transition and an additional 26.5 percent after it.[13] The means and medians analysis found similar quality improvements, although the frequency of interruptions results was not statistically significant for the posttransition period.[14]

Figure 3.6 Quality of Electricity Distribution before, during, and after Private Sector Participation

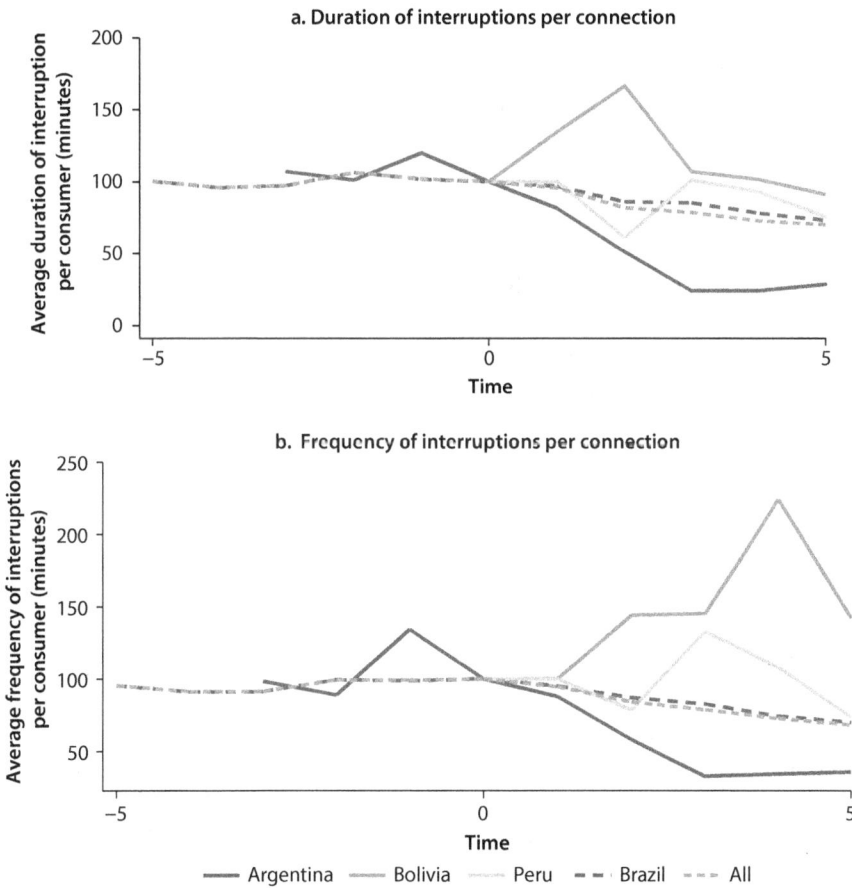

Note: The average line for all countries appears erratic because of the relative scarcity of data. $t = 0$ is the base year, the last year in which the utility was publicly owned for at least six months. The y-axis is normalized at 100 when $t = 0$.

Both the average duration of interruptions per consumer and the average frequency of interruptions per consumer fell during both the transition and posttransition periods. Combining these two indicators yields an overall quality measure that shows improvement in both periods.

Summary

The change in ownership did not change the growth trend for number of connections, energy sold, or coverage.[15] Employment fell during both periods, but primarily during the transition. Growth in labor productivity accelerated during the transition, followed by a deceleration during the posttransition period. Distributional losses and quality improved during both periods. Average prices in real local currency increased somewhat over both periods, although results for dollar price changes were less robust given Brazil's currency devaluation in 1999.

Impact of Private Sector Participation on Water and Sewerage

Growing dissatisfaction with the performance of national water monopolies, combined with political pressure for devolution across all areas of government, created the conditions for a move toward decentralized control of water infrastructure in the 1980s and 1990s. In general, water sector reforms comprised three components: decentralization, regulation, and private sector participation.

Chile was the first country to modernize its water sector, passing new legislation as early as 1988. By 1991, both Argentina and Mexico were beginning to conduct a series of experiments with private sector participation. In a second wave, Peru, Colombia, and Bolivia enacted ambitious legislation in the mid-1990s. During the second half of the decade, reform began to take root in Brazil and Central America. By the end of the 1990s, few countries had not completed reforms, had major reforms in process, or were actively considering reforms.

As part of the reform process, many countries created national regulatory agencies for water, similar to the Water Services Regulation Authority (Ofwat) model developed in the United Kingdom. The responsibilities of these agencies typically included determination of tariffs, approval of investment plans, oversight of quality of service, and protection of consumers. In some cases (for example, Peru), the agencies did not have final authority to determine tariffs. In the larger federal countries (Argentina, Brazil, and Mexico), regulatory functions were often organized at the state or provincial level. The regulatory agencies were seen as a precursor to private participation in the sector, although the ultimate scope of private participation was modest relative to initial expectations.

Historically, the water and sewerage sectors have not been well analyzed in Latin America. In contrast to electricity distribution and telecommunications, firms tend to be based at the local or regional government level, making the private participation process slower and more fragmented. Despite the slow process, at least 11 percent of the water used by households in the region is supplied by private firms Andrés and others (2007).

For the analysis in this section, data were collected for 49 firms that underwent a change in ownership in the previous 15 years. Two complementary methodologies were used to learn about the effects of changes in ownership: a means and medians analysis and an econometric analysis.

Output and coverage measures improved, but only consistent with the trend. The number of employees dropped substantially during the last years under public management, significantly increasing labor productivity, especially during the transition period. Labor productivity rates accelerated during the transition but decelerated in the posttransition period. Efficiency—measured by distributional losses—improved, mainly after the transition. Prices for both water and sewerage rose, although the increases for sewerage were generally not robust because of the small sample size. Two measures were used to measure quality: the continuity of the water service and the number of water samples that passed a potability test. Both measures improved in both periods, but potability improvements occurred mainly during the transition.

Output and Coverage

The number of water and sewerage connections increased during the transition and posttransition periods, but these improvements were consistent with existing trends. Similar results were found for both water and sewerage coverage. Water production increased somewhat in both periods, but after controlling for trends, a slight deceleration occurred in the posttransition period.

Two variables were used to measure output: the number of residential connections (for both water and sewerage) and the amount of water produced (in cubic meters) each year. The number of connections for both water and sewerage increased substantially during both the transition and posttransition periods (figure 3.7, panels a and b); the econometric analysis found increases of 15–20 percent for each period (see appendix D). The means and medians analysis found similar results.

A closer look at the results, however, shows that the increases can be accounted for by the existence of a trend. After controlling for firm-specific time trends, the econometric analysis found no significant changes in the number of water or sewerage connections. The econometric analysis found no significant changes in growth rates during the transition; after the transition, the average annual growth rate fell 1 percent for both water and sewerage.[16]

The second output indicator is the number of cubic meters of water produced a year (see figure 3.7, panel e). The econometric analysis found that water production increased 4.1 percent during the transition period and an additional 1.5 percent after the transition. However, taking trends into account—by controlling for firm-specific time trends or looking at changes in growth rates—erases those gains. In fact, the econometric analysis found no significant change in water production during the transition and a small drop after the transition.[17] As shown later, a possible explanation for this

Figure 3.7 Indicators of Water and Sewerage Output and Coverage before, during, and after Private Sector Participation

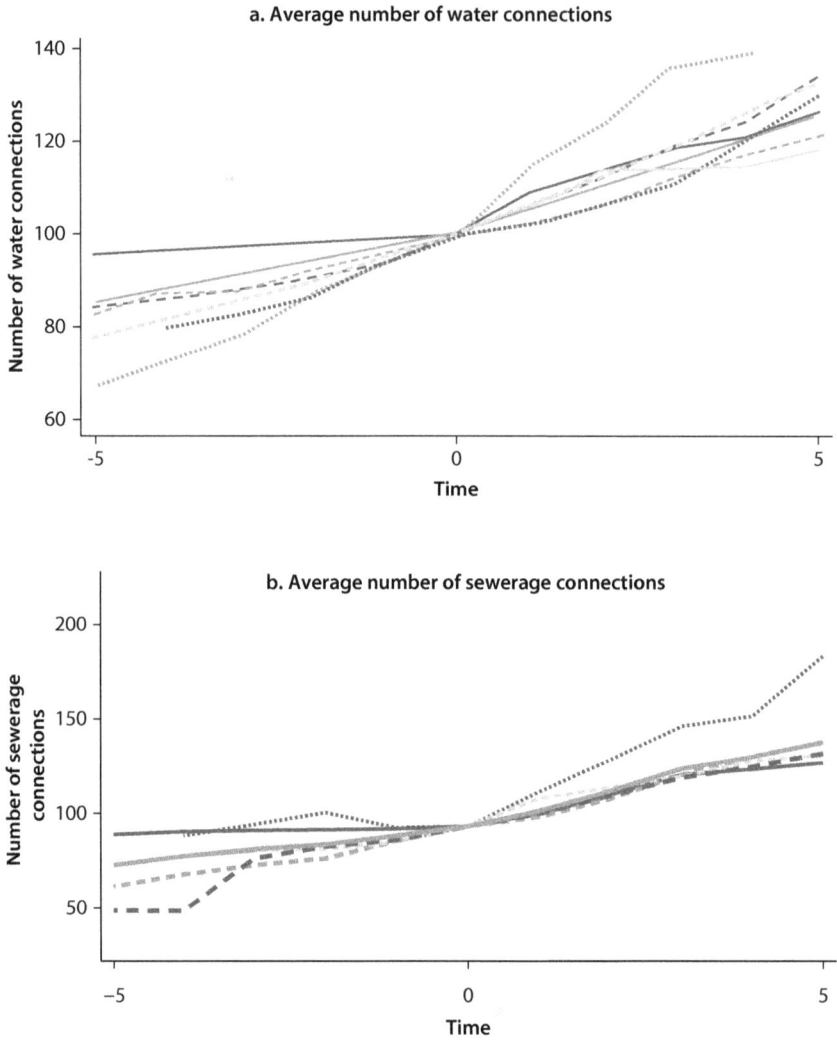

a. Average number of water connections

b. Average number of sewerage connections

figure continues next page

Figure 3.7 Indicators of Water and Sewerage Output and Coverage before, during, and after Private Sector Participation *(continued)*

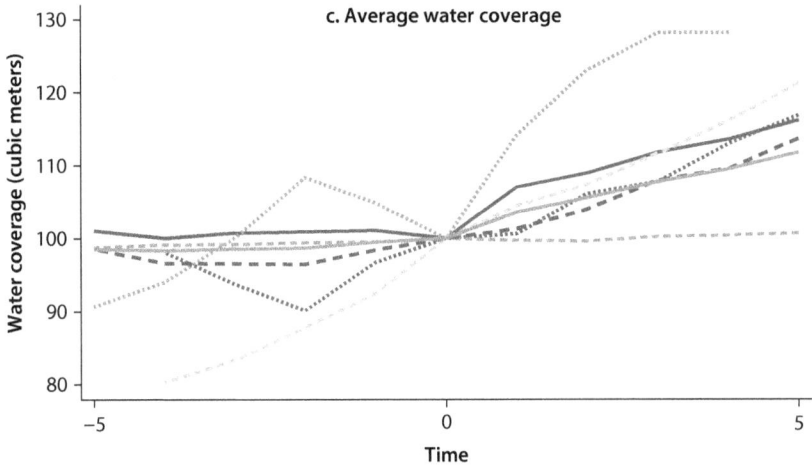

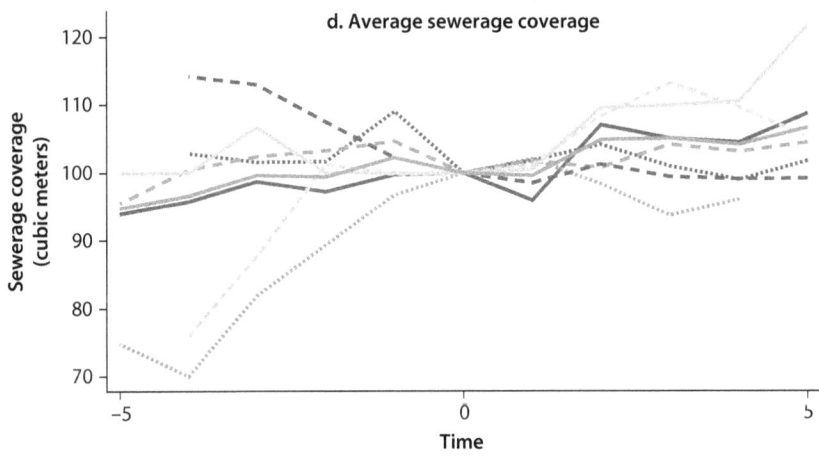

c. Average water coverage

d. Average sewerage coverage

figure continues next page

Figure 3.7 Indicators of Water and Sewerage Output and Coverage before, during, and after Private Sector Participation *(continued)*

e. Average water production

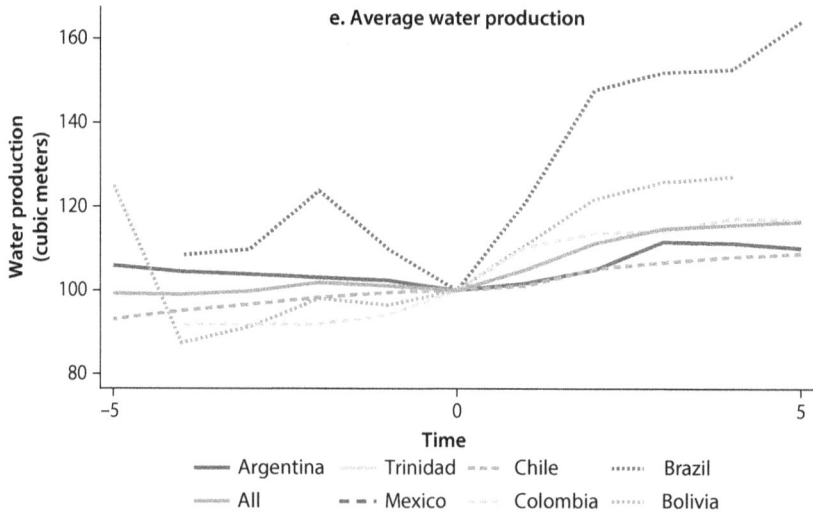

Note: $t = 0$ is the base year, the last year in which the utility was publicly owned for at least six months. The y-axis is normalized at 100 when $t = 0$.

deceleration is the improvement in efficiency caused by the reduction in distributional losses.

Coverage in both water (figure 3.8) and sewerage improved during the transition and posttransition periods. According to the econometric analysis, these improvements were statistically significant and ranged from 2.5 to 6.7 percent. The means and medians analysis found increases of 6.9–11.1 percent. These improvements were apparently driven by trends, however, and would have occurred even in the absence of private sector participation. After controlling for firm-specific time trends, the econometric analysis found no significant changes. Growth rates showed no significant changes during the transition period, combined with a small drop in the average annual growth rate of 0.4 percentage points for water and 0.8 percentage points for sewerage after the transition. Not surprisingly, these results are quantitatively similar to the results found for the number of connections.

Water coverage levels are relatively high in most countries—more than 90 percent. Mexico stands out as an exception, with less than 80 percent coverage. For sewerage, actual coverage levels are lower—closer to 60 percent for some countries. Chile is an outlier, with close to 100 percent sewerage coverage.

Employment and Labor Productivity

The number of employees declined during the transition and posttransition periods, not accounting for time trends. Both types of analyses found significant drops in employment during both periods, although the decline during

Figure 3.8 Water Distribution before and after Private Sector Participation

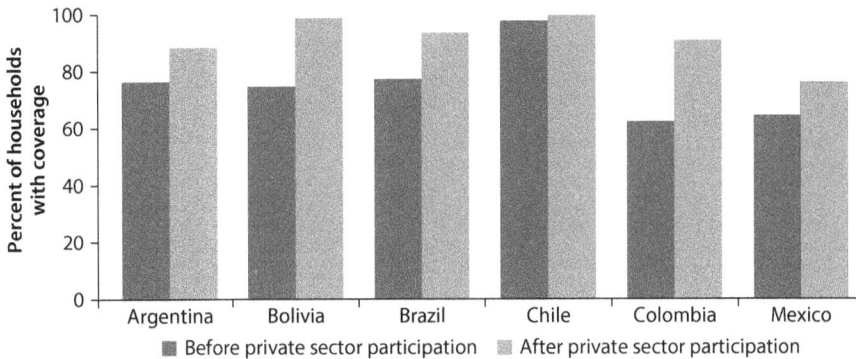

Source: Andrés and others 2008.
Note: The y-axis is the number of connections per 100 inhabitants.

the transition seems to have been greater (figure 3.9, panel a). The means and medians analysis found a 26.3 percent drop during the transition and an 11.7 percent drop after the transition. The econometric analysis found a 16.5 percent drop during the transition and a 17.6 percent drop after the transition.[18]

Given that most SOEs had excess personnel, the declines during the transition period should not be surprising. Many governments opted to trim the labor force before the ownership change, in an attempt to increase the value of the firm. Argentina had by far the most employees; it also experienced the largest absolute reduction in employee numbers.

Labor productivity—measured by the number of water connections per employee—increased greatly during both the transition and posttransition periods (figure 3.9, panel b). The econometric analysis found that water connections per employee increased 30.7 percent during the transition and another 42.5 percent after the transition. The means and medians analysis found similar increases.

Controlling for trends tells a somewhat different story. According to the econometric analysis, the average annual growth rate of connections per employee increased 4.7 percentage points during the transition. This increase was followed by a drop of 3.7 percentage points after the transition. There was thus a temporary acceleration in labor productivity growth (largely because of employment changes) during the transition before the annual growth rate returned to roughly 1 percentage point above the pretransition level. The means and medians analysis identified similar changes: an 11.6 percentage point increase during the transition followed by a 9.6 percentage point decrease after the transition. There was no statistically significant difference between the pretransition and posttransition growth rates in the means and medians analysis.

Prices

Water prices in dollars showed little change during the transition period (because of Brazil's devaluation) and rose after the transition. Water prices in real local

Figure 3.9 Employment and Labor Productivity in the Water Distribution Sector before, during, and after Private Sector Participation

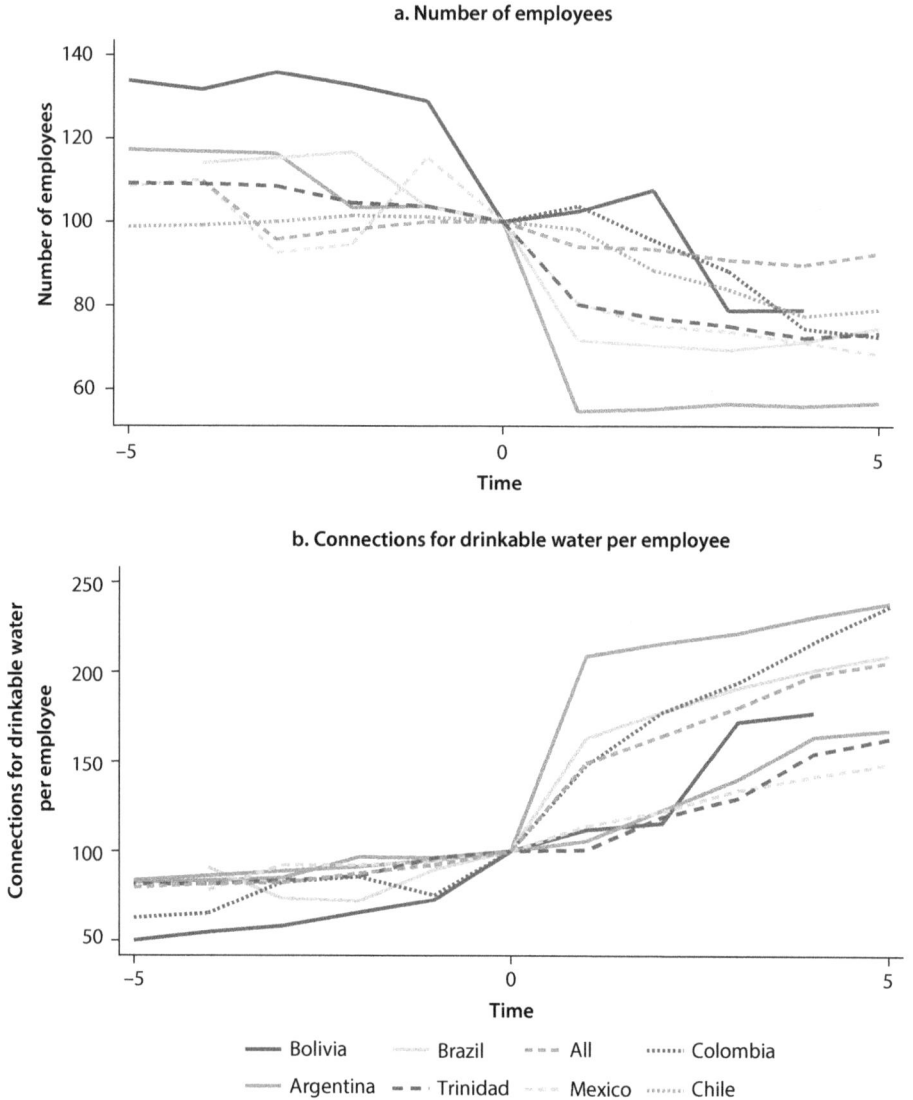

a. Number of employees

b. Connections for drinkable water per employee

Legend: Bolivia, Brazil, All, Colombia, Argentina, Trinidad, Mexico, Chile

Note: $t = 0$ is the base year, the last year in which the utility was publicly owned for at least six months. The y-axis is normalized at 100 when $t = 0$.

currency increased fairly substantially in both the transition and posttransition periods. Because of the small sample size, not much can be said about sewerage prices; however, a significant price increase in real local currency occurred during the posttransition period.

Water prices increased before and after transition in both dollars and real local currency (figure 3.10). Brazil's currency devaluation in 1999 accounted for the main difference between the two types of currencies. As a result of the devaluation, Brazil's water prices fell in dollars and mainly rose in real local currency. Given that the Brazil devaluation skewed the results for dollar prices so that they appeared artificially low, it is preferable to look at changes in real local currency.

According to the econometric analysis, water prices in dollars did not change significantly during the transition but increased 10.2 percent after the transition. In contrast, water prices showed statistically significant increases in real local currency of 15.7 percent during the transition and 23.7 percent after the transition. In the means and medians analysis, there were no significant changes between adjacent periods in dollars, but there was a statistically significant increase between the pretransition and posttransition periods. In real local currency, the

Figure 3.10 Average Price of Water and Sewerage before, during, and after Private Sector Participation

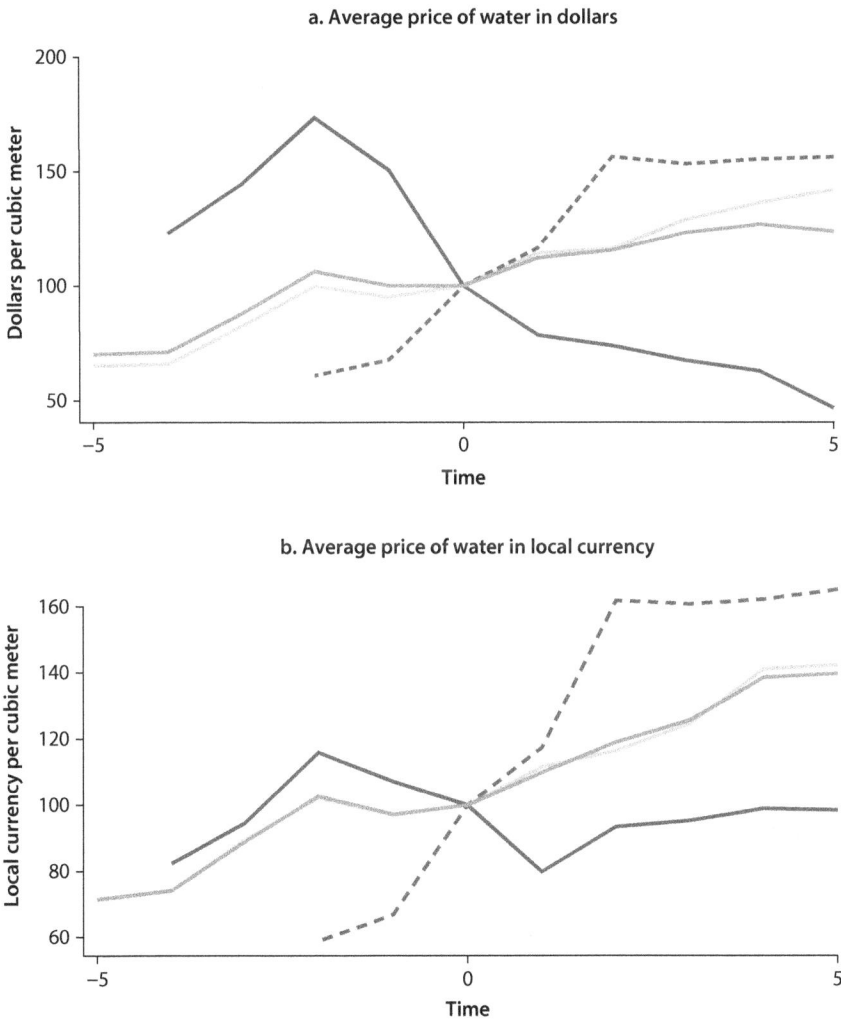

a. Average price of water in dollars

b. Average price of water in local currency

figure continues next page

Figure 3.10 Average Price of Water and Sewerage before, during, and after Private Sector Participation *(continued)*

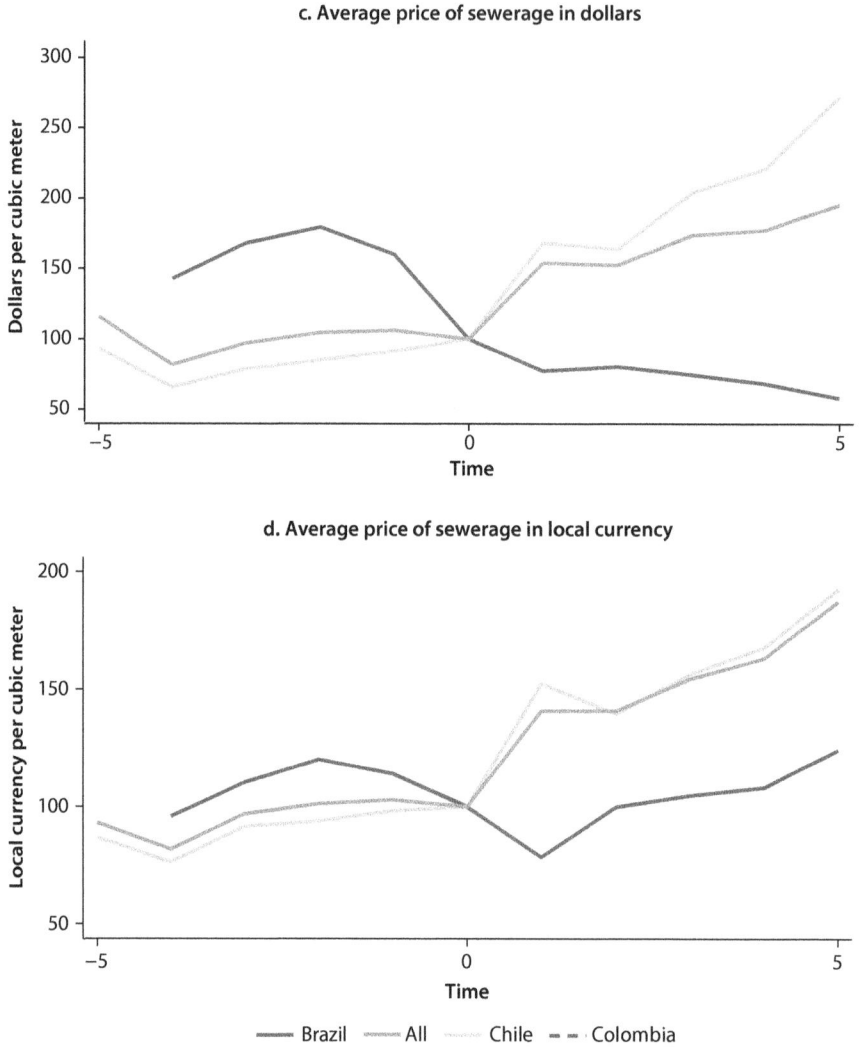

c. Average price of sewerage in dollars

d. Average price of sewerage in local currency

― Brazil　――― All　········· Chile　― ― Colombia

Note: $t = 0$ is the base year, the last year in which the utility was publicly owned for at least six months. The y-axis is normalized at 100 when $t = 0$.

means and medians analysis found significant price increases in each period. When Brazil was excluded from the sample, the means and medians analysis found statistically significant increases of 32.6 percent during the transition and 16.9 percent after the transition.

Sewerage prices seem to have behaved in a similar fashion as water prices (see figure 3.10, panels c and d). Because of the small number of observations, however, the only statistically significant change was the 24.9 percent increase in real local currency prices after the transition period in the econometric analysis.

Distributional Losses

Distributional losses fell substantially during both the transition and posttransition periods (figure 3.11). Indeed, the econometric analysis found a 3.8 percent drop in the percentage of water lost during the transition period followed by a 14.4 percent drop during the posttransition period. The means and medians analysis found results of a slightly larger magnitude (an 8.1 percent decline in the transition period followed by an 18.3 percent decrease in the posttransition period). Trends are not controlled for, because a natural trend is not expected and figure 3.11 does not signal a trend in the period before private sector participation.

Quality of Service

Improvements in service continuity appear to have occurred during both the transition and posttransition periods; no improvements occurred during the pre-transition period (figure 3.12). The means and medians analysis found that average continuity improved 27.8 percent during the transition and 14.8 percent after the transition Presumably because of the relatively small sample size, the econometric analysis found a statistically significant improvement (of 7.7 percent) only in the posttransition period.

Although the number of observations was small, it seems evident that water potability improved (see figure 3.12, panel b). Most of the changes occurred during the transition: according to the econometric analysis, potability improved 6.1 percent during the transition and 1.2 percent in the posttransition period. Given that potability numbers were already close to 100 percent for many countries (with the exception of Colombia), it is not surprising that improvements in the posttransition period were modest.

Figure 3.11 Losses in Water Distribution before, during, and after Private Sector Participation

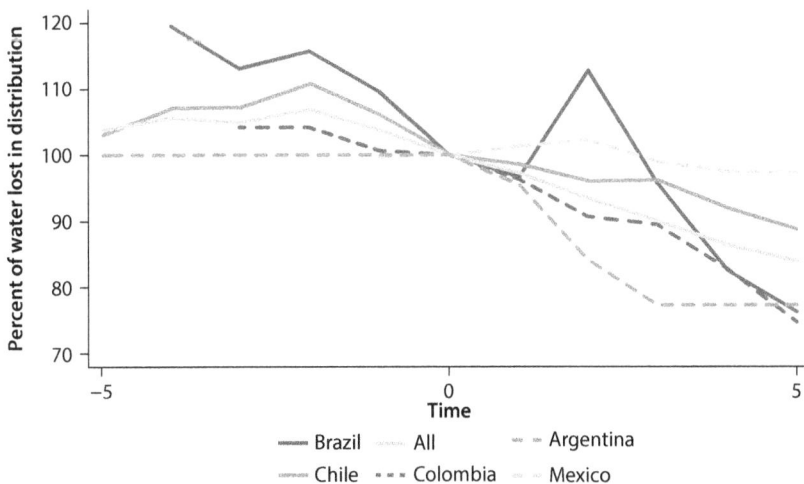

Note: $t = 0$ is the base year, the last year in which the utility was publicly owned for at least six months. The y-axis is normalized at 100 when $t = 0$.

Figure 3.12 Service Continuity and Quality of Water before, during, and after Private Sector Participation

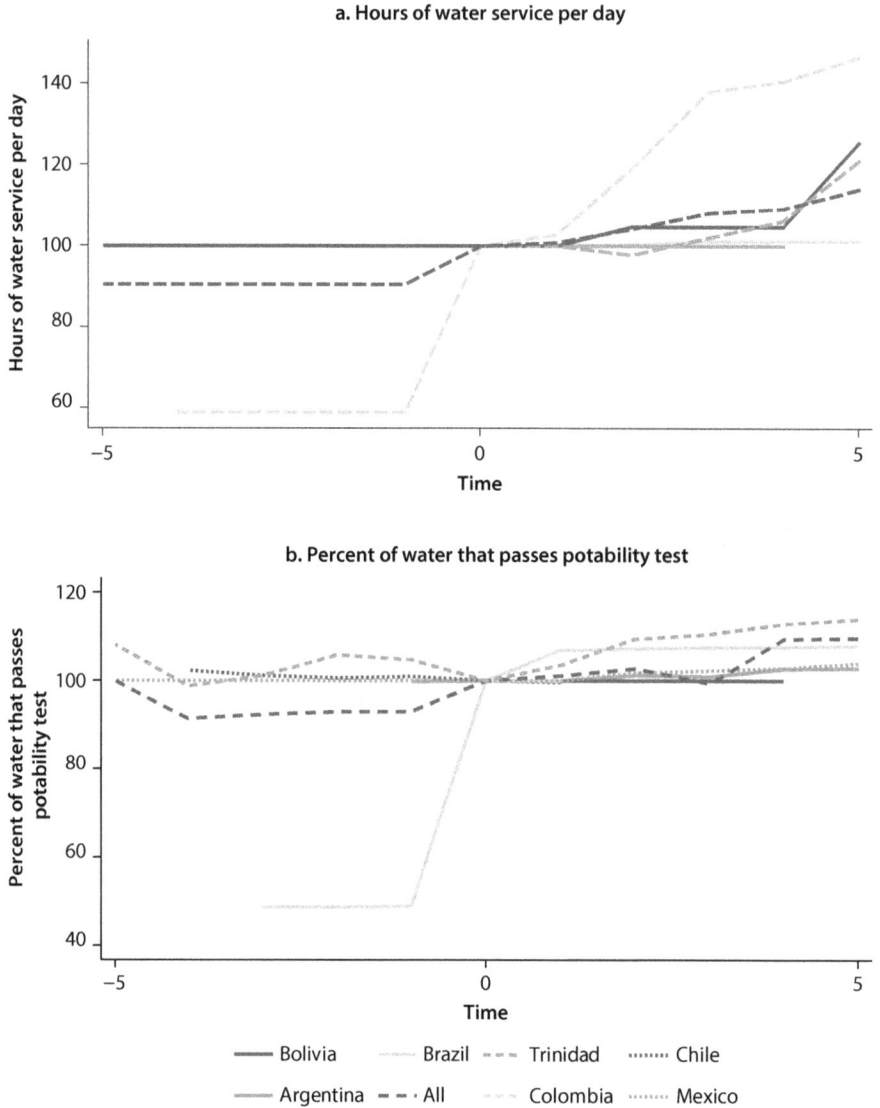

a. Hours of water service per day

b. Percent of water that passes potability test

Bolivia   Brazil   – – Trinidad   ········ Chile
Argentina   – – · All   Colombia   ········ Mexico

Note: t = 0 is the base year, the last year in which the utility was publicly owned for at least six months. The y-axis is normalized at 100 when *t* = 0.

Summary

Output and coverage of water and sewerage improved following the change in ownership, but the improvements were consistent with the existing trend. The number of employees dropped substantially during the last years of public management. These changes significantly increased labor productivity, especially during the transition period. However, labor productivity rates accelerated during the transition and decelerated in the posttransition period. Efficiency—measured by distributional losses—improved mainly after the transition. Prices for both water and sewerage rose, although the increases for sewerage were generally not robust because of the small sample size. Two measures were used for quality: the continuity of water service and the number of water samples that passed a potability test. Both measures improved in both periods, but potability improvements occurred mainly during the transition.

Impact of Private Sector Participation on Fixed-Line Telecommunications

During the 1980s and the 1990s, the state owned fixed-line telecommunications companies, which operated as monopolies in national markets. After Chile's experience in the 1980s, most countries in the region privatized their telecom companies (Andrés and others 2008). The new owners generally had to comply with requirements such as network expansion and quality standards. In exchange, they were granted a monopoly period, after which new firms could enter the market. In most countries, liberalization of the long-distance market took place within a few years after privatization. It may therefore be that the impacts attributed to private sector participation were actually caused by liberalization.

This section analyzes a data set constructed by the International Telecommunication Union (ITU) (2008) that covers 16 fixed-line telecommunication companies that were privatized.[19] Two complementary methodologies were used to examine the effects of changes in ownership: a means and medians analysis and an econometric analysis. The period under analysis is separated into three parts: the period before private sector participation (pretransition), a three-year transition period, and the period after private sector participation (posttransition).

Output

Two variables are used to measure output: the number of connections and the number of local minutes consumed each year.

Number of connections. The number of connections increased during all three periods for almost all countries (figure 3.13). Both the means and medians analysis and the econometric analysis confirmed that there were statistically significant increases in the number of connections between the pretransition, transition, and posttransition periods (see appendix tables D.4 and D.6). The econometric analysis found a 29 percent increase in the number of connections during the transition period and an additional 64 percent increase during the posttransition period.

Figure 3.13 indicates that growth in the number of connections accelerated, possibly temporarily, in the first few years of private ownership. The means and medians analysis found that average annual growth in the number of connections increased 6.9 percent in the pretransition period, 12.7 percent during the transition period, and 7.2 percent in the posttransition period. The econometric analysis found that the average annual growth rate increased 2.7 percentage points during the transition; there was no statistically significant change from that level after the transition.[20] After controlling for trends, it seems that an increase

Figure 3.13 Number of Fixed-Line Connections and Average Minutes Consumed before, during, and after Private Sector Participation

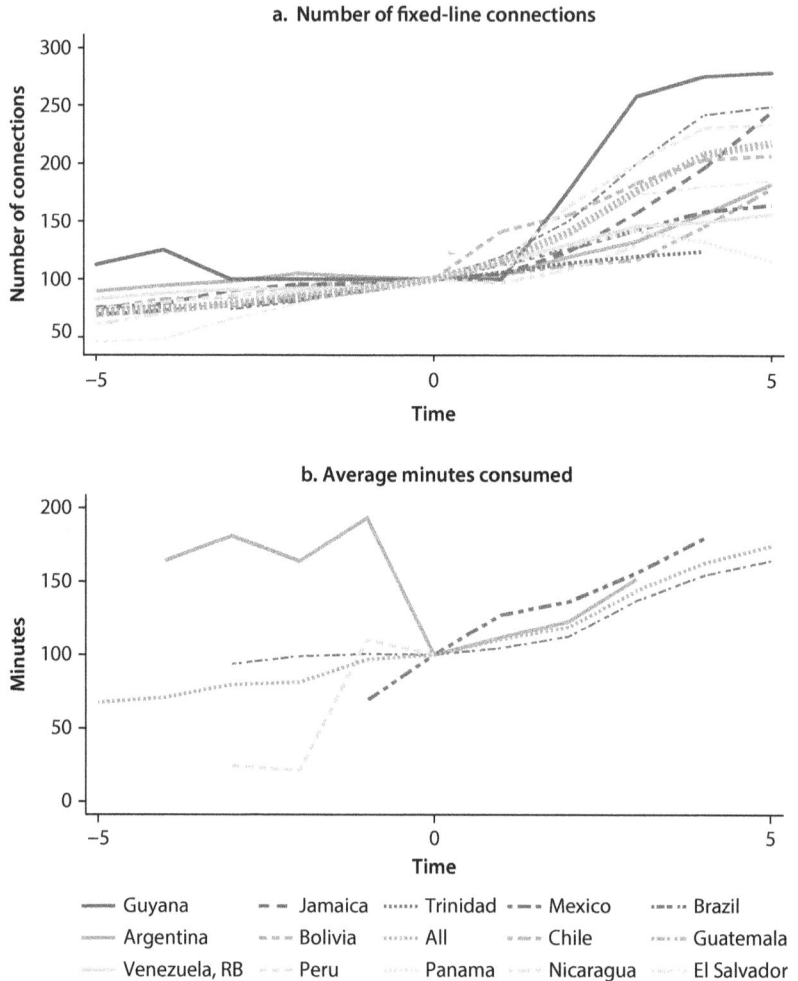

a. Number of fixed-line connections

b. Average minutes consumed

—— Guyana	— — Jamaica	······ Trinidad	—··— Mexico	···—·· Brazil
—— Argentina	— — Bolivia	······ All	·—·— Chile	—··—·· Guatemala
······ Venezuela, RB	— — Peru	······· Panama	···—·· Nicaragua	······· El Salvador

Note: t = 0 is the base year, the last year in which the utility was publicly owned for at least six months. The y-axis is normalized at 100 when *t* = 0.

occurred during the transition but that growth rates returned to normal levels after the transition.

One possible explanation for the surge in the number of connections during and shortly after the transition is that newly privatized companies took action to meet pent-up demand. According to the ITU, waiting lists for connections in the year before the reform numbered 780,000 in Argentina (26 percent of connections in operation), 308,247 in Peru (46 percent of connections in operation), and 175,000 in El Salvador (54 percent of connections in operation). Another contributing factor was the spread of mobile telecommunications, especially during the second half of the 1990s, which likely reduced the demand for new fixed connections.

In principle, private ownership in fixed-line telecommunications could shift priorities away from network expansion, because shareholders are likely to be reluctant to expand the network unless doing so is profitable or required by the contract (Ros 1999). In practice, private sector participation led to network expansion.

Number of minutes. The second output indicator is the number of minutes consumed a year. Except in Argentina, this indicator generally increased, with growth particularly strong after the transition (figure 3.13). These results are not surprising given the greater number of connections discussed above. The means and medians and econometric analyses generally confirm what can be seen in figure 3.13, although the results are not always robust because of the relatively small number of observations. The econometric analysis found statistically significant increases of 8.2 percent in the transition period and 37.6 percent during the posttransition period.[21]

When time trends are taken into account in the econometric analysis, there was no significant change during the transition period, whereas the posttransition period showed an increase of 14.2 percent over transition levels. In contrast, the regressions found statistically significant increases in growth rates of 6.9 percentage points during the transition period and 5.3 percentage points during the posttransition period. Hence, the preponderance of evidence suggests that the number of minutes of fixed-line telecom services increased in both the transition and posttransition periods after controlling for the trend.

Coverage

Consistent with the output measures, coverage (or teledensity, defined as the number of connections per 100 inhabitants) increased substantially during the periods under study (figure 3.14). The econometric analysis found an

Figure 3.14 Coverage of Fixed-Line Telecommunications before, during, and after Private Sector Participation

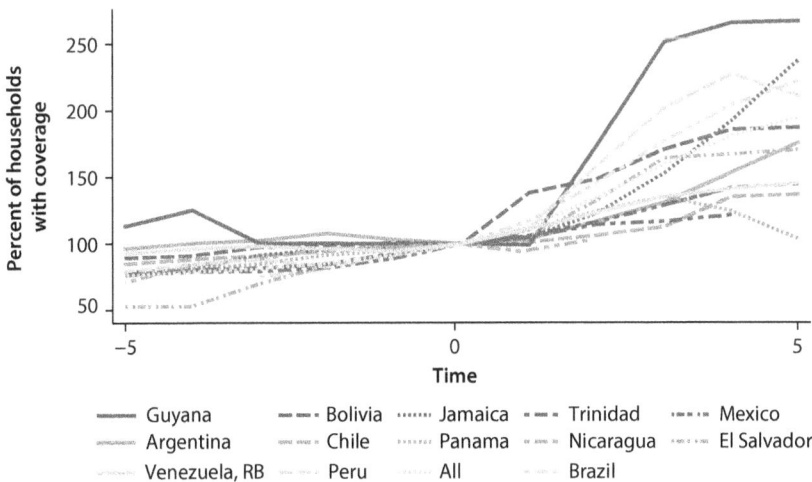

Note: $t = 0$ is the base year, the last year in which the utility was publicly owned for at least six months. The y-axis is normalized at 100 when $t = 0$.

increase of 18.3 percent during the transition period and an additional increase of 52.3 percent during the posttransition period. The means and medians analysis also found substantial statistically significant increases.

The econometric analysis found that the annual growth rate increased 3.7 percentage points during the transition period and registered no additional changes after the transition. The means and medians analysis found that the average annual growth rate increased 6.1 percentage points during the transition period and fell 5.9 percentage points (relative to transition rates) during the posttransition period.[22]

Figure 3.15 compares coverage levels across countries. Although considerable heterogeneity exists, most countries had coverage levels of 10–20 connections per 100 inhabitants.

The number of connections increased during both periods, but after controlling for trends, only the transition period showed abnormally high growth rates. After controlling for trends, the number of minutes increased in both periods, whereas increases in coverage occurred mainly in the transition period.

Labor and Labor Productivity

The number of employees declined during the transition and posttransition periods, not accounting for time trends. The average number of employees in fixed-line telecommunications companies had been declining steadily since before the transition period. This average decline masks considerable differences across firms and countries, however (figure 3.16). The econometric analysis found that employment declined 9.2 percent during the transition period and another 23.2 percent after the transition period.[23] A natural trend in employment is not expected, but employment growth rates became increasingly negative during the transition and posttransition periods. The econometric

Figure 3.15 Coverage Levels of Fixed-Line Telecommunications before and after Private Sector Participation

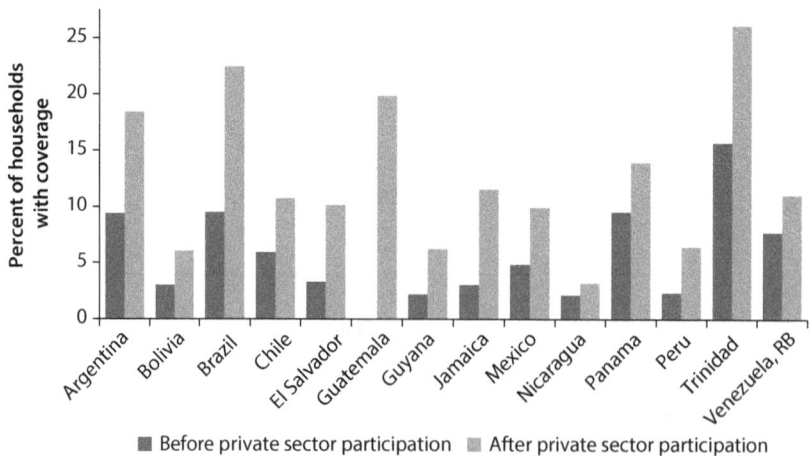

Source: Andrés and others 2008.

Figure 3.16 Number of Employees in the Fixed-Line Telecommunication Sector before, during, and after Private Sector Participation

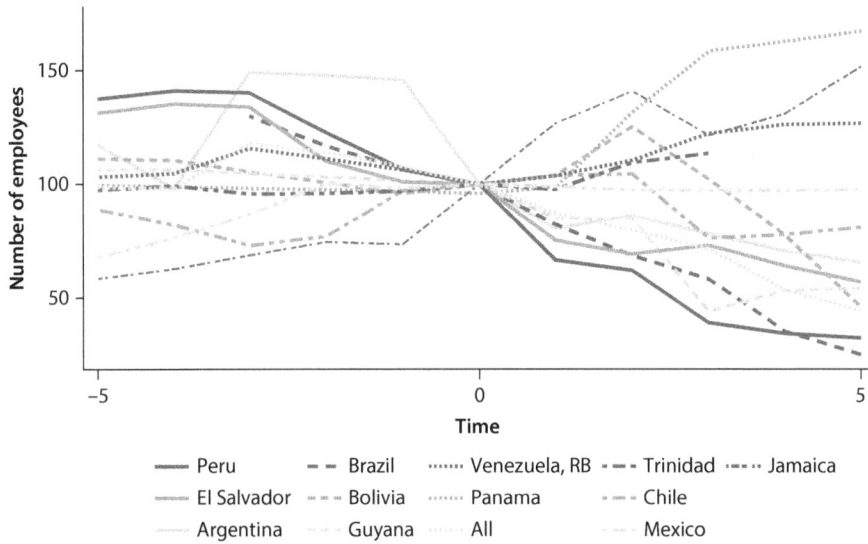

analysis found that during the transition, the annual growth rate of employment was 4.1 percentage points lower than during the previous period; annual growth fell an additional 2.6 percentage points after the transition.

One reason for the decline in employment during the transition period is that governments decided to trim the labor force before the ownership change, with the intention of increasing the value of the firm and bringing employment to a more sustainable level. Investors proved indifferent to these policies, and in the end the value of the firm remained at the same level or even declined when the government applied layoff programs in advance. One explanation is selection issues, which provide incentives for good employees to leave and bad employees to remain with the company (Chong and López-de-Silanes 2003).

Two indicators were used to measure labor productivity: connections per employee and minutes per employee. As a consequence of the increase in the output measures and the general negative trend in the number of employees, labor productivity improved substantially, especially after the transition (figure 3.17). Almost all countries in the data set at least doubled labor productivity within five years of reform. The single exception was Panama, which already had relatively high teledensity (at the time of the reform, Panama's teledensity was 13 percent; teledensity was 3 percent in Nicaragua, 4 percent in Guatemala, and 6 percent in El Salvador).[24]

According to the econometric analysis, the number of connections per employee increased 35.1 percent during the transition (compared with the pre-transition period) and a whopping 106.9 percent after the transition. The results of the means and medians analysis were even more impressive: the increase during the transition was 65.6 percent, and the increase after the transition was 117.9 percent (see appendix table D.4). All changes were statistically significant.

Figure 3.17 Labor Productivity in Fixed-Line Telecommunications before, during, and after Private Sector Participation

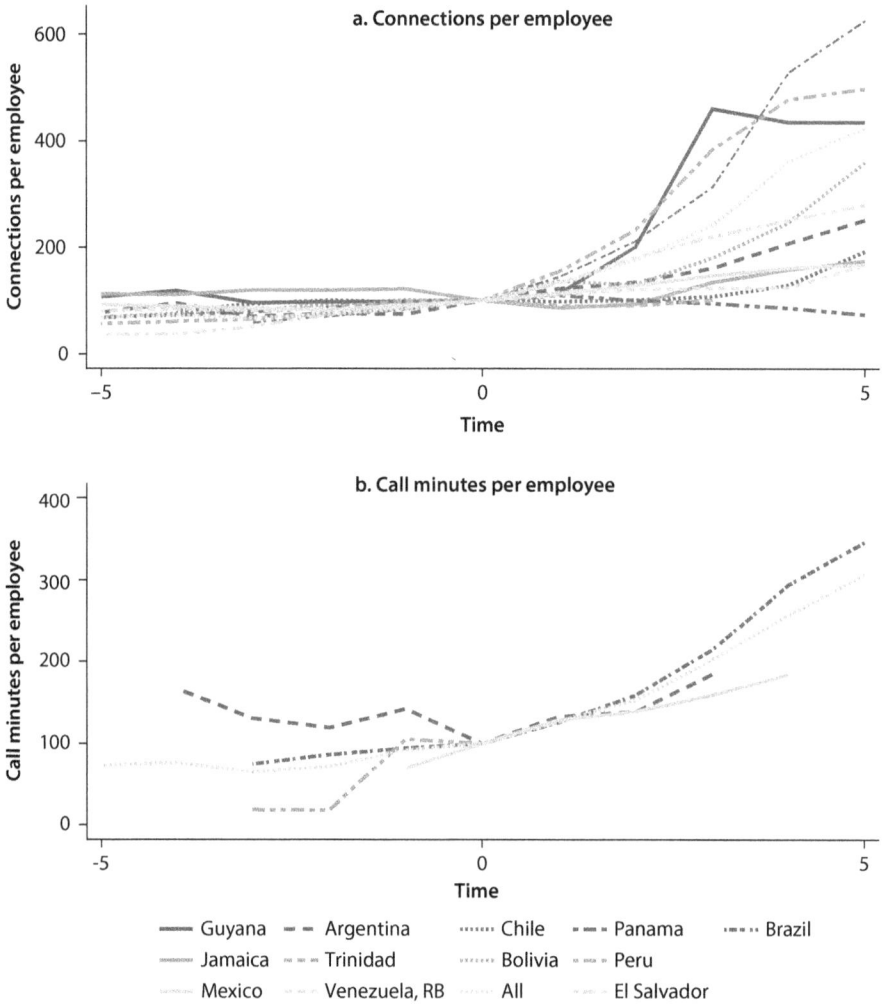

a. Connections per employee

b. Call minutes per employee

Guyana	Argentina	Chile	Panama	Brazil
Jamaica	Trinidad	Bolivia	Peru	
Mexico	Venezuela, RB	All	El Salvador	

Note: $t = 0$ is the base year, the last year in which the utility was publicly owned for at least six months. The y-axis is normalized at 100 when $t = 0$.

Fewer data were available for minutes per employee, but the econometric analysis still found impressive statistically significant improvements: 32.0 percent during the transition and an additional 92.9 percent after the transition. The means and medians analysis found even larger increases: 43.2 percent during the transition and 117.2 percent after the transition.

Controlling for trends dramatically reduces the impact of private sector participation on labor productivity (see appendix D). It is appropriate to look at the changes in trends given the underlying indicators: in the previous sections, it was argued that the output indicators follow natural trends, but the number of employees does not. One way to examine trend changes is through growth rates.

In this case, the annual number of connections per employee rose by 7 percentage points during the transition period and 3.3 percentage points after the transition. Minutes per employee increased 8.5 percentage points during the transition period and registered no additional statistically significant changes during the posttransition period.

Actual (not normalized) labor productivity measures show large variance across countries. Brazil is by far the most productive country, with more than 1,000 connections per employee during the posttransition period. The next-closest country, Bolivia, had less than half that number. The number of minutes per employee in Brazil vastly exceeds that of other countries.

Prices

Three measures of fixed-line telecommunications prices were analyzed, in both dollars and real local currency: the average price of a three-minute local call, the average monthly charge for residential service, and the average charge for installing a residential line. The average price of a three-minute local call mainly increased during public ownership. One exception was Chile, which experienced a steep decline in prices leading up to the ownership change. On average, however, prices increased during the first part of the transition, reaching a high point during the last year of public ownership. Prices then began to fall, but not as rapidly as the increases of previous years (figure 3.18). Trends in U.S. dollars and real local currency followed roughly similar patterns, although the 1999 devaluation in Brazil introduced some variation.

The econometric analysis found that average prices in both dollars and real local currency for a three-minute call increased roughly 45 percent. There were no significant changes during the posttransition period. The means and medians analysis did not find any statistically significant changes during either period.

Monthly charges for residential service increased significantly during and after the transition, in both dollars and real local currency. The changes were largest during the transition: prices rose 75.9 percent in dollars and 62.6 percent in real local currency. After the transition, both dollar and real local currency prices were roughly 22 percent higher than transition levels. The means and medians analysis also increased significantly (see appendix table D.4). Judging from figure 3.18 and the econometric trend analysis, it appears that residential monthly charges experienced an abnormal increase during the transition before returning to a slower rate of growth similar to the pretransition period.

The analysis of average installation charges for a residential line produced somewhat mixed results, although the preponderance of evidence suggests that prices declined during the transition and posttransition periods. Panels e and f of figure 3.18 show a big drop in installation charges during the transition and more modest declines after that. The means and medians analysis found a large statistically significant drop during the transition period; the drop during the posttransition period was not significant. The econometric analysis found the reverse: the drop during the transition was not significant, whereas the drop during the posttransition period was significant and roughly

Figure 3.18 Price of a Fixed-Line Telecommunications Service before, during, and after Private Sector Participation

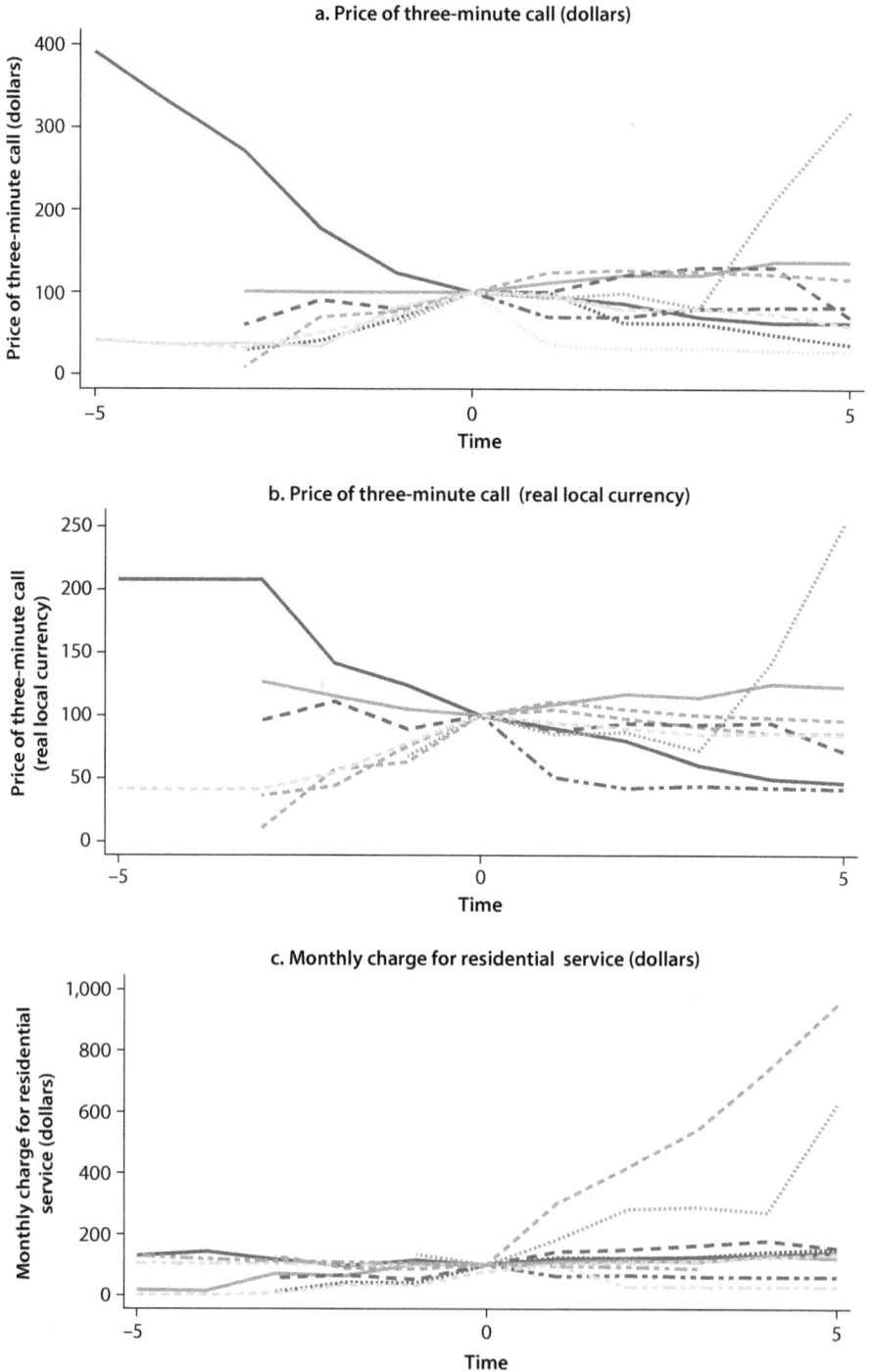

a. Price of three-minute call (dollars)

b. Price of three-minute call (real local currency)

c. Monthly charge for residential service (dollars)

figure continues next page

Figure 3.18 Price of a Fixed-Line Telecommunications Service before, during, and after Private Sector Participation *(continued)*

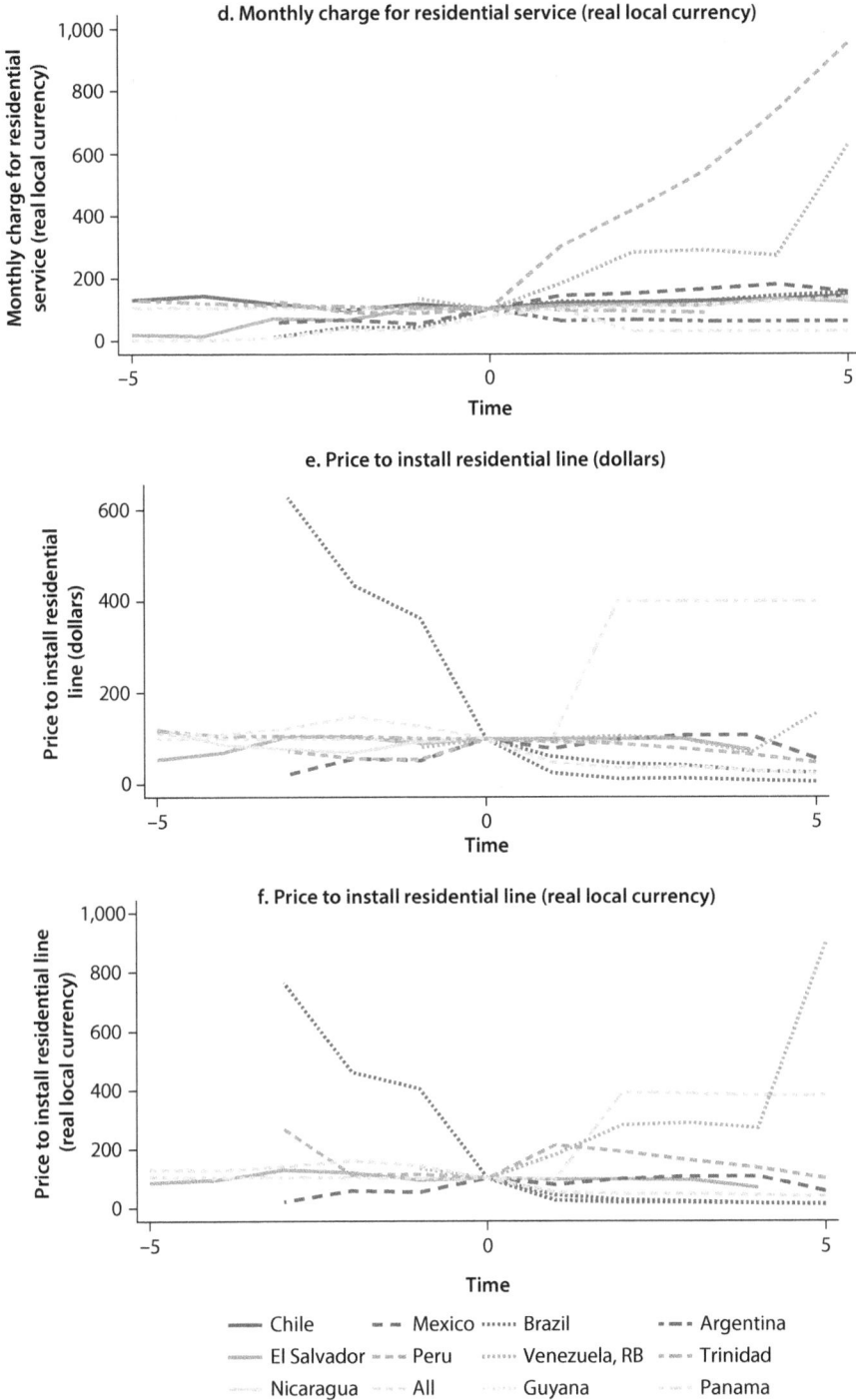

d. Monthly charge for residential service (real local currency)

y-axis: Monthly charge for residential service (real local currency) — 0, 200, 400, 600, 800, 1,000

x-axis: Time — −5, 0, 5

e. Price to install residential line (dollars)

y-axis: Price to install residential line (dollars) — 0, 200, 400, 600

x-axis: Time — −5, 0, 5

f. Price to install residential line (real local currency)

y-axis: Price to install residential line (real local currency) — 0, 200, 400, 600, 800, 1,000

x-axis: Time — −5, 0, 5

Legend:
— Chile   – – Mexico   ⋯⋯ Brazil   –·· Argentina
El Salvador   –·– Peru   ⋯⋯ Venezuela, RB   –·– Trinidad
Nicaragua   – – All   ⋯⋯ Guyana   Panama

Note: $t = 0$ is the base year, the last year in which the utility was publicly owned for at least six months. The y-axis is normalized at 100 when $t = 0$.

Uncovering the Drivers of Utility Performance • http://dx.doi.org/10.1596/978-0-8213-9660-5

25 percent in both dollars and real local currency. There were no significant changes in the growth rate.

Service Quality

The percentage of incomplete calls was chosen as the most feasible measure of efficiency. Although considerable heterogeneity exists across countries, the average percentage of incomplete calls declined (figure 3.19) Despite a relatively small number of observations, the econometric analysis confirmed that there was a statistically significant drop of 29.7 percent in the posttransition period. Neither the econometric results from the transition period nor the results of the means and medians analysis were statistically significant.

Figure 3.19 Quality of Fixed-Line Communications before, during, and after Private Sector Participation

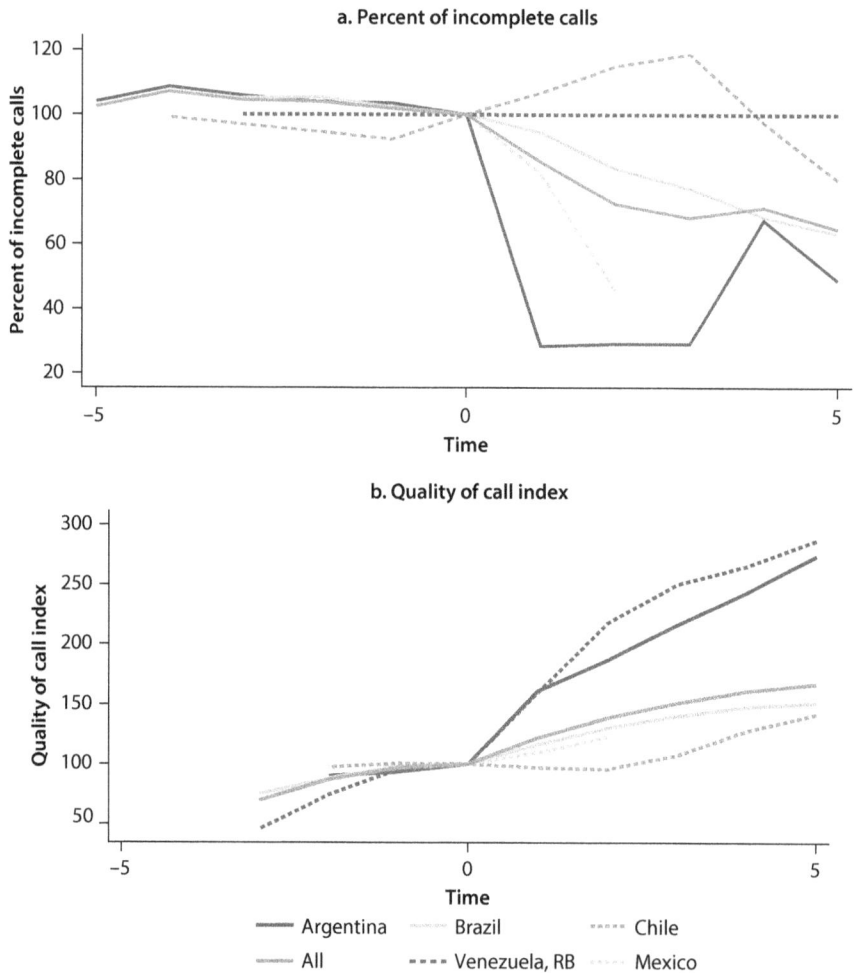

Note: $t = 0$ is the base year, the last year in which the utility was publicly owned for at least six months. The y-axis is normalized at 100 when $t = 0$.

The network digitization percentage was selected as a proxy for quality in fixed-line telecommunications. Network digitization increased during the transition and posttransition periods, with the largest increase coming during the transition, not controlling for time trends. The econometric analysis found increases of 36.3 percent during the transition and 58.1 percent after the transition. Similarly, the means and medians analysis found increases of 75.4 percent in the transition and 69.5 percent during the posttransition period.

A natural trend is not assumed, but it is still interesting to control for trends and examine growth rate changes. The econometric analysis found that after controlling for firm-specific time trends, there was a statistically significant increase of 4.9 percent during the transition period; there was no significant change after the transition. The econometric growth analysis found a 5.6 percentage point decline in the average annual growth rate after the transition but no significant change during the transition.

A quality index was created that combines the percentage of completed calls and the share of the network that was digitized. This index steadily increased across all periods. Quality levels after the transition were generally comparable across countries (see figure 3.19). Network digitization increased during both periods, with the largest increase coming during the transition.

Summary
The change in ownership in the fixed-line telecommunication sector generally increased output and coverage, even after controlling for firm-specific time trends in the sector. Employment fell and labor productivity increased during the transition and posttransition periods; efficiency (the percentage of incomplete calls) improved during the posttransition period. Prices showed mixed results: the price of a local call increased during the transition, residential monthly charges increased in both periods, and installation charges decreased in both periods. Quality—as measured by network digitization—improved.

Impact of Contract Design

This section deepens the analysis by introducing a number of private sector participation contract and process variables. The variables come from a World Bank data set of nearly 1,000 infrastructure transactions in LAC between 1989 and 2002 (see appendix B). This data set was merged with the data sets containing performance information on utilities in order to identify whether private sector participation characteristics such as the sale method, investor nationality, and award criteria affect the performance variables discussed in previous sections.

The main aim of this section is not to advocate a certain type of contract design but to emphasize that private sector participation is not simply a yes-no decision. Indeed, different contract design variables can have different effects on each performance outcome. The results in this section show that, depending on the priorities of a country, some contract characteristics may be more important than others.

There are many reasons to suspect that characteristics of the private sector participation process and regulatory environment would affect firm performance during and after the transition to private ownership. Large unexplained differences in performance across firms were found. For instance, large declines in employment occurred during both the transition and posttransition periods in the electricity distribution sector. However, some firms experienced much larger declines than others. These large performance differences suggest that differences in private sector participation procedures or the regulatory environment may have played a significant role.

The three sectors were pooled to maximize the amount of variation in the data set.[25] (For more details on the data and methodology, see appendix A.[26]) Results from two time periods are analyzed: changes between the period before the transition to private ownership and the transition period and changes between the transition and posttransition periods. Overall changes are not reported. Rather, the changes shown are relative to the base case for each variable (table 3.2). For instance, when it is reported that the number of connections per 100 households increased from 5.8 to 6.8 when an auction process was used, this change is relative to cases in which auctions were not used—"no auction" being the base case.

The effect of contract characteristics can be summarized as follows:

- *Sale method.* Auctions were associated with lower sector employment and higher quality, by fairly large amounts. They were associated with price increases during the transition and price decreases after the transition, as well as reductions in distributional losses after the transition.

- *Investor nationality.* The presence of only foreign investors was associated with a decline in output during both periods, lower coverage during the transition, lower sector employment during the transition, and lower distributional losses after the transition. Average dollar prices seem to have increased during both periods, and prices in real local currency first decreased then increased. When both foreign and local investors were involved, employment fell during both periods, distributional losses fell after the transition, prices in dollars first fell then rose, and quality improved.

Table 3.2 Base Case for Regulatory and Contract Variables

Category	Variable	Base case
Sale method	Auction	No auction
Investor nationality	Foreign only; foreign and local	Local only
Award criteria	Highest price; best investment plan	Other criteria
Tariff regulation	Rate of return; price cap	Other regulation

Source: Andrés and others 2008.

- *Award criteria*. When concessions were awarded according to the best invest-ment plan, employment fell substantially during both periods, prices in dollars rose after the transition, and prices in real local currency fell during the transi-tion. When concessions were awarded based on the highest price, the number of connections fell slightly during the transition, coverage first fell slightly then increased, the number of employees fell substantially, and prices in real local currency fell moderately during both periods.

- *Tariff regulation*. Price-cap tariff regulation was associated with slight increases in output and quality and slight declines in sector employment and labor productivity all during the transition. Distributional losses increased after the transition, and prices in real local currency increased during both periods. Rate of return regulation was associated with a moderate increase in the number of connections and a slight increase in coverage during the transition, as well as lower sector employment during both periods. Distributional losses fell after the transition, and prices in dollars first increased then decreased.

Three messages emerge from this analysis:

- Contract characteristics matter: the way private sector participation pro-cessses are undertaken can create significant performance differences.
- Each contract characteristic affects each performance variable differently. A certain contract characteristic could have a positive influence on one per-formance variable and a negative or insignificant impact on another.
- Some contract variables have greater impacts than others.

Conclusions

Private sector participation in LAC was associated with significant improvements in sector performance, including consistent improvements in efficiency and quality and reductions in the workforce. There do not appear to have been significant impacts on output and coverage. Prices tended to increase somewhat, although the picture is highly variable across sectors.

The differences between publicly and privately operated distribution utilities showed up primarily with regard to labor productivity, distribution losses, quality of service, and tariffs. Other indicators, such as coverage and operational expendi-tures, were similar in public and private utilities. Although private sector partici-pation had positive effects, the bottom decile of performers in the public utility group underperformed the average private utility, and the bottom decile of per-formers in the private utility group underperformed the average public utility.

Both groups of utilities had similar starting values for labor productivity and distribution losses. Following the change in ownership, the performance of the privatized group improved substantially. Labor productivity ended up being twice as high in private utilities. In the case of distribution losses, private utilities improved their performance 12 percent whereas public utilities saw their performance deteriorate 5 percent. With regard to continuity of service, both groups started at about 24 interruptions a year. Private utilities reduced this number to about 12, whereas public utilities reduced it to about 19. Similarly, public utilities saw the average duration of their outages increase almost 50 percent, compared with a reduction of almost 30 percent at private utilities, from similar starting values.

The results of private sector participation depend on the way the reform is designed. Key dimensions include sale method, award criteria, nationality of the firm, and details of the subsequent regulatory framework, including the degree of autonomy of any regulatory body and the principles used to set tariffs. Each of these aspects can significantly affect the incentives faced by the private party and, hence, the enterprise behavior reviewed above.

Notes

1. This chapter draws heavily on Andrés and others (2008).

2. The four main types of private participation in infrastructure are management and lease contracts, concessions, greenfield projects, and divestitures. In this chapter, the terms *private participation in infrastructure* and *privatization* are used interchangeably to cover all four types.

3. An exception is Panama, where only about 40 percent of the population expressed discontent with private sector participation in 1998 (Andrés and others 2007).

4. As shown in the chapter 2, there is significant variation in performance within both groups. The top 10 percent of performers in the public utility group outperformed the average private utility, and the average private utility outperformed the bottom 10 percent of the private utility group.

5. The transition period is defined as starting two years before the award of the concession—an approximation of when the reform was announced—and ending one year after the award. The pretransition period or the period before private sector participation refers to the three years before the transition period. The posttransition period or the period after private sector participation refers to the four years after the transition.

6. These increases were statistically significant by both the means and median analysis (appendix table D.1) and the econometric analysis (appendix table D.3).

7. In the rest of the chapter, "average" for a given variable refers to the simple average within the country.

8. Several reasons may account for this decline, as discussed later in this chapter. First, the average consumption per household may have declined, because of the increase in prices. Second, the composition of the average household may have changed. Among households that were not connected after a concession was awarded, most were probably low-income families, with below-average energy consumption. Third, distributional technical and commercial losses may have fallen, reducing the volume of energy sold.

9. These increases were statistically significant in both the means and median analysis (appendix table D.1) and the econometric analysis (appendix table D.3).

10. Statistically significant drops were found by both the means and median analysis (appendix tables D.1 and D.2) and the econometric analysis (appendix table D.3).

11. The means and medians analysis found similar results: the mean number of employees during the transition was 38 percent lower than before the transition, and the mean number of employees after the transition was 14 percent lower than during the transition (see appendix table D.1).

12. The increases were found to be statistically significant by both the means and median analysis (appendix tables D.1 and D.2) and the econometric analysis (appendix table D.3).

13. All of these declines in interruptions were statistically significant.

14. The means and medians analysis found a 23 percent drop in the duration of interruptions between the pretransition and transition periods and a 25 percent drop between the transition and posttransition periods. Both of these declines were statistically significant. The frequency of interruptions fell 26 percent between the pretransition and posttransition periods; no statistically significant change occurred between the transition and posttransition periods (see appendix table D.1).

15. The results for the output, coverage, and labor productivity indicators are reported after controlling for time trends. A natural increase is expected for each of these variables, regardless of whether ownership is public or private.

16. When actual (as opposed to normalized) water connection numbers are considered, Argentina and Chile have the largest water distribution companies. For sewerage, Argentina, Chile, and Colombia have companies of roughly the same size. In contrast, the electricity, water and sewerage companies in Brazil and Mexico fall at the small end of the spectrum (Andrés and others 2008).

17. The only significant result of the means and medians analysis was a drop of roughly 3 percent in the mean amount of water produced between the transition and posttransition periods.

18. Although a natural trend in employment is not expected, the numbers after controlling for trends are reported in appendix C.

19. As of 2009, only six countries remained with public telecommunications companies: Colombia, Costa Rica, Ecuador, Honduras, Paraguay, and Uruguay. For a description of the data set, see appendix B.

20. Results from the econometric analysis that controls for firm-specific time trends tell a somewhat different story. The number of connections fell 4.9 percent during the transition, then increased 12.0 percent after the transition (with respect to transition levels). This model specification is less useful in this case, however, given the fluctuating nature of the underlying data.

21. The means and medians analysis did not find a statistically significant difference between the pretransition and transition periods. Based on two observations, the analysis found that the average number of minutes was 40 percent higher during the posttransition period than during the transition period (see appendix table D.4).

22. The econometric analysis that controlled for firm-specific time trends found that coverage fell 6.3 percent during the transition and then increased 9.5 percent during the posttransition period. This model specification may be less applicable, however, given the shape of the underlying data (that is, the time trend analysis becomes less accurate when there is more than one shift in the presumed trend).

23. The means and medians analysis found that employment fell 14.5 percent during the transition and 18.2 percent more after the transition. All of these changes were statistically significant.

24. Panama actually had more connections in 1998 than in 2003. In 1998, 419,000 subscribers had fixed connections; at the end of 2003, only 380,000 had fixed connections. Not surprisingly, mobile telecommunications proliferated during this time. In fact, the number of mobile subscribers surpassed the number of fixed-line subscribers, jumping from 49,000 in 1998 to 834,000 in 2003 (ITU 2004).

25. The models were run for each sector separately (these tables are available upon request); results were qualitatively similar to the results presented here (see Andrés and others 2008 for details).

26. The econometric analysis included several regression specifications using different combinations of independent variables (that is, for each performance variable, the impact of each contract variable was tested while controlling for different combinations of other contract variables). Controlling for other contract variables addresses collinearity issues, but it tends to reduce the number of statistically significant results. Multiple regression specifications can also produce a range of results. For this reason, the following sections mention either a range of impacts or mixed results. Andrés and others (2008) report the minimum and maximum percentage changes in each performance variable disaggregated by the contract variables.

References

Andrés, L., V. Foster, and J. L. Guasch. 2006. "The Impact of Privatization on the Performance of the Infrastructure Sector: The Case of Electricity Distribution in Latin American Countries." Policy Research Working Paper 3936, World Bank, Washington, DC.

Andrés, L., J. L. Guasch, M. Diop, and S. L. Azumendi. 2007. "Assessing the Governance of Electricity Regulatory Agencies in the Latin American and the Caribbean Region: A Benchmarking Analysis." Policy Research Working Paper 4380, World Bank, Washington, DC.

Andrés, L., J. L. Guasch, V. Foster, and T. Haven. 2008. *The Impact of Private Sector Participation in Infrastructure: Lights, Shadows, and the Road Ahead.* Washington, DC: World Bank.

Boix, C. 2005. "Privatization and Public Discontent in Latin America." Background paper commissioned for Marianne Fay and Mary Morrison, 2007, *Infrastructure in Latin America and the Caribbean: Recent Developments and Key Challenges.* Directions in Development. Washington, DC: World Bank.

Briceño-Garmendia, C., A. Estache, and N. Shafik. 2004. "Infrastructure Services in Developing Countries: Access, Quality, Costs and Policy Reform." Policy Research Working Paper 3468, World Bank, Washington, DC.

Calderón, C., and L. Servén. 2004. "The Effects of Infrastructure Development on Growth and Income Distribution." Policy Research Working Paper 3400, World Bank, Washington, DC.

Chong, A., and F. López-de-Silanes. 2003. "The Truth about Privatization in Latin America." Latin American Research Network, Research Network Working Paper R-486, Inter-American Development Bank, Washington, DC.

De Ferranti, D., G. E. Perry, F. H. G. Ferreira, and M. Walton. 2004. *Inequality in Latin America: Breaking with History?* Washington, DC: World Bank.

Fay, M., and M. Morrison. 2006. *Infrastructure in Latin America and the Caribbean: Recent Developments and Key Challenges.* Washington, DC: World Bank.

Harris, C. 2003. "Private Participation in Infrastructure in Developing Countries: Trends, Impacts and Policy Lessons." Working Paper 5, World Bank, Washington, DC.

ITU (International Telecommunications Union). 2008. "World Telecommunication/ICT Indicators Database." CD-Rom, 12th edition. Geneva: ITU.

_____. 2009. "World Telecommunication/ICT Indicators Database." Geneva.

Martimort, D., and S. Straub. 2005. "The Political Economy of Private Participation, Social Discontent and Regulatory Governance." Background paper commissioned for Marianne Fay and Mary Morrison, 2007, *Infrastructure in Latin America and the Caribbean: Recent Developments and Key Challenges.* Directions in Development. Washington, DC: World Bank.

Ros, A. 1999. "Does Ownership or Competition Matter? The Effects of Telecommunications Reform on the Network Expansion and Efficiency." *Journal of Regulatory Economics* 15 (1): 65–92.

Schwartz, J., L. Andrés, and G. Dragoiu. 2009. "Crisis in Latin America: Infrastructure Investment, Employment and the Expectations of Stimulus," *Journal of Infrastructure Development* 1(2) (December): 111–31.

World Bank. 2007. Private Participation in Infrastructure Projects: PPP Database. Washington, DC. http://ppi.worldbank.org/.

CHAPTER 4

Regulatory Institutional Design and Sector Performance

This chapter explores the governance of independent regulatory agencies (IRAs) in the water and electricity distribution sectors and the link between the governance of IRAs and the performance of both sectors. The first part of the chapter analyzes the institutional design of regulatory agencies. It compares the different governance modes of IRAs based on various measures of autonomy, transparency, accountability, and tools. Measures of agencies' governance are the result of both formal and informal practices of IRAs. The second part of the chapter describes the methodology and presents the results on the correlation between institutional design and sector performance.

The analysis first focuses on the institutional design of IRAs. It attempts to determine the inputs or characteristics that contribute to greater autonomy and accountability. The presence of these features does not, of course, guarantee that either autonomy or accountability improves.

The second phase of this work involves the application of techniques used in qualitative comparative politics to address issues of causality, sequencing, and complex interaction effects that better explain IRAs in policy making. The approach is used to capture aspects of the governance of IRAs that can be assessed against sector performance.

Most of the literature on the governance of IRAs in Latin America and the Caribbean (LAC) has been conducted with the goal of comparing countries in the region in terms of formal attributes of IRAs. Analysis of causality is at best limited.

IRAs are more widespread in LAC than in other developing regions (Sosay and Zenginobuz 2005). Created within the context of wide private sector participation programs, they were the chosen institutional arrangement to insulate decision making in various economic sectors, such as infrastructure, from political intervention (Thatcher 2007). After the unbundling of the electricity industry, regulatory agencies were assigned the task of enforcing concession contracts and protecting consumers. Between 1993 (when

Argentina established the National Electricity Regulatory Agency) and 2001 (when Barbados established the Fair Trading Commission), 70 percent of the countries in the region established separate entities regulating electricity markets, with different degrees of independence (Andrés and others 2007).

There is a growing consensus that institutions matter for growth and development (Aron 2000; Rodrick 2004). This chapter emphasizes the positive externalities associated with the presence and good governance of an independent regulatory agency.

Benchmarking

Benchmarking Regulatory Institutional Design

Studies of regulatory agencies in the infrastructure sector have considered the U.S. model of independent commissions as their benchmark of comparison and analysis. An institutional design model that emphasizes agencies that make decisions independently of the executive branch, are subject to the accountability of the parliament, and have budgeting autonomy has emerged as the paradigm of an infrastructure regulator.

The literature has dealt with the design of regulatory agencies in two ways: by focusing only on independence and by considering accountability and transparency as well. The first attempts to evaluate infrastructure regulatory agencies assessed the independence of central banks (Stern and Cubbin 2005; Oliveira and others 2005). For this reason, the original emphasis was on agencies' independence; less attention was paid to other aspects, such as accountability and transparency.

The evolution of the subject and the initial stages of agencies' functioning changed the original approach and introduced more comprehensive strategies to assessment. A different approach (OECD 1999) involves the consideration of mechanisms to achieve high-quality regulation, such as cost-benefit analysis of regulations and administrative simplification.

Stern and Holder (1999) develop a framework for assessing the governance of economic regulators in several sectors in six developing Asian economies. Gilardi (2002) develops an independence index covering regulators from five sectors in seven European countries. He also proposes three ways of evaluating independent regulators. Johannsen (2003) measures the formal independence of energy regulators in eight European countries. Gutiérrez (2003) develops a regulatory framework to assess the evolution of regulatory governance in the telecommunications sector between 1980 and 2001 in 25 LAC countries. They attempt to measure informal regulation. Three comprehensive approaches to assessing the governance of regulatory agencies have been developed by Brown and others (2006), Correa and others (2006), and Andrés and others (2007). Correa and others provide a detailed analysis of Brazilian regulatory agencies. Brown and others develop a framework to assess the effectiveness of a regulatory system. Andrés and others develop a framework for LAC that is discussed more in detail in this chapter.

This chapter defines regulatory governance as the institutional design and structure of the agency that allows it to carry out its functions as an independent regulator. Based on selected literature on the subject, the chapter defines and assesses regulatory agencies' governance according to four main characteristics: autonomy from political authorities and autonomy of their management and regulatory competencies; transparency before institutional and noninstitutional stakeholders; accountability to the three branches of government (executive, legislative, and judiciary); and tools and capacities for the conduct of the regulatory policy and the improvement of its institutional development.

The governance of IRAs is measured by a main aggregated index and other indexes covering different aspects of governance.[1] Indexes were built with data from a survey completed by 19 countries of the electricity distribution and water and sanitation sectors.[2] Responses from the survey covered 43 electricity and 28 water regulatory agencies, which cover more than 90 percent of consumers in the region. All LAC countries except Chile and Colombia have introduced regulatory agencies in which the agency has both regulatory and oversight responsibilities, with different degrees of independence from the government.[3]

Regulatory agencies are viewed here as both public bodies that are part of the public administration (and as such in charge of the delivery of public services) and instruments with which to implement regulatory policies. The analysis therefore draws on both the literature on infrastructure agencies' designs and notions and tools of public sector governance applied to decentralized structures of government.

Figure 4.1 presents the framework used to assess the governance of IRAs. Only an institutional perspective of accountability, as defined by the relationships of the agency with the executive, legislative, and judiciary branches of government, is considered. Autonomy is divided into political, managerial, and regulatory autonomy; transparency is divided into social and institutional transparency; and tools are divided into regulatory and institutional tools.

Variables for agencies' governance reflect not only formal aspects (procedures and tools established in the agency's statute or laws) but also the practices that derive from their implementation (informal regulation). Indicators for the informal elements of autonomy, accountability, and transparency represent the operationalization of some aspects of these variables. The variable "tools" is excluded from this analysis, because the mere existence of these instruments implies their implementation.

The first variable of agencies' regulatory governance is autonomy, defined as the procedures, mechanisms, and instruments aimed at guaranteeing the independence of the agency from political authorities (political autonomy), the autonomous management of its resources (managerial autonomy), and the regulation of the sector (regulatory autonomy). Political autonomy represents the level of independence of the agency from government authorities. It is measured by indicators that reflect the autonomy of the agency's decision making. Managerial autonomy involves the freedom of the agency to determine the administration of its resources. It is measured by indicators that reflect

Figure 4.1 Framework for Assessing Governance of Independent Regulatory Agencies

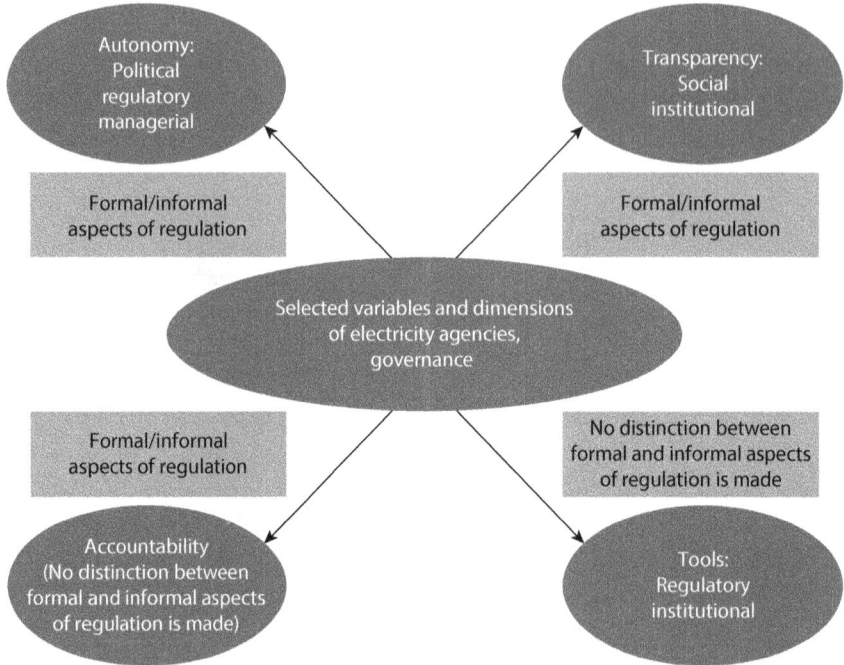

Source: Andrés and others 2007.

the powers of the agency to determine its organizational structure and the use of its budget. Regulatory autonomy is defined by the extension of the agency's regulatory powers in the electricity sector. It is represented by indicators that capture agencies' responsibilities in electricity regulation.

The second aspect of an agency's governance is accountability, defined as the procedures, mechanisms, and instruments aimed at guaranteeing an adequate level of control of the agency's budget and performance by political authorities (the parliament). The accountability of the agency before the parliament is prioritized for two reasons. First, the institutional design model adopted is that of a U.S. independent commission, where agencies are subject to congressional oversight. Second, the history of political interference of LAC line ministries in utilities underscores the importance of including other political stakeholders, such as the parliament, in the regulatory process. An institutional perspective of accountability is considered only as defined by the relationships of the agency with the three branches of government (executive, legislative, and judiciary); the variable is further disaggregated.

The third variable is transparency, defined as the procedures, mechanisms, and instruments aimed at guaranteeing the disclosure and publication of relevant regulatory and institutional information, the participation of stakeholders in the agency's regulatory decisions and decision making, and the application of rules aimed at governing the integrity and behavior of agency officials. Two dimensions of transparency are examined: social transparency and institutional transparency. *Social transparency* is composed of indicators related to the involvement of noninstitutional actors in the agency's policy making, including their access to the agency's information. *Institutional transparency* is composed of indicators related to the transparent management of the agency that are not directly linked to stakeholder involvement. It includes issues such as the publication of the agency's annual report, the use of norms of ethics, and the existence of public examinations for hiring employees.

The fourth variable is tools, defined as the instruments and mechanisms that contribute to the strengthening of different aspects of an agency's functioning and the quality of its regulations. This variable includes not only regulatory tools (for example, mechanisms for tariff revision, regulatory accountability, and instruments for monitoring technical standards) but also instruments aimed at improving the institutional quality of the agency (for example, audits of agencies' accounts, electronic files for consumer complaints, performance-based payments for employees, and regulatory quality standards). This is the only variable whose analysis does not consider its formal and informal aspects; the mere existence of agencies' tools implies their implementation.

Benchmarking Governance at the Regional Level

LAC presents a wide spectrum of institutional design in its regulatory agencies. A regional analysis of regulatory governance indicates the prevalence of autonomy over the other variables, with tools as the index's component with the lowest score. Most independent regulators in the electricity sector have a board of directors appointed by the president with the authorization of the parliament, a separate status from the line ministry, and separate budgeting (although there are different levels of autonomy in the management of funds). The lowest levels of autonomy can be found in agencies in charge of both regulation and sector planning, where the government, through the line minister and other ministers, is part of the agency's decision-making process.

The top ranking of the autonomy variable and the lower scores given to transparency and institutional and regulatory tools might be explained by the lack of progress in improving the institutional quality of the agencies (represented in the Infrastructure Regulatory Governance Index [IRGI] by several components of the transparency and tools variables). With some exceptions, the process that started with the creation of regulatory agencies has not been expanded or improved. For instance, few agencies publicize their job openings or have developed public examinations for hiring employees. On the tools side, few agencies use regulatory quality standards (such as cost-benefit analysis to assess the impact of regulations) or performance-based payment of employees.

Figure 4.2 presents the distribution of the aggregated index for each sector. Agencies in the electricity sector show better performance than agencies in the water sector, not only in the general indexes but also in specific measures.

Figure 4.2 Aggregated Index of Regulatory Governance

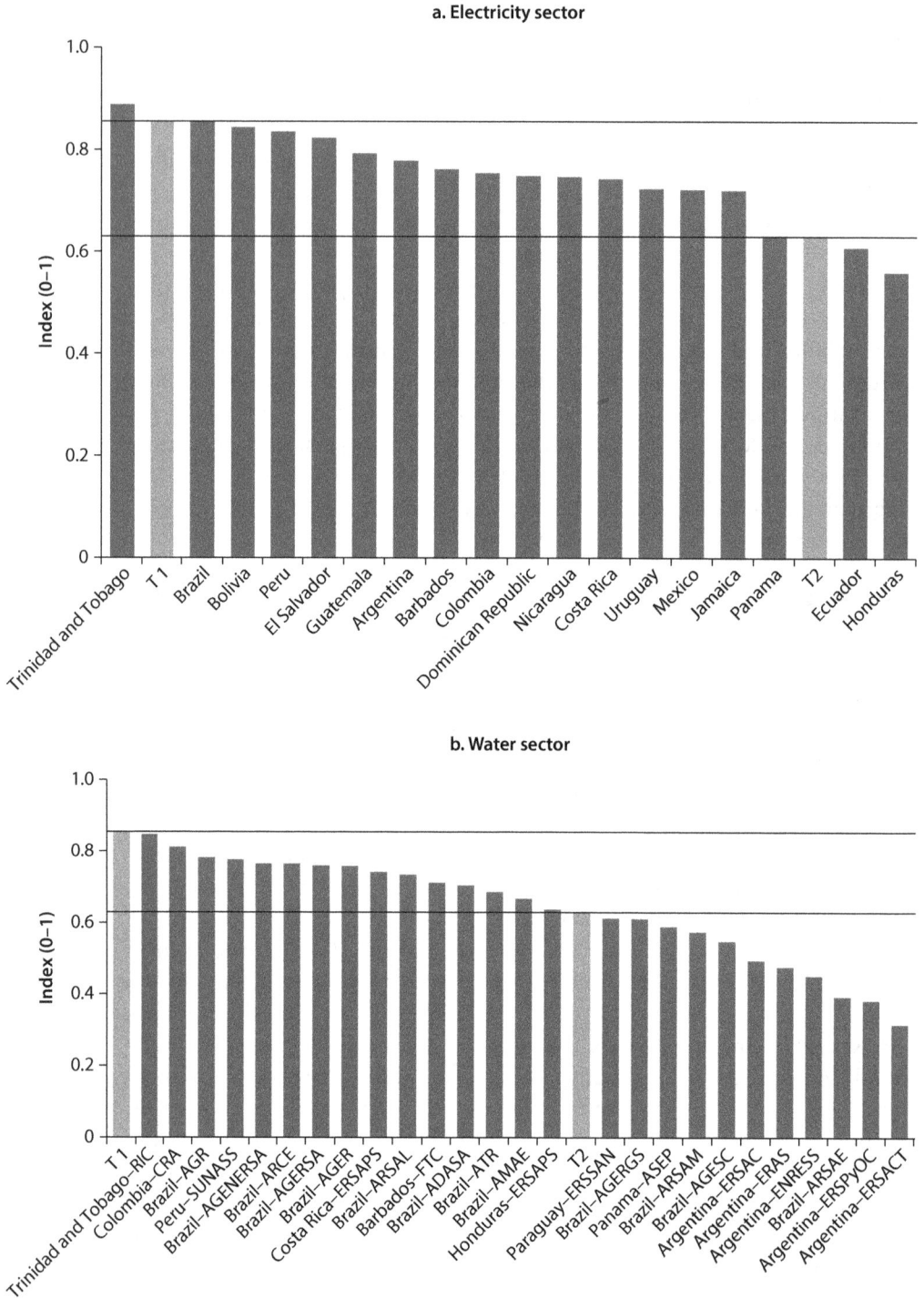

a. Electricity sector

b. Water sector

Source: World Bank 2008 and World Bank 2009.

Box 4.1 Multiagency Regulatory Schemes

Agencies included in the index are agencies that exhibit a design similar to that of a formal independent regulator. Although several agencies embody the institutional patterns of a formal IRA, the region's most salient characteristic is a board composed of independent members. Members appointed to the board should not be government ministers, state secretaries, or other officials whose autonomy could be compromised by holding a policy-formulation position.

Chile's National Energy Commission (NEC) does not follow these criteria. Its board is composed of the ministers of mining, finance, defense, and planning and the secretary general of the presidency. This circumstance makes Chile a stand-alone case incomparable to the other IRAs. Moreover, tariffs in Chile are not determined by the NEC but by the minister of finance, the only authority that approves electricity tariffs in the country. Regulatory competencies in Chile are complemented by the Superintendencia de Electricidad y Combustibles, which is responsible for the enforcement of regulations as well as quality and technical standards.

Colombia and the Dominican Republic have similar institutional designs. These cases were nevertheless included in the analysis, for several reasons. The board of Colombia's National Energy and Gas Regulatory Commission includes five independent experts, who balance the influence of public sector officials, such as the ministers of mining and energy, finance, and the national director for planning. Moreover, the country's score is the result of the combination of the complementary roles of the Regulatory Commission (in charge of the main economic regulation responsibilities) and the Superintendencia de Servicios Publicos Domiciliarios (responsible for enforcing standards and regulations). In the Dominican Republic, only the Superintendencia de Electricidad was included, because it is the only electricity regulator with policy-formulation responsibility.

Benchmarking Governance at the Agency Level

Agencies were grouped into three tiers based on their performance on several indicators (figure 4.3). Tier 1 encompasses agencies that have conditions conducive to developing good regulatory governance. The responses of agencies in this tier are similar to the highest value for each survey question. Tier 2 encompasses agencies that meet only the minimum conditions considered necessary to implement the independent regulator model. Agencies in this tier have fewer responsibilities than agencies in Tier 1 and lower levels of autonomy from the line minister. They also have fewer sophisticated mechanisms for publishing their decisions and policies. Tier 3 includes agencies that do not meet the minimum conditions to implement the benchmark model of regulatory governance.

Consistent with the regional analysis, autonomy is the variable with the highest score for Tier 2 and Tier 3 countries. Bolivia's Superintendencia de Electricidad,[4] Nicaragua's Comisión Nacional de Energía, and the Dominican Republic's Superintendencia de Electricidad have the highest scores.

The variable with the third-highest score is accountability. Trinidad and Tobago's Regulated Industries Commission has the highest score. The main difference between the best and worst performers in accountability is greater

Figure 4.3 Indicators of Regulatory Governance in Electricity Distribution

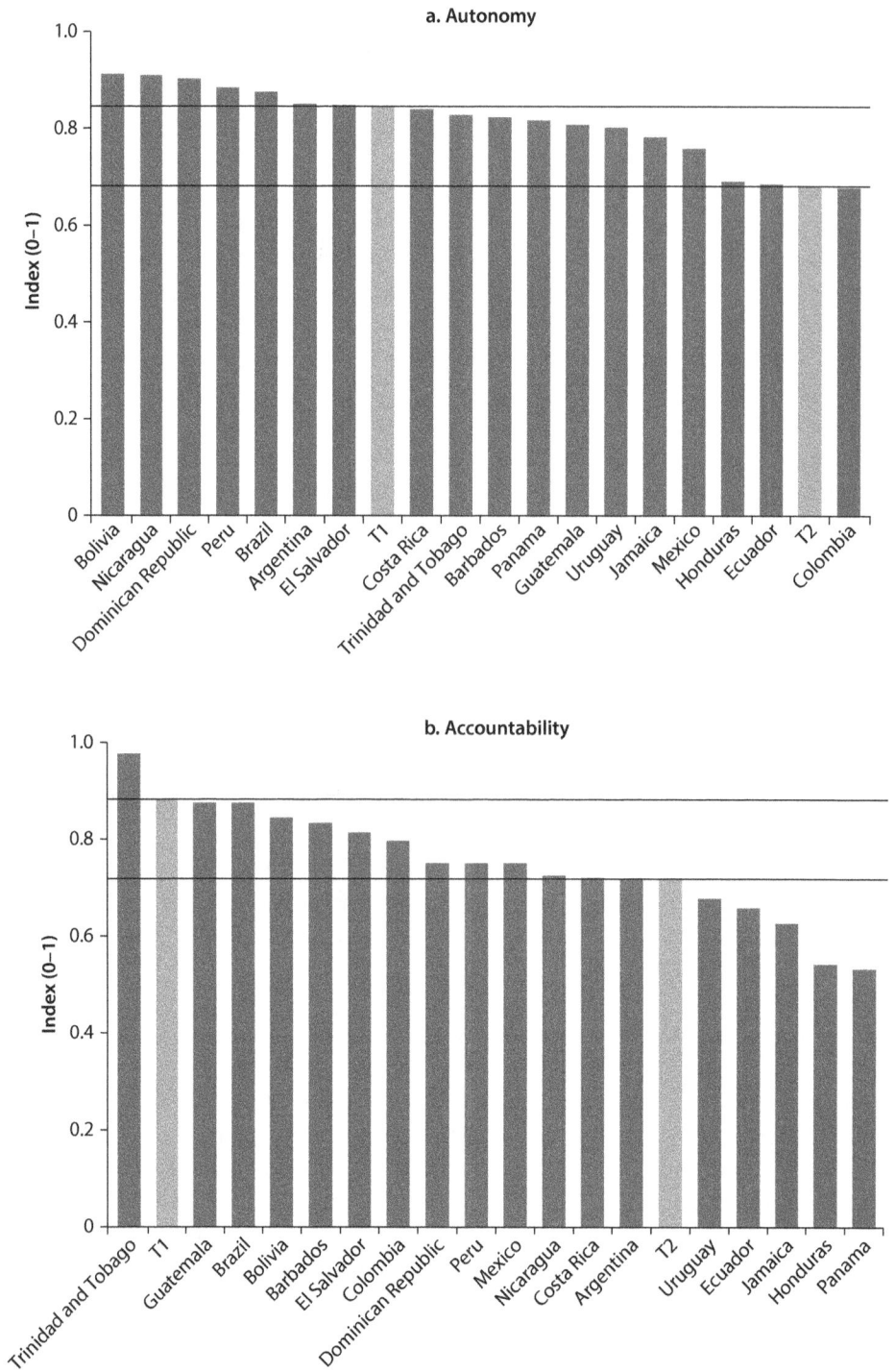

a. Autonomy

b. Accountability

figure continues next page

Figure 4.3 Indicators of Regulatory Governance in Electricity Distribution *(continued)*

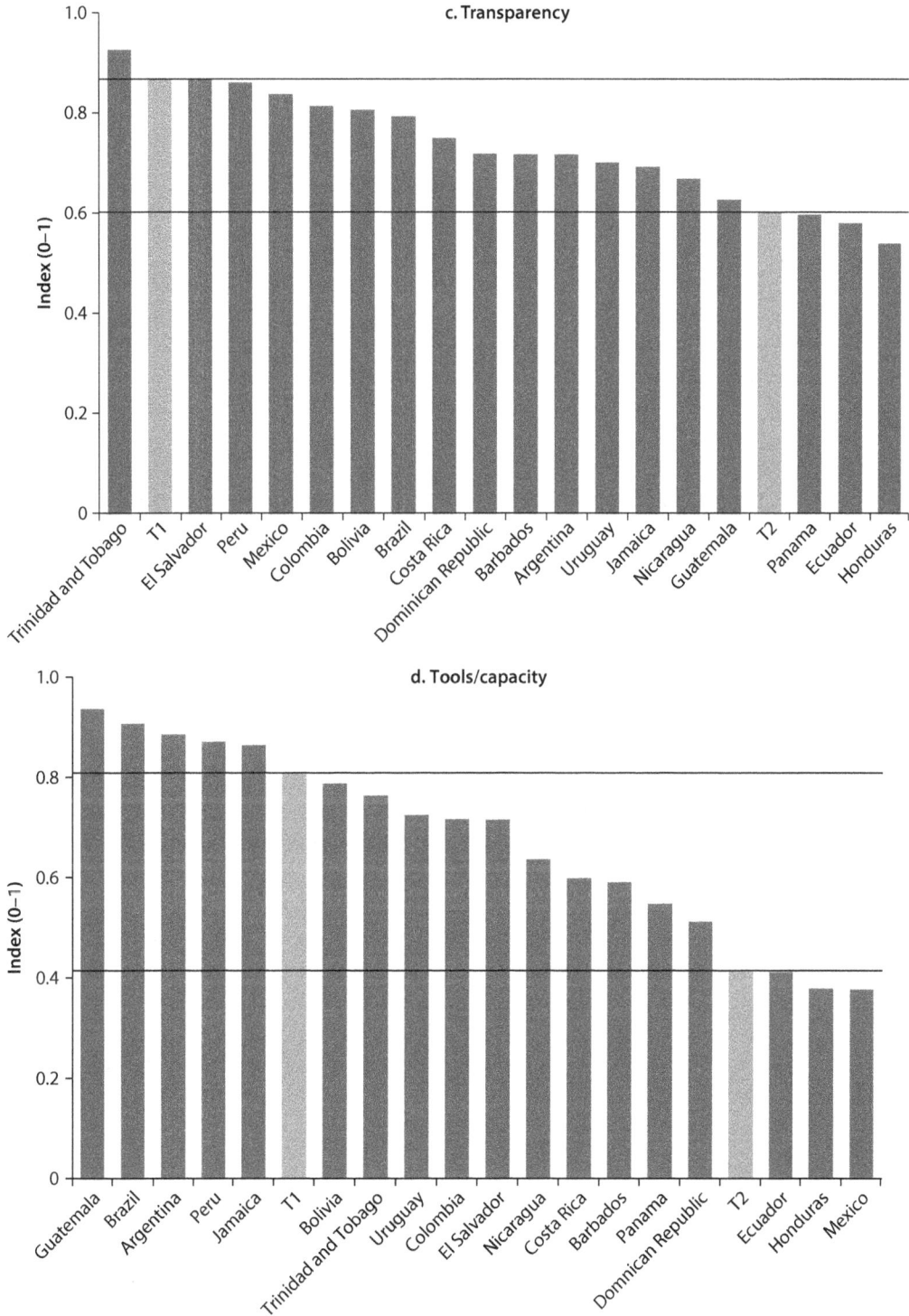

c. Transparency

d. Tools/capacity

Source: World Bank 2008.

obligations to the executive by weak performers. Countries at the top of the aggregated measure of regulatory governance, except Bolivia and Peru, have a more balanced distribution of obligations between the executive and the parliament and are not fully accountable to the executive. In contrast, countries at the bottom of this distribution are heavily dependent on the executive, to which they are, in most cases, fully accountable.

The variable with the third-highest score is transparency. Trinidad and Tobago's Regulated Industries Commission has the highest score; Honduras' Comisión Nacional de Energía has the lowest score. Differences in scores between best and worst performers are narrower than for other measures (an exception is Ecuador among the worst performers). Both best and worst performers have collective decision-making structures, mechanisms to allow participation of stakeholders in rule-making processes, and adequate mechanisms to report their activities to the required institutions and to publish their annual reports. The only area in which the poorly performing countries have lower scores is public consultations.

The variable with the lowest score is tools. This variable captures not only tools related to the application of the agencies' regulatory policies such as benchmarking or the methodology for tariff revision but also instruments aimed at improving institutional and managerial quality (for example, the publication of the agency's annual report or the use of performance-based payments). Guatemala's Comisión Nacional de Energía Eléctrica has the highest ranking. Honduras' Comisión Nacional de Energía and Mexico's Comisión Nacional Reguladora de Energía have the lowest scores for this variable. The main factors that explain the differences between best and worst performers in terms of the tools variable are the use of benchmarking, the extent and number of regulatory instruments, the publication of the agency's annual report, the registration of users' claims, the utilization of regulatory quality standards, and the existence of a structure of posts and salaries.

Differences between IRAs in water and electricity are wider in informal transparency, formal accountability, tools, regulatory autonomy, social transparency, regulatory tools, and institutional tools. Although it might be expected to have higher scores in most of the indicators in the electricity sector than in the water sector, it could also be expected to have better results in the water sector in aspects where the sector is considered to be stronger, such as social public involvement in rule making. In fact, the measure of social transparency shows one of the largest differences, with average scores in countries above Tier 1 higher in the electricity than in the water sector. Similar results are seen in informal transparency (figure 4.4).

Factors Accounting for Differences in Governance

This section disaggregates the variables. Autonomy is broken down into political, managerial, and regulatory autonomy; transparency into social and institutional transparency; and tools into regulatory and institutional tools. Accountability considers only an institutional perspective regarding

Figure 4.4 Indicators of Regulatory Governance in Water Distribution

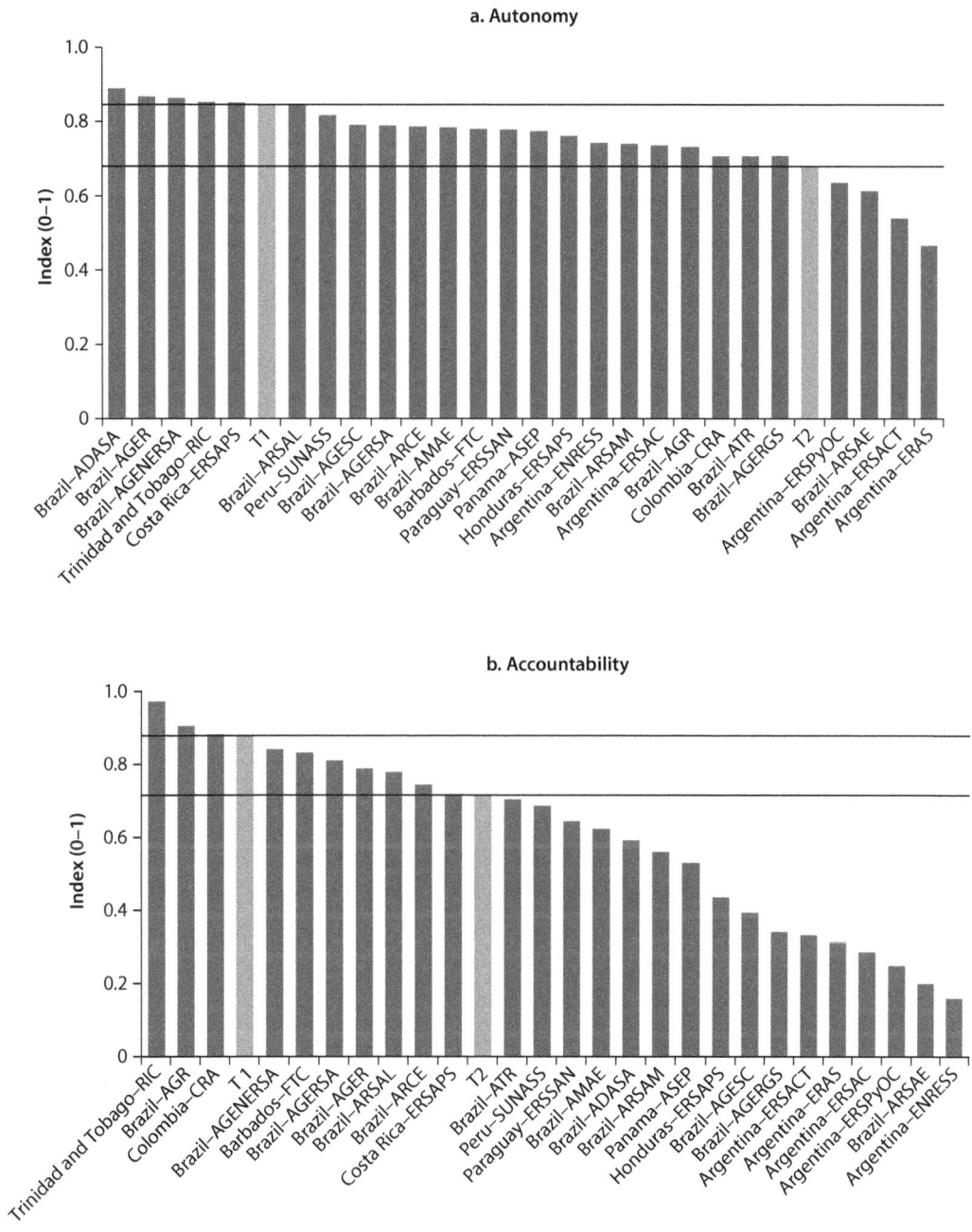

a. Autonomy

b. Accountability

figure continues next page

Figure 4.4 Indicators of Regulatory Governance in Water Distribution *(continued)*

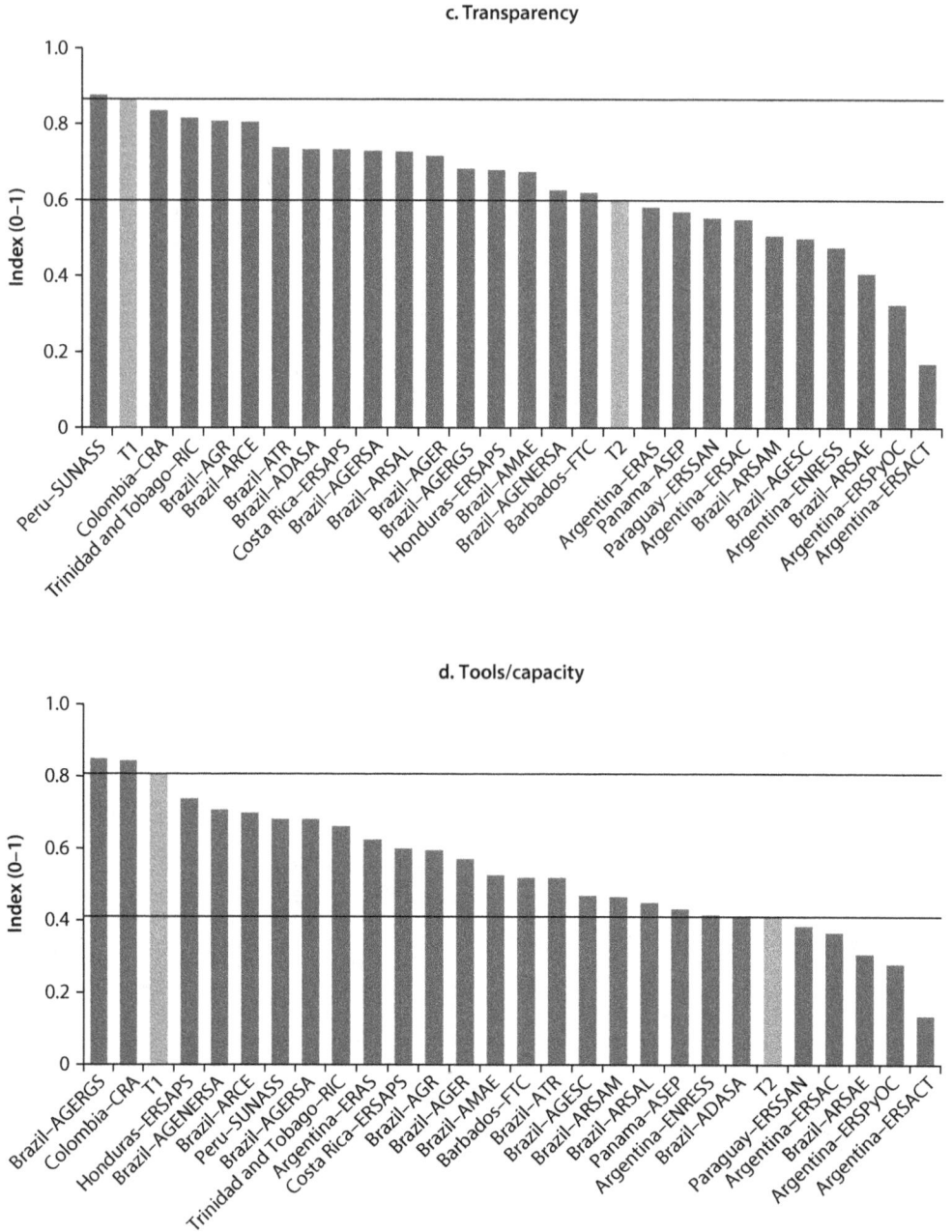

c. Transparency

d. Tools/capacity

Source: World Bank 2009.

the relationships between the agency and the other branches of government; no further division is made of its indicators.

Political Autonomy

Political autonomy measures the independence of the agency's decision making from the authorities in charge of policy formulation (namely, the line minister). It includes the mechanism for selecting agencies' directors, the renewability of directors' mandates, the number of directors who have not completed their terms, the reasons why directors leave their positions, the interference of the minister in the agency's decisions, and the composition of the agency's budget.

The number of countries with Tier 3 agencies is larger for this variable than for any other (see appendix E). Only Brazil is in Tier 1. Tier 3 countries represent a wide variety of agencies. The scores of best performers are significantly different from countries at the bottom of that index. Regulatory agencies in Brazil, the Dominican Republic, and Bolivia have a separate status from the line ministry, separate roles for the agency and government authorities, and a budget composed exclusively of a regulation tax charged to electricity distribution companies. Directors leave mostly because of retirement, voluntary leave, or the completion of their appointments; the line minister has a low level of influence over the agency's affairs, according to sources at the agency.

In contrast, agencies at the bottom of this ranking have no autonomy from the line minister. The sector ministry is part of the agencies and chairs their boards; their budgets are composed exclusively of government funds, without any type of income from companies (regulation tax).

Managerial Autonomy

Managerial autonomy involves the freedom of the agency to determine the use of its budget and the organization of its resources. It includes aspects such as the ability of the agency to determine its organizational structure, the freedom to make its own decisions on personnel, the autonomy to determine its own expenses, and the type of legal regime that applies to its employees (private law, civil service law, or both). It also includes other aspects related to tools that contribute to improving its management, such as the existence of its own structure of posts and salaries and performance-based payment of employees.

Argentina, Barbados, Brazil, Guatemala, Jamaica, Peru, and Trinidad and Tobago have desirable conditions to manage their resources. Agencies in these countries have adequate mechanisms and procedures to guarantee an autonomous administration of the agency by its authorities. In contrast, agencies in Colombia and Honduras have less managerial freedom to determine their organizational structure or the use of their resources.

Results in this section are not an indication of the effectiveness of the agency's management but of powers aimed at allowing the agency an autonomous administration. Countries at the top of the distribution have full powers in all the aspects mentioned in the first paragraph of this section. Brazil is among the leading countries in managerial autonomy.

Uncovering the Drivers of Utility Performance • http://dx.doi.org/10.1596/978-0-8213-9660-5

Regulatory Autonomy

Regulatory autonomy includes characteristics such as responsibility for regulation of the sector (the agency, parliament, the executive, or some combination of the three); the type of powers (consultative, oversight, pricing, and rule making); responsibilities regarding particular issues (tariffs, service quality, consumer complaints, companies' investment plans, wholesale market, anticompetitive behavior, technical standards); and powers to enforce its decisions.

Most countries in the region are in Tier 1; only four are in Tier 3. Countries with desirable conditions in regulatory autonomy have full responsibilities for tariffs, service quality, standards, and investments, as well as the power to implement sanctions and regulations. In contrast, countries that do not meet the minimum requirements in terms of the extension of their regulatory prerogatives have little responsibility for specific regulatory issues and no power to enforce regulations.

The changes experienced by regulatory agencies in political versus regulatory autonomy explain the importance of linking political independence to the expansion of agencies' regulatory powers. An agency can have the highest level of independence from political authorities but no relevant power in the regulation of the sector, making independence an abstract characteristic of the agency's functioning with no real impact on regulation. The same conclusion was observed in an assessment of European electricity regulators, which found that even if regulatory agencies shared the same regulatory objectives, there were significant variations in the means the regulators had to pursue those objectives (Johannsen 2003).

Social Transparency

The social aspects of transparency are related to the involvement of stakeholders in the agency's decision-making and rule-making processes and their access to the agency's information. Social transparency includes the participation of stakeholders in the agency's rule-making process, the publication by the agency of its decisions, the organization by the agency of public consultations, the existence of advisory committees in the agency's structure, the existence of a website, and the registration of users' claims. Agencies' positions in social transparency are presented in appendix E.

This standard of governance is headed by Trinidad and Tobago, followed by Colombia, the Dominican Republic, Peru, El Salvador, and Bolivia. Differences between countries at the top and bottom of social transparency center on three main aspects. The first aspect is the participation of the stakeholders in the agency's rule-making process. Although public consultations or public hearings are aimed at allowing the involvement of stakeholders in the agency's main decisions, the rule-making process is the mechanism through which regulatees are invited to contribute their opinions in the elaboration of the agency's regulations. In contrast to countries at the top, countries at the bottom of the distribution either lack provisions to involve stakeholders in the rule-making process or have provisions but fail to involve stakeholders in that process.

The second aspect is the existence of advisory committees integrated by different stakeholders in the structures of best performing agencies. These committees are supposed to play an important role in the agency's decision making by representing and promoting different interest groups (mainly consumers).

The third aspect is the registration of users' claims. Best-performing agencies register consumer claims through both paper-based and electronic mechanisms, allowing faster resolution of the cases and easier access to files by regulatees (both at the agency and through the website).

Institutional Transparency

Institutional transparency is composed of indicators related to the transparent management of the agency that are not directly linked to involvement of stakeholders. It includes aspects such as the nature of the agency's decision making (collective or individual), the existence of quarantine rules for directors, the agency's reporting instruments (annual report and public hearing before parliament), the publication of the agency's institutional strategy and annual report, the publication of the agency's audit accounts and job openings, the existence of norms of ethics, the record of the board's meetings, and the use of public examinations to hire employees.

Several factors place agencies at the top of the index. The first factor is related to the existence of collective decision making by a board of directors. As opposed to a single decision-making structure, a board composed of directors with varied technical backgrounds allows for more comprehensive and diverse debates on regulatory issues than a decision made by a single policy maker. The second factor is related to the publication of information such as job vacancies, an annual report, an institutional strategy, and audited accounts. The third factor is a record of the board's meetings and the existence of quarantine rules for directors who leave the agency.

Agencies with good institutional transparency tend to possess characteristics related to administrative modernization. For instance, publication of the organization's institutional strategy, annual report, and job vacancies are indicators of agencies concerned not only with sector-based policies related to transparency (such as the conducting of public hearings) but also with mechanisms and procedures aimed at making them more effective as administrative bodies.

Accountability

Accountability was not disaggregated. Its indicators represent different institutional elements (for example, reporting obligations to the executive and the parliament and the ability to appeal its decisions before the executive and the judiciary) of the agency's relationships with the executive, the legislative, and the judiciary. Hence, the institutional aspect of agencies' accountability design is considered.

Regulatory Tools

More than three-quarters of the regulatory agencies in the region (78 percent) use benchmarking, mainly to determine tariffs; a smaller percentage of countries have the full complement of tools listed in the survey. Many countries are in Tier 1, reflecting the importance LAC agencies give to the development of several tools to implement their regulatory decisions. Brazil, El Salvador, Guatemala, and Peru lead the countries in Tier 1. Leading countries in this dimension make use not only of benchmarking but also of tools to conduct regulatory policies, such as a database for regulatory accountability, a methodology for tariff revision, a methodology for annual tariff readjustment, instruments for monitoring quality and technical standards, a methodology for monitoring technical standards, a methodology for defining interconnection tariffs, and five-year revisions of these tools. Most countries in the region have developed specific legislation to regulate consumers' rights.

Institutional Tools

The region shows better performance in regulatory than in institutional tools. There are large disparities between countries at the top and the bottom of this measure. Top performers use certain regulatory quality standards tools (cost-benefit analysis, regulatory impact analysis, and administrative simplification) as well as performance-based payment of their employees; publish both annual reports and institutional strategies; and, with the exception of Peru, have a structure in place for posts and salaries. In contrast, weak performers lack regulatory quality standards, do not offer incentives to their employees, and have not developed institutional strategies. In addition, the registration of consumer complaints is facilitated through paper-based mechanisms rather than electronically.

Regulatory Governance and Sector Performance

This section combines the data on infrastructure agencies' governance with data collected at the company level to assess the impact of regulatory agencies on utility performance. This work fills a gap in the literature on the subject, as previous attempts to interrelate agency governance and utility performance focused on a limited number of factors, narrowing the scope and explanatory potential of the research.[5]

The analysis assesses the relationship between two strands of literature. The first is related to the impact of private sector participation on sector performance. The second is related to measuring the governance of regulatory agencies. Little is known about the relationship between the two.

A few papers focus on the relationship between regulatory characteristics and performance. Sirtaine and others (2004) create a regulatory quality index based on three key aspects of regulatory quality: legal solidity, financial strength, and decision-making autonomy. Despite their small sample sizes, three of the four models show that the regulatory quality variables are statistically significant and explain 20–25 percent of the internal rate of return of private investment in infrastructure projects in LAC. Estache and Rossi (2008) explore the causal relation between the establishment of a regulatory agency and the performance of the electricity distribution sector. They analyze a unique dataset comprising firm-level information on a representative sample of 220 electric utilities from 51 developing countries and transition economies between 1985 and 2005. Their results indicate that regulatory agencies are associated with more efficient firms and higher consumer welfare.

The analysis presented here is based on unique databases (for descriptions, see appendix B). It merges the performance data described in chapter 2 with the regulatory governance analyzed in this chapter. Every country except Colombia was matched with its own regulatory agency (Colombia was assigned only one score, because it has two different agencies with regulatory functions). The following sections describe the results with different specifications.[6]

Existence of a Regulatory Agency

A dummy was defined with a value equal to one starting in the year when the regulatory agency was established.[7] Two specifications were run. The first ran the ownership dummies and the dummy for the existence of a regulatory agency (see appendix table F.1). These specifications allowed for the identification of the impact of ownership after controlling for the existence of a regulatory agency and the effect of the existence of regulation when controlling for ownership. The second set of specifications interacted the ownership dummies with the dummy for existence, allowing complementarities between the two phenomena to be identified (see appendix table F.2).

Most of the results presented in chapter 3 hold when controlling for the existence of a regulatory agency. However, their magnitude is slightly reduced. For instance, the effect on labor productivity is reduced by one fourth. Similar to quality of service, the result during the transition becomes nonsignificant. In contrast, the results for the posttransition period on the impact of the change in ownership remain significant, with a 10 percent reduction in the electricity distribution sector and a 17 percent reduction in the water sector with respect to the results that did not control for the existence of an agency.

With respect to the existence of a regulatory agency, controlling for the change in ownership revealed the significant positive impact of most indicators. For instance, the presence of a regulatory agency is associated with increases in labor productivity of 19.4 percent in electricity distribution and 18.2 percent in water distribution. Similarly, utilities reported 18.9 percent less average duration and 17.3 percent less frequency of interruptions. With respect to operational expenditures, utilities regulated by an agency had 27.4–32.1 percent lower expenditures. Residential tariffs were 13.5 percent higher given the presence of a regulatory agency, industrial tariffs were 4.6 percent lower, and the cost recovery ratio was 13.3 percent higher.

Experience of the Regulatory Agency

Experience was defined as the years since the establishment of the regulatory agency. As expected, these results are correlated with the results on the existence of a regulatory agency. These estimations also support the hypothesis of gradual improvement of utilities' performance given the presence of a regulatory agency.

Most of the results on the change in ownership hold when controlling for the experience of the regulatory agency, but the magnitude of the effect declines. For instance, after controlling for the change in ownership, labor productivity rose 1.4 percentage points with respect to the parameters obtained when the model does not control for experience. Distributional losses fell 1.8 percentage points a year according to the same comparison. Together these quality indicators resulted in annual improvement of 9.0 percentage points. Operational expenditures 1.6–5.5 percentage points a year. Residential tariffs improved 2.6 percentage points a year, and industrial tariffs fell 1.3 percentage points. Consequently, the cost recovery ratio improved significantly.

Aggregated Measure of Regulatory Governance

The models include various measures of regulatory governance developed in the previous sections. The IRGI is based on seven indicators: formal/informal autonomy indexes, formal/informal transparency indexes, formal/informal accountability indexes, and the tool index. The IRGI ranges between 0 and 1, with an average value of 0.483 and a standard deviation of 0.343. The purpose of these models is to test not only the existence of regulatory agencies but also their governance. The mere existence of a regulatory agency has a significant impact on performance. This section tests whether there are additional effects of good regulatory governance.[8]

Most of the results on changes in ownership from chapter 3 hold when controlling for the regulatory governance of a regulatory agency, although there is some reduction in the magnitude of their effect when the IRGI is added to the model. A one standard deviation increase in the IRGI is associated with an 8.7–9.1 percent increase in labor productivity and a 7.5–8.2 percent reduction in the duration and frequency of interruptions. Operational expenditures fell more than 10 percent, and residential tariffs increased 5.7 percent. Consequently, there was an improvement in the cost recovery ratio.

Principal Components of the Governance of Regulatory Agencies

Principal component analysis was used to break down the IRGI into its components, thus minimizing the loss of information associated with possible correlation of some of the seven indicators.[9] Principal component analysis may be helpful when there are multiple variables and a relatively small number of observations. An additional advantage of principal component analysis is that once patterns in the data are identified, the number of dimensions can be reduced without much loss of information.[10]

The results are presented by examining the impact on performance of an increase of one standard deviation for each factor.[11] Factor 1 reflects informal governance aspects in a regulatory agency, which are correlated with informal autonomy, informal transparency, informal accountability, and tools and capacities. Factor 2 reflects formal aspects of regulatory governance, which are highly correlated with formal transparency and formal accountability. Factor 3 reflects formal aspects of autonomy and the formal power of the agency to determine the tariff structure and level, which is highly correlated with the tariff regulatory and formal autonomy indexes.

Most of the coefficients for the three principal components are significant and had the expected signs. However, each component had a distinct effect on each of the performance indicators. For instance, a one standard deviation change in the formal component had a large effect on improving labor productivity (15.9 percent) and reducing the frequency of interruptions (13.8 percent) and residential tariffs (19.0 percent). A one standard deviation improvement in formal autonomy and the characteristics of the agency in terms of setting tariffs was associated with higher labor productivity (11.4 percent) and a reduction in the average duration of interruptions (17.2 percent). It was also associated with a 42.8–49.3 percent reduction in operation expenditure, with consequent improvements in the cost recovery ratio. Factor 1 had less influence than the other two factors: only 3 of 11 coefficients were significant.

Conclusions

Regulatory agencies in LAC were created to isolate regulatory decisions from political intervention, a feature reflected in their governance design. About 75 percent of the agencies in the region have final decision responsibilities in determining the structure and levels of tariffs.

The region has encountered difficulties in implementing safeguards to guarantee the autonomous management of agencies, however. The largest number of weak performers (agencies in Tier 3) was found for informal aspects of agencies' governance and political autonomy. Informal aspects of agencies' governance account for 14 percent of the variance in governance variables; they reflect informal autonomy, transparency, accountability, and tools. Almost 40 percent of agencies do not meet minimum governance conditions. Among these agencies, almost 70 percent do not meet the minimum governance requirements to guarantee the insulation of the agency from political influence. Many agencies fall into Tier 3 on informal accountability, which assesses the degree of an agency's accountability to the executive.

Regulatory agencies in the region do not perform well on institutional non-regulatory, mechanisms aimed at improving transparency and overall institutional quality. For the most part, governance does not reflect the use of regulatory quality standards, such as administrative simplification, or cost-benefit analysis in the assessment of regulations. Moreover, 30 percent of agencies do not publish their jôb vacancies, and almost half do not use public examinations to hire employees.

Regulatory governance matters for sector performance. The existence of a regulatory agency matters, the experience of the regulatory agency matters, and the governance of the agency matters. Significant improvement in utility performance occurs as a result of a regulatory agency, even in the case of SOEs.

Notes

1. The measurement of agencies' governance is not an indicator of the effectiveness of the use of their regulatory instruments (such as the methodology to calculate tariff readjustment) or the quality of stakeholders' involvement in public consultations. It aims to capture the institutional conditions necessary to achieve good regulation regardless of their scope and impact on the sector's performance (Correa and others 2006).

2. The countries are Argentina, Bolivia, Brazil, Chile, Colombia, Costa Rica, the Dominican Republic, Ecuador, El Salvador, Guatemala, Honduras, Jamaica, Mexico, Nicaragua, Panama, Paraguay, Peru, Trinidad and Tobago, and Uruguay.

3. Chile and Colombia split regulatory responsibilities in two agencies, one in charge of the main regulatory functions (the National Energy Commission) and one in charge of enforcement of the regulatory framework, particularly in terms of the imposition of sanctions and the observance of service quality standards (Superintendencia).

4. In 2009, the government of Evo Morales announced the elimination of Superintendencias as sector regulator in Bolivia and the creation of Autoridades de Fiscalizacion y Control Social. Article 138 of supreme decree 29894, published February 7, 2009, stated that with the exception of the hydrocarbons regulator, all regulators that formed part of the sector regulatory system or the renewable natural resources regulatory system would disappear within 60 days from the date of the decree's publication and their functions taken over by the corresponding ministries or a new regulatory authority. Their levels of autonomy as IRAs were reduced as the law made them directly accountable to the line minister.

5. Previous research on governance has focused on the existence of an agency, a legal framework, or particular aspects of its governance (mainly autonomy), emphasizing formal attributes. In terms of performance, only electricity generation per capita was used as an indicator related to governance (Stern and Cubbin 2005). Estache and Rossi (2008) study the relationship between the establishment of an agency and the efficiency of the utilities as well as the welfare of consumers.

6. All specifications were run using a semilogarithmic functional form of these models for each of the indicators. First, a dummy for the existence of a regulatory agency as well as its interactions with the ownership dummies was added. Next, the square of experience of the regulatory agency was included. Following this, the Infrastructure Regulatory Governance Index (IRGI) to the specifications was added as well as its interactions with ownership. Finally, the regulatory index was decomposed through a principal component approach, and three principal components were introduced in the models.

7. There are some differences between the year the agency was created (in general by law) and the year it was established. The governance data report both dates. The regressions used the year the agency was established; similar results were obtained using the year the agency was created.

8. This section reports the results of an increase of one standard deviation in governance. The data are cross-sectional. Hence, the underlying assumption is that once the agency was created, it followed a similar institutional design. Its governance is therefore assumed to be constant.

9. Principal component analysis develops a composite index by defining a real-valued function over the relevant variables objectively. When different characteristics of a set of events are observed, the characteristic with greater variation explains a larger proportion of the variation in the dependent variable than the variable displaying less variation. Therefore, the issue is one of finding weights to assign to each of the concerned variables, determined by the principle that the objective is to maximize variation in the linear composite of these variables. This approach allows patterns in data to be identified, and it allows the data to be presented in a way that highlights similarities and differences.

10. See Andrés and others (2008) for details on factor scores and their eigenvalues.

11. The standard deviations for the three principal components were 1.51, 1.41, and 1.28.

References

Andrés, L., J. L. Guasch, and S. L. Azumendi. 2008. "Regulatory Governance and Sector Performance in Electricity Distribution in Latin America." In *Regulation, De-Regulation, and Re-Regulation: Institutional Perspectives*, edited by M. Ghertman and C. Menard. London: Edward Elgar.

Andrés, L., J. L. Guasch, M. Diop, and S. L. Azumendi. 2007. "Assessing the Governance of Electricity Regulatory Agencies in the Latin American and the Caribbean Region: A Benchmarking Analysis." Policy Research Working Paper 4380, World Bank, Washington, DC.

Aron, J. 2000. "Growth and Institutions: A Review of the Evidence." *World Bank Research Observer* 15 (1): 99–135.

Brown, A. C., J. Stern, B. Tenenbaum, and D. Gencer. 2006. *Handbook for Evaluating Infrastructure Regulatory Systems.* Washington, DC: World Bank.

Correa, P., C. Pereira, B. Mueller, and M. Melo. 2006. *Regulatory Governance in Infrastructure Industries: Assessment and Measurement of Brazilian Regulators.* Washington, DC: World Bank, Public-Private Infrastructure Advisory Facility.

Estache, A., and M. A. Rossi. 2008. "Regulatory Agencies: Impact on Firm Performance and Social Welfare." Policy Research Working Paper 4509, World Bank, Washington, DC.

Gilardi, F. 2002. "Policy Credibility and Delegation to Independent Regulatory Agencies: A Comparative Empirical Analysis." *Journal of European Public Policy* 9 (6): 873–93.

Gutiérrez, L. H. 2003. "The Effect of Endogenous Regulation on Telecommunications Expansion and Efficiency in Latin America." *Journal of Regulatory Economics* 23 (3): 257–86.

Johannsen, K. S. 2003. *Regulatory Independence in Theory and Practice: A Survey of Independent Energy Regulators in Eight European Countries.* Energy Research Programme and the Danish Research Training Council, Copenhagen.

OECD (Organisation for Economic Co-operation and Development). 1999. *OECD Guiding Principles for Regulatory Quality and Performance.* Paris: OECD.

Oliveira, G., E. Machado, L. Novaes, L. Martins, G. Ferreira, and C. Beatriz. 2005. *Aspects of the Independence of Regulatory Agencies and Competition Advocacy.* Getulio Vargas Foundation, Rio de Janeiro.

Rodrick, D. 2004. "Getting Institutions Right." *CESifo DICE Report: A Journal for International Comparisons* 2: 10–15.

Sirtaine, S., M. E. Pinglo, J. L. Guasch, and V. Foster. 2004. "How Profitable Are Infrastructure Concessions in Latin America? Empirical Evidence and Regulatory Implications." Trends and Policy Options 2, World Bank, Latin America and Caribbean Region, Finance, Private Sector and Infrastructure Department, Washington, DC. http://rru.worldbank.org/documents/other/topic60_latinamerica.pdf.

Sosay, G., and U. Zenginobuz. 2005. "Independent Regulatory Agencies in Emerging Economies." Munich Personal RePEc Archive, Paper 380.

Stern, J., and J. Cubbin. 2005. "Regulatory Effectiveness: The Impact of Regulation and Regulatory Governance Arrangements on Electricity Industry Outcomes." Policy Research Working Paper 3536, World Bank, Washington, DC.

Stern, J., and S. Holder. 1999. "Regulatory Governance: Criteria for Assessing the Performance of Regulatory Systems: An Application to Infrastructure in Developing Countries of Asia." *Utilities Policy* 8: 33–50.

Thatcher, M. 2007. "Regulatory Agencies, the State and Markets: A Franco-British Comparison." Working Paper RSCAS 2007/17, European Union University.

World Bank. 2008. LAC Electricity Regulatory Governance Database. Washington, DC.

———. 2009. LAC Water Regulatory Governance Database. Washington, DC.

CHAPTER 5

Corporate Governance of State-Owned Enterprises

Governments and international donors no longer adopt a "one model fits all" approach to address the management framework of state-owned enterprises (SOEs). They recognize that public enterprises face different problems from private operators, related to deficiencies in service provision and financial shortcomings unique to the environment in which they operate. Addressing issues such as performance-based management, the role of incentives, the professionalization of senior management, and policies regarding transparency of utilities' information systems requires a pragmatic, case-specific approach to reform.

As a result of work by the Organisation for Economic Co-operation and Development (OECD) on corporate governance and concepts and tools of the New Public Management theories, policy makers now view SOEs as corporations driven by incentives that reward efficiency and transparency. The notion of corporate governance as applied to public enterprises tries to reflect as closely as possible the incentives that private enterprises face. In the case of SOEs, corporate governance refers to the organization of decision making in a public corporation.

The OECD's *Guidelines of Corporate Governance in SOEs* (OECD 2005) emphasize the importance of a legal framework that clearly establishes the separate roles of the state as owner, regulator, and policy formulator. The institutional setting for SOEs should ensure a level playing field with respect to private enterprises in order to avoid distortions and inefficiency. The OECD Guidelines also stress the importance of an explicit legal mandate that regulates the provision of public service obligations, the sources of funding, and the scope of governance. They recommend the development of an ownership policy that defines the overall objectives of state ownership and the state's role in the corporate governance of SOEs and explains how the state will implement its ownership policy. It also recommends clear and equitable rules for all shareholders, particularly small investors. It emphasizes the need for a board of directors composed of officials with good qualifications, reasonable levels of autonomy, and effective mechanisms of accountability.

Two main approaches can be observed in the literature on corporate governance of SOEs. The first approach emphasizes improved corporate governance of SOEs as a prerequisite to private sector participation. This approach assumes that the resemblance to a private enterprise with higher levels of autonomy in the management of funds that is subject to corporate law and eventually listed in the stock markets aligns internal incentives. Consequently, this approach improves performance, clearing the way to private sector participation. Critics of this view emphasize the approach's focus on one of the several ways of organizing state corporations.

The second approach adopts a more comprehensive, less dogmatic view of the governance of SOEs. It considers improvement in the governance of SOEs as an end in itself rather than merely a strategy for eventual private sector participation. It presents SOEs with various strategies for improving performance, including but not limited to private sector participation.

According to Whincop (2005), government corporations SOEs face three main problems. The first is related to the alignment of the interests of the government corporations' managers with those of its ultimate owners, the citizens (the agency costs of management). The constituency to which a government corporation is ultimately accountable—the people—stands in a dual relation to the government corporation. On the one hand, the people are the government corporations' residual claimants, as shareholders in a business corporation. On the other hand, they are frequently the principal recipients of the goods and services the government corporation provides. This dual relation between the government corporation and the public makes it difficult to concretize the meaning of acting in the best interests of the public. The second problem is associated with the alignment of the interests of the body wielding delegated governance power over managers with the interests of its ultimate owners (the agency costs of governance). Questions arise regarding the extent to which the people wielding this power are inclined to use it for political advantage. The third problem is the reduction of social costs associated with anticompetitive behavior by the government corporation.

Whincop explores how the governance of government corporations can be evaluated in terms of three objectives—management costs, anticompetitive behavior costs, and costs of governance—which he evaluates from a "constituency" perspective. He examines the major players whose interests may be affected by the governance of the government corporation and their relation to the ultimate principal, the public at large. Principal players are managers, empowered political agents, and active stakeholders, including customers and employees.

Vagliasindi (2008, 2009) develops a detailed review of the substantial body of research on theoretical models of board effectiveness and ownerships structures. The literature (which is on the private sector) stresses the importance of independent directors. In the case of SOEs, even more than in private enterprises, the appointment of directors with technical expertise and a reasonable level of independence acquires central relevance. Vagliasindi also emphasizes the importance of external governance (by, for example, the government agency in charge of ownership decisions) and regulation.

Schwartz (2006) examines the organizational model in state water utilities. He applies the two main organizational approaches—the bureaucratic model and the New Public Management model—to public water utilities in Mexico. He defines the bureaucratic model as one based on the preeminence of the law and rules, composed of civil servants with stability and civil service careers in public administration, and organized around the principles of hierarchy and levels. The New Public Management framework proposes higher levels of decentralization of and autonomy for government entities; the use of performance-based instruments, such as performance-based payments; and accountability focused on results. Schwartz challenges conventional wisdom about the effectiveness of New Public Management, finding that well-performing public utilities tend to display stronger adherence to the Weberian ideal type than poorly functioning public service providers. He concludes that the two strategies are better viewed as complementary than opposing, as both focus on reducing patronage and depoliticizing the management of the utility (bureaucratic model) and emphasize the levels of service that must be delivered by the utility (New Public Management model).

Both approaches lack empirical evidence about the impact of governance on performance. For instance, no assessment has been conducted of the contributions of corporatization to access to finance or productivity or the role of shares in not-for-profit enterprises. There is, however, some evidence on performance contracts, presented below.

Methodology and Framework of Analysis

This chapter focuses on the governance of SOEs in the water and electricity distribution sectors of Latin America and the Caribbean (LAC). As in the previous chapter, the focus is on governance design rather than effectiveness. Figure 5.1 summarizes the framework of analysis.

The data collected reflect the corporate arrangements that shape 45 state-run companies in the region, including both public companies with full state ownership and companies in which the state owns at least 51 percent of total shares (only a few utilities are in this category). Governance of SOEs is measured through six indexes. The Corporate Governance Index, the main index, is an aggregate index based on the other five indexes (legal soundness, board competitiveness, professional management, performance orientation, and transparency and disclosure) plus a binary measure based on the listing of the company on the stock exchange.

The data were collected through a survey implemented in 110 utilities in the electricity and water sectors. The benchmark used was a corporatized public enterprise for which access to finance and auditing requirements were similar to private enterprises. The benchmark was adjusted to allow sector specificities, such as the mechanisms for appointing the board of directors, economic regulation, and performance-based orientation.

Figure 5.1 Framework for Assessing Corporate Governance of State-Owned Enterprises

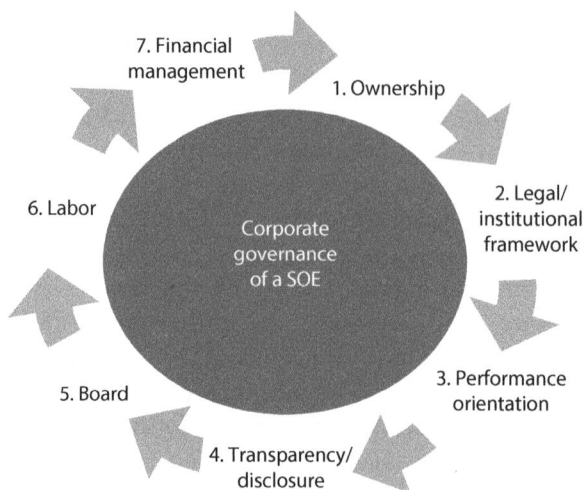

Source: Andrés, Guasch, and Lopez Azumendi 2011.

Also included in the study were the selection, appointment, salary, and educational levels of staff. Previous approaches emphasized only the role of the board and its relationship with shareholders. For SOEs providing infrastructure services, the role of the staff is a vital aspect of good management. Most utilities are not profit oriented and do not focus on revenues as a measure of good performance. A good bureaucracy may also limit political intervention. An index that reflects the professionalism of the staff (as measured by educational levels, hiring criteria, and rewards) may therefore provide a good proxy for the performance of the enterprise. Table 5.1 describes the components of this framework of analysis.

As in chapter 4, three tiers were created. Tier 1 encompasses enterprises that have "desirable" conditions for developing good corporate governance. Utilities' responses in this tier are close to the highest value for each of the questions. Their corporate governance design meets high standards. Tier 2 encompasses SOEs that meet only the minimum conditions considered necessary to implement a corporate governance program. Utilities in Tier 2 have weaker institutional design and less sophisticated mechanisms than utilities in Tier 1. Tier 3 includes utilities that do not meet the minimum conditions to implement the benchmark model of corporate governance.

Results of Corporate Governance Benchmarking

This section presents the results on the aggregated index and each of the individual indexes. The scores for each enterprise are aggregated to the country level. Although this approach simplifies the presentation, it conceals significant

Table 5.1 Analytical Framework for Assessing Corporate Governance of State-Owned Enterprises

Ownership/legal framework	Board/chief executive officer (CEO)	Management/ staff	Transparency disclosure	Performance orientation
Components				
Ownership structure, tax regime, corporatization, regulatory bodies and functions, restructuring, procurement, public listing	Appointments process (authority, criteria); origin and background of directors; deliberative or executive roles; salary levels; scope of responsibilities; assessment of performance	Educational levels, training, criteria for hiring, mechanism for rewarding employees, salary levels	Website's contents, participation of civil society in decision-making, annual performance report, auditing of company's accounting, financial disclosure standards, involvement of consumers and civil society representatives in company's decision making, criteria for appointing senior management, criteria and mechanisms for hiring employees	Assessment of performance of company and its decision-making authorities, criteria, tools and mechanisms, evaluation authorities, and systems for rewarding employees
Benchmark				
Focus on company that has corporate structure, is subject to the same conditions as the private sector, and has the possibility of accessing private and public financing	Emphasis on board of directors and CEO appointed based on meritocratic criteria, with reasonable level of independence, and whose performance is assessed regularly	Benchmark is company that hires its employees through external competition, rewards employees' performance, and has salary levels close to private sector levels	Emphasis on decision-making process in which civil society has a say in the company's decisions (accountability effect) and there is a strong focus on the publication of institutional and performance information. Involvement of private auditors and the publication of financial information through best international practices is prioritized. Importance also given to ways company hires employees (open process).	Model of a state-owned enterprise with a focus on performance-based management. Benchmark compensates lack of incentives provided by the profitability of a private company with a framework in which the performance of public companies is properly assessed.

Source: Andrés, Guasch, and Lopez Azumendi 2011.

heterogeneity in the governance structures of utilities within a country (Brazil and Colombia, for example, are home to both best-performing and worst-performing utilities).

Aggregate Index of Corporate Governance

The aggregated measure of corporate governance ranks companies in the region based on account information from all five components of the framework: legal soundness, board competitiveness, professional management, performance-orientation, and transparency and disclosure (figure 5.2). The results reveal that Colombia, Peru, and Brazil, have the best-performing SOEs in the region. None of them is above Tier 2, however.

Figure 5.2 Aggregate Index of Corporate Governance in Selected Countries in Latin America and the Caribbean

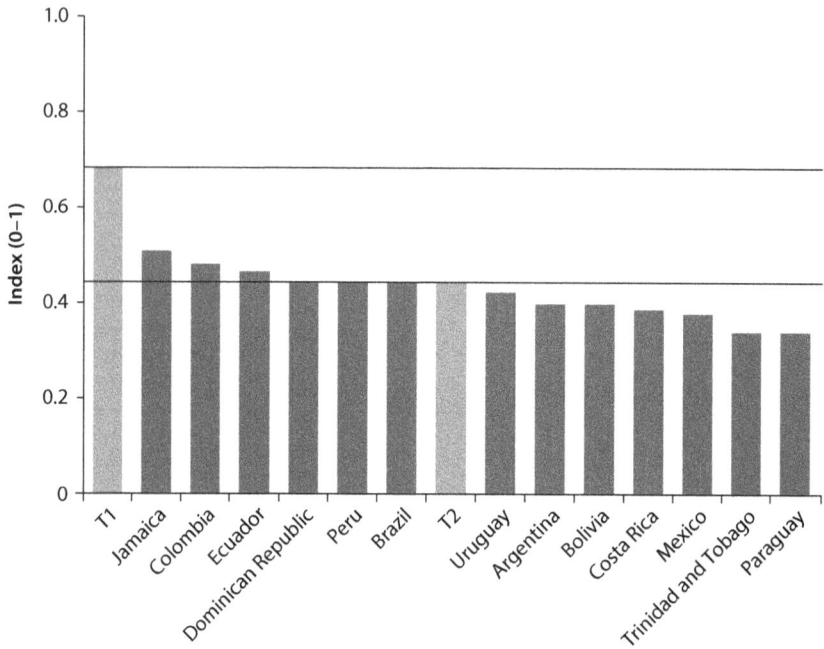

Source: World Bank 2009.

Component 1: Ownership and Legal Framework

A legal framework in which companies are corporatized and subject to similar standards as private companies was prioritized in the assessment of governance (figure 5.3). Priority was also given to companies whose policies are established and monitored by a specialized government agency. The index gives higher scores to companies regulated by independent commissions or agencies and subject to the same tax obligations as private enterprises. Companies that are publicly listed also receive higher scores, because companies subject to the standards of the stock commission are assumed to have better corporate governance.

Corporatization. The majority of the companies in the sample have been corporatized. The most common modality is to subject SOEs to the same legal framework as a limited liability enterprise (sometimes known as *sociedades anónimas* or *capital variable companies* in LAC). SABESP (Brazil) is the only company in the sample that is publicly listed, and, hence, subject to more quality controls by authorities and investors.

Corporatized enterprises are subject to corporate law. Their institutional design is closer to a private company than a unincorporated enterprise. About 70 percent of SOEs can declare bankruptcy in case of insolvency, have a board of directors, and have a shares structure of ownership. Only 35 percent of SOEs require the pursuit of profits.

Uncovering the Drivers of Utility Performance • http://dx.doi.org/10.1596/978-0-8213-9660-5

Figure 5.3 Index of Legal Soundness in Selected Countries in Latin America and the Caribbean

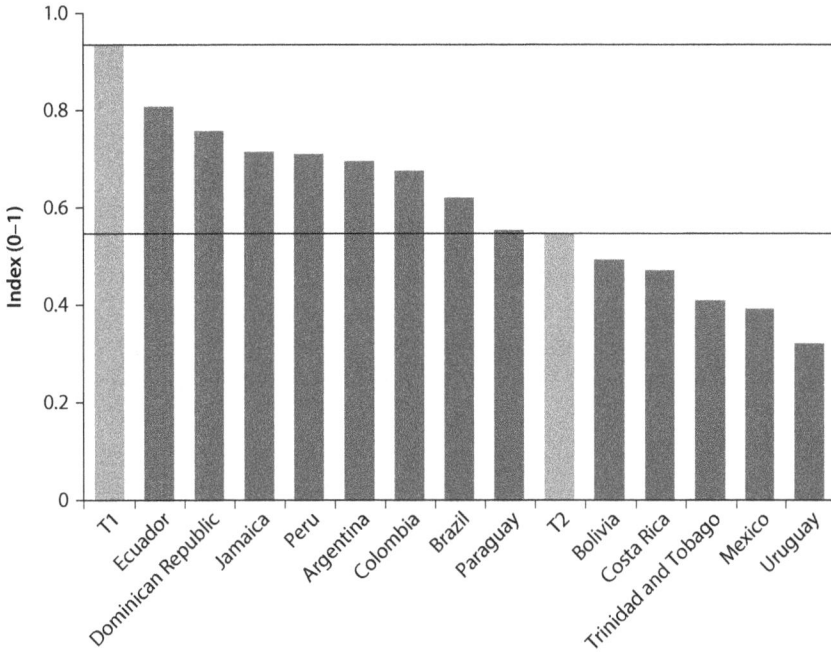

Source: World Bank 2009.

The landscape of companies with shares is diverse. Companies like Aguas de Rio Negro S.A. (Argentina) have not issued shares, even though the company is organized as a private enterprise. Other companies have distributed dividends but at very low levels. In Peru, shares have been used to reimburse users for the money spent on extending the network. Some companies that have not issued shares have earned significant profits. Empresas Publicas de Medellin, for example, transferred about $200,000 to the municipality of Medellin, the company's shareholder.

Ownership structure. Almost half of the sample of SOEs has some private sector participation, but in most cases the percentages are very small (exceptions are SABESP, with 49.7 percent private ownership, and Aguas de Saltillo, with 49.0 percent private ownership). Some alternative mechanisms for private sector participation include share ownership by employees, trade associations, citizens, and users, although they usually account for no more than 10 percent of shares. In Agua y Saneamiento Argentinos S.A., for example, employees represented by the unions are the largest private shareholders. The National Association of Coffee Producers of Colombia owns shares in the Centrales Eléctricas Norte de Santander S.A. E.S.P., and the Association of Manufacturers of Pichincha (Cámara de Industriales de Pichincha) owns shares in Eléctrica de Quito S.A.

Role of authorities. Ownership rights are usually exercised by the sector or line minister. In some cases, ministers of finance and auditing bodies also possess ownership rights. Where SOEs are subsidiaries of larger state enterprises, ownership rights are exercised by a holding company.

Only 23 percent of the utilities sampled have an agency specifically in charge of policies.[1] The rest have a wide range of policy formulation authorities. The sector ministry or some ministerial agency constitutes the most frequent policy formulation authority.

Regulatory role. Economic regulation—particularly the relationship between tariffs and the quality standards of service provision—is a critical aspect of the sustainable management of SOEs. Only a very specific division of roles between the state as policy formulator, provider, and regulator can provide a framework for enforcing economic sustainability and quality of service. In the survey, 72 percent of respondents claimed that the regulator has final decision power in the sector in specific aspects such as tariffs, quality standards, and service expansion. The survey results suggest that the involvement of the government is heavier when it comes to critical issues such as tariff levels and expansion of service and lighter when it is related to more technical, less controversial, aspects of service, such as technical standards and service quality. The distribution of competencies between regulatory agencies and the line ministry shows that the line ministry makes the critical decisions.

Tax regime. Ideally, SOEs should be subject to the same tax obligations as private enterprises. More than half of the SOEs in the sample receive tax exemptions or discounts; only 43 percent reported receiving no fiscal privileges. Exemptions and discounts usually come from differential treatment of income and value added taxes. In practice, SOEs that are not exempt from income tax do not pay income taxes, because they generate no revenues or capitalize revenues as reserves.

The legal soundness index benchmarks SOEs based on their legal framework. Priority was given to a legal structure that levels the playing field for SOEs and private enterprises. The results were surprising, as companies well known for good performance, such as Agua y Drenaje de Monterrey, rank low on this index, and companies known for operational gaps rank high. Overall, companies with a limited liability framework and subject to similar rules as private enterprises score high, and companies with the legal typology of government departments or private enterprise but subject to public rules score low.

The majority of SOEs in LAC have been corporatized and adopted the legal typology of a private enterprise. Several are integrated by shares and have varying degrees of private sector participation. SABESP and Aguas de Saltillo are the companies with the highest levels of private sector participation that have implemented a share structure that provides benefits to shareholders.

Various commissions and agencies regulate SOEs in LAC. Their influence seems to be greater on issues such as quality standards. Line ministries seem to be the most influential actors in regulation.

Component 2: Board and Chief Executive Officer

This section focuses on the composition, qualifications, and performance of the board of directors and chief executive officers (CEOs) of SOEs (figures 5.4 and 5.5). It prioritizes a board in which political discretion is low, members are selected based on predefined criteria (particularly related to merit), and performance is assessed based on different governance arrangements. The greater the emphasis on transparency and accountability of the decision-making authorities of an SOE, the greater the possibilities of improving performance.

The weak results indicate the prevalence of political authorities in the appointment of boards of directors, the low percentage of directors who come from within the SOE or from the ranks of private independent experts, and the lack of board selection criteria. At only 36 percent of utilities does the law establish the need to select directors based on certain criteria. Among utilities that have an established procedure, sector experience and a university degree seem to be the most common requirements. In only 2 percent of cases is political independence a precondition for board eligibility.

The appointment of directors constitutes an interesting example of the differences between SOEs and private enterprises. In for-profit private enterprises, shareholders are interested in appointing a CEO and executive directors with the skills to improve financial performance. Hence, the selection process, whether conducted through the human resources department or based on

Figure 5.4 Index of Board Competitiveness in Selected Countries in Latin America and the Caribbean

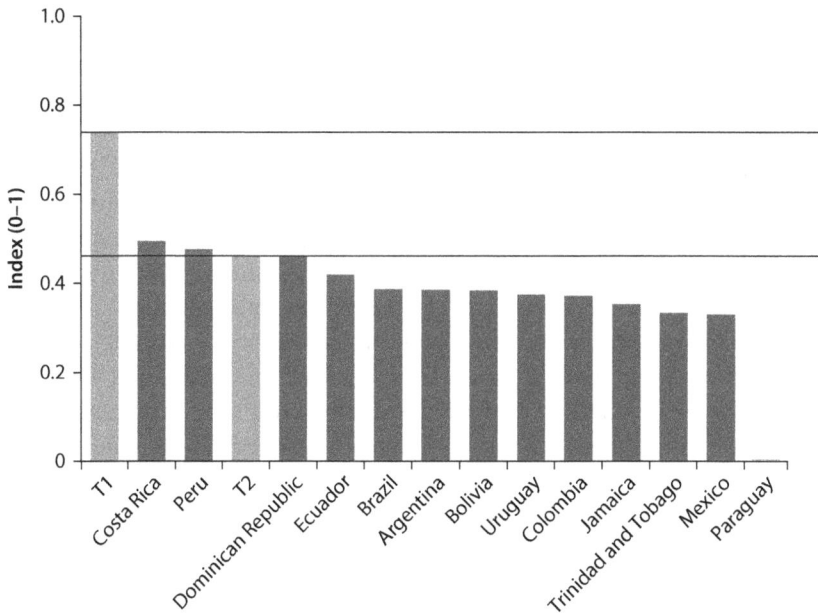

Source: World Bank 2009.

Figure 5.5 Index of Chief Executive Officer Competitiveness in Selected Countries in Latin America and the Caribbean

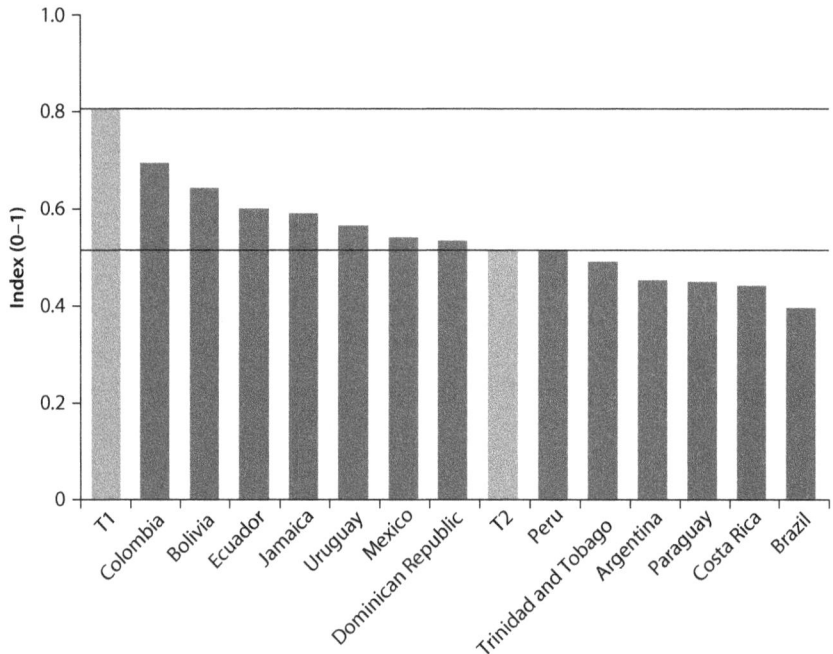

Source: World Bank 2009.

the sole decision of shareholders, emphasizes the candidates' ability to increase the company's revenue. For SOEs, the selection criteria should focus on reducing political discretion in the appointment of decision-making authorities and creating the incentives for good performance. Very few companies have developed specific criteria, beyond legal requirements, to select independent, qualified directors to the board.[2]

Of critical importance for SOE management is performance evaluation. Although responsibility for the achievement can adopt different criteria, the board of directors and CEO are ultimately responsible for the conduct of business. Private companies and SOEs measure performance differently. Profit maximization is the main criterion for rewarding or dismissing directors of private enterprises. All the company's policies are aligned around this objective; its organizational structure and strategies also reflect this orientation. In contrast, at some state enterprises, the dispersion and conflicting interests of stakeholders prevent the formulation of consistent strategies and policies. As a result, assessment of the performance of the companies' authorities is more challenging.

The survey attempted to capture the way directors are evaluated. A significant number of SOEs indicated that their directors were evaluated. Answers to the rest of the survey questions remain unclear. When asked about the methodology/criteria used for assessing directors, only 17 percent of SOEs identified specific criteria. Most indicated that although directors are assessed, there are no specific criteria, confirming the existence of ad hoc mechanisms of evaluation. Very few SOEs identified a particular mechanism against which performance is evaluated. As in private enterprises, directors are assessed at the end of the fiscal year. In some cases, after approval of the accounting and financing reports, the president of the country approves the performance of directors by decree. Strikingly, companies that declared having specific criteria to set objectives responded that they do not have a particular mechanism (especially written) to evaluate directors.

Component 3: Management/Staff

The management/staff index measures the composition and characteristics of the enterprise's staff by education, type of training, legal status, salary and benefit levels, hiring, and incentives (figure 5.6). Employees are a central part of SOEs in the infrastructure sector. They can buffer an SOE from political interference, as a professional and well-organized bureaucracy can oppose measures that hinder their career prospects.

Staff education levels. Most SOE employees work in operations.[3] Thirty-seven percent of all workers are skilled workers, and 31 percent are unskilled workers. Twenty-four percent are nonoperational (administrative) workers. About 15 percent of employees in SOEs have university degrees. The average age in the sample is 44.

Figure 5.6 Index of Professional Management in Selected Countries in Latin America and the Caribbean

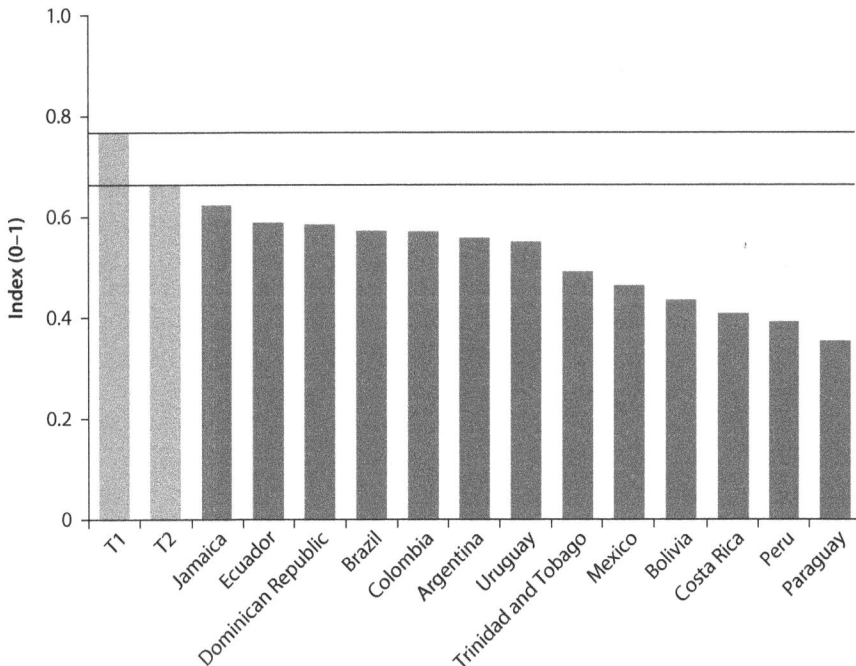

Source: World Bank 2009.

Uncovering the Drivers of Utility Performance • http://dx.doi.org/10.1596/978-0-8213-9660-5

The sample shows diverse educational backgrounds among both board members and staff. At 70 percent of utilities, all board directors have a university degree; at 30 percent, some directors have a university degree. Fifteen percent of companies indicated that all board members had graduate degrees, 55 percent indicated that some board members have a graduate degree, and 30 percent indicated that no members of the board had graduate degrees.

Educational levels are higher among CEOs and managers. At 56 percent of utilities, the CEO has a graduate degree or some graduate education, at 38 percent the CEO has only an undergraduate degree, and at 6 percent the CEO does not have a degree. At 78 percent of utilities all managers have a university degree; at 22 percent some managers have a university degree. With respect to graduate studies, 12 percent of the companies said that all their managers have a graduate degree, and 58 percent reported that some managers did so. At 30 percent of SOEs, none of the managers of the companies had pursued graduate studies.

A common assumption regarding the management of SOEs is that rigid labor schemes prevent the restructuring of the labor force. In the sample, two-thirds of the utilities hired employees under the same laws governing private companies; the remaining utilities did so under civil service rules. The majority of the labor force is hired on a permanent basis; 84 percent of employees were hired under a regime that provides some degree of stability or a special regime, such as a labor agreement or *convenio colectivo de trabajo*. Managers and employees receive training; training of members of the board of directors is rare. Managers benefit most from capacity building.

A crucial aspect related to the proficiency of the human resources of state companies is the mechanism for selecting employees. Political discretion and the influence of trade unions were frequently cited in the past as drivers of overstaffing and low capacity. But the majority of survey respondents identified external competition as the primary way of selecting personnel, particularly for higher-level positions up to the managerial level. A third of unskilled workers are selected through a noncompetitive process. Others mechanisms for hiring staff include internal competition and combinations of internal competition with external selection.

A similar situation can be seen in the case of nonoperational workers, 25 percent of whom are selected based on discretion and 25 percent of whom are selected by unions. Half of the SOEs surveyed indicated that they selected their managers based on discretion rather than competition. These figures are not necessarily an indication of political intervention or undue influence of other stakeholders. They may reflect the need for professionals that the CEO, the board, or both trust.

Performance evaluation. In addition to open and merit-based selection processes, staff of SOEs would benefit from a system of incentives that rewards good performance. The survey asked about the criteria for rewarding performance and the ways in which performance is rewarded. Criteria include years in the company, performance, and the discretional determination of rewards for employees. Rewards include promotion, salary increases, and bonuses.

The majority of SOEs reward their staff based on years in the company and performance. A significant number of companies use only discretion or a combination of discretion and performance/years in the company to reward their employees. Very few companies, including EPM in Colombia and Aguas de Saltillo in Mexico, pay bonuses for achieving certain revenue targets.

Incentive payments in the public sector have been used to motivate civil servants and to increase efficiency and effectiveness. There is no empirical evidence on the consequences of this type of reform. The anecdotal evidence on its use in SOEs is mixed. In the sample, only 20 percent of companies have some type of performance-based payments.

On average, employees earn more than board members. Remuneration of board members is similar to the private sector (and higher than in the public administration) at 30 percent of SOEs surveyed and similar to the public sector at 34 percent of SOEs. Among employees, 84 percent perceive that their salaries are similar to private sector levels or at least higher than public sector levels; 16 percent believe that their salaries are equivalent to public sector salaries. Salary benefits follow the same trend: 90 percent of SOEs pay their employees benefits that are similar to or higher than the private sector or between private and public sector levels.

Component 4: Transparency and Disclosure

The transparency index measures the existence of mechanisms that allow transparent disclosure of the company's financial and nonfinancial information, the involvement of civil society in decision making, and the independent auditing of accounts (figure 5.7). The tier analysis indicates that the majority of SOEs meet only the minimum conditions for achieving the open disclosure of their performance and accounts. No SOE in the sample met the desirable criteria.

Quality of companies' websites. All but one company has a website. Websites include the annual report, financial accounts, corporate structure (chart), and mechanisms to receive consumers' claims and suggestions. Issues such as performance statistics (coverage, quality of service, costs, and so forth); job openings; the names and backgrounds of directors; procurement processes (stages, prices, and so forth); or information for consumers or students were rarely included on the websites.[4]

Involvement of consumers and society in formulation of company policies. Civil society participation can be an important factor in reducing political discretion in the management of the company. Although inclusion of civil society members on the board is an important way of achieving transparency, the focus here is on mechanisms through which some decisions are subject to the scrutiny of society. Among companies that involve civil society, 90 percent do so on a voluntary basis (that is, the company is not obliged to request the views of users or other stakeholders on various aspects of service delivery). Both mandatory and nonmandatory mechanisms include consultations on issues such as tariff increases and infrastructure works for contracts over a specific threshold.

Figure 5.7 Index of Transparency and Disclosure in Selected Countries in Latin America and the Caribbean

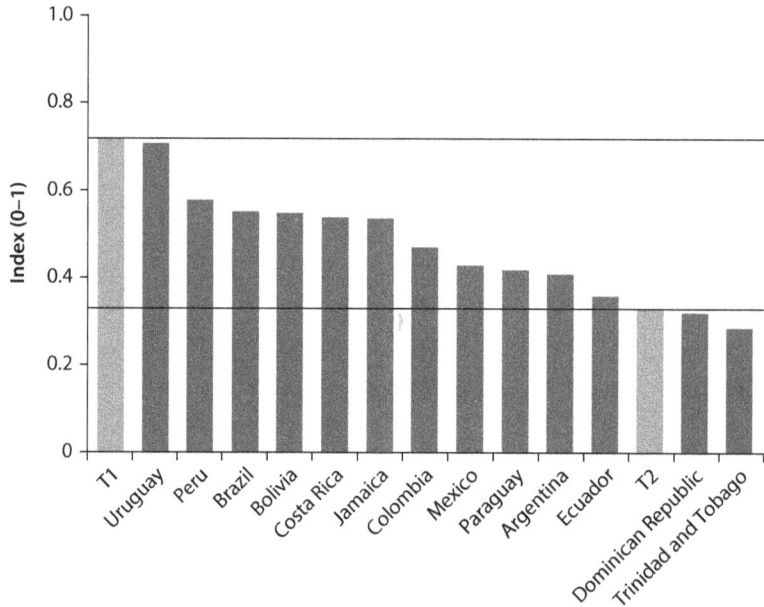

Source: World Bank 2009.

Publication of annual reports. Annual reports serve as accountability mechanisms, because companies must describe their achievements. The majority of SOEs surveyed publish annual reports of their performance. These reports range from the simple enumeration of works developed during the fiscal year to complete, detailed reports.

Auditing of financial accounts. Although traditionally subject to public sector scrutiny, a significant number of SOEs are also audited by private auditors. The majority of enterprises sampled are audited by both government audit agencies and private auditors: only 5 percent of SOEs are audited exclusively by the government, and 30 percent are audited only by private auditors. Forty percent use international accounting standards to report financial information. The majority of SOEs also publish their audited accounts. Eighty percent of companies that do so use their website and other means, such as newspapers and printed publications. Only 22 percent of companies in the sample do not publish their audited accounts.

Integration of the board. Just 7 percent of boards of directors include consumers or members of civil society. At 23 percent of utilities, board members are appointed with the intervention of the parliament or the private sector.

Component 5: Performance Orientation
Performance-oriented management facilitates the identification of objectives and, consequently, increases efficiency, particularly for SOEs, where incentives for performance are difficult to create because of the lack of private investors.

Three dimensions of the performance orientation of SOEs are examined: the process of setting objectives, the instruments used to set objectives and its enforcement, and the authority that conducts these assessments (figure 5.8).

Objective setting. Answers from SOEs were not sufficiently clear about the ways performance objectives are established. The majority of responses focused on the instruments through which the evaluation takes place. A few were explicit about targets and the process of identification and establishment.[5]

Instruments. The strategic plan or business plan seems to be the most common mechanism used by SOEs to set objectives; the annual report is the way companies inform stakeholders about the fulfillment of these achievements. Some companies also use public hearings as a way for board members to explain the results of the enterprise. It is not clear from the responses what constitutes a performance agreement and what constitutes a business strategy. Three companies specifically recognize the use of a performance contract to guide the strategic direction of the enterprise. Other mechanisms that complement business plans are the balance scorecard and evaluation systems linked to national or local development strategies.

Evaluation authorities. The line ministry, the regulator, and auditing agencies seem to be the principal centers of accountability for state enterprises. In some

Figure 5.8 Performance Orientation Index in Selected Countries in Latin America and the Caribbean

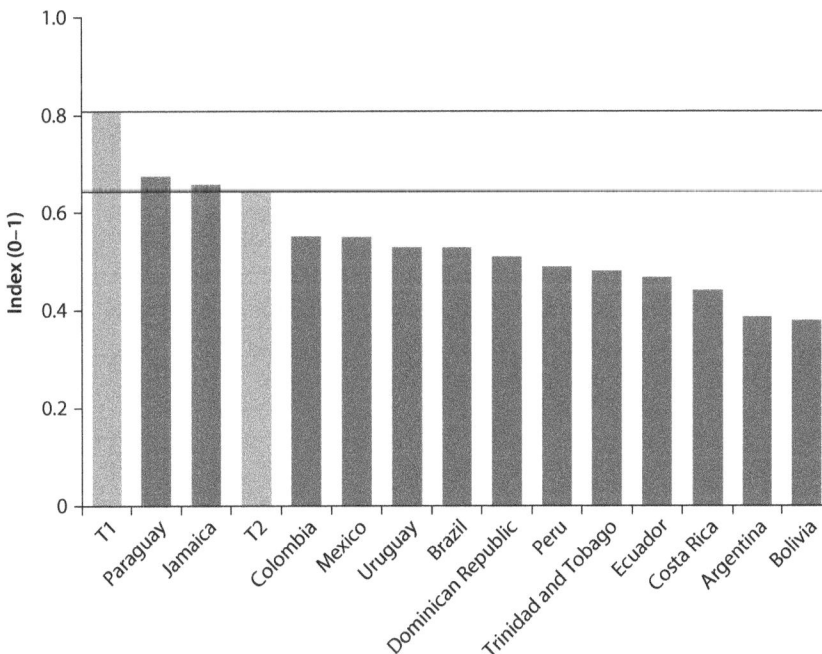

Source: World Bank 2009.

cases, the company is self-assessed by its board of directors. Some companies are subject to the control of a specific agency, such as the Solidarity Fund of Ecuador or the SOE Oversight Council of Paraguay. The parliament has little say in the accountability of SOEs. Greater involvement of the parliament in the discussion of management issues related to SOE performance could serve as a counter-weight to the political discretion of the executive.

Assessment of board of members and staff. SOEs have weak mechanisms for evaluating the performance of board members. Not surprisingly, executive directors—who are responsible for managing the enterprise—seem to be subject to higher levels of scrutiny than members of the board. Thirty percent of executive directors are not assessed based on particular criteria. Arrangements to evaluate the performance of the CEO range from informal, ad hoc mechanisms to more detailed systems. At most utilities, the board approves the CEO's performance. At some utilities, specific criteria are established; other utilities lack procedures to evaluate CEO performance. The most detailed mechanisms include memorandums of understanding between the government and the executive director or the assessment of performance against the performance agreement or other mechanism through which the company is evaluated (such as the balance scorecard).

Corporate Governance and Performance

This section explores the relations between various dimensions of corporate governance and the operational performance of utilities in the water and electricity distribution sectors of LAC. The dimensions described in the previous section are correlated with the level and growth rates of the main performance indicators. Appendix G presents the detailed results.

Legal Framework
A legal arrangement in which companies are corporatized and subject to similar standards as other private companies receives a higher score. Results suggest that greater legal soundness is associated with low distributional losses, low coverage, high labor productivity, and high tariffs. The stronger the legal framework, the lower the average quality of service and the higher the average tariffs. For water utilities, greater soundness is associated with higher labor productivity; in electricity distribution, the opposite trend is observed. The main other results hold for both sectors.

Board of Directors and Chief Executive Officer
A higher score is given to companies in which political discretion over the board of directors is low, board members are selected based on predefined criteria, and member performance is assessed based on different governance arrangements. The results suggest that the higher the scores on these dimensions, the lower the distributional losses and the lower the service coverage. The higher the qualifica-tions of the board, the higher the level of average tariffs. Growth rates of these

performance indicators seem not to be significantly affected by the competitiveness of the board or the CEO; however, when the sectors are analyzed separately, the change in performance in the water sector seems to be more sensitive to these dimensions. In the water sector, these dimensions are associated with greater continuity of service. The measure of CEO competitiveness is more closely correlated with positive changes in coverage and lower average tariffs; board competitiveness is more closely correlated with positive changes in labor productivity and micrometering. For the electricity sector, the results were not significantly different from zero.

Management/Staff

For the sample as a whole, only labor productivity is correlated with good management. In the water sector, better management is also associated with lower distributional losses and better continuity of service, sewerage coverage, and micrometering.

Transparency and Disclosure

The transparency index measures the existence of mechanisms that allow for publication of the company's financial and nonfinancial information, the involvement of civil society in decision making, disclosure of financial information, and independent auditing of accounts. Utilities with greater transparency and disclosure standards are associated with higher levels of service coverage and lower average tariffs. In the electricity sector, utilities with higher transparency indexes have higher coverage and lower tariffs. The results are stronger in the water sector, where transparency is correlated with greater efficiency; lower volumes of nonrevenue water; and higher potability, metering, and coverage.

Performance Orientation

The performance orientation index measures the existence of internal and external mechanisms for evaluating performance. As expected, this index is highly correlated with labor productivity and (low) distributional losses, as well as significant changes in coverage. Most of these results hold when each sector is assessed separately.

Aggregated Corporate Governance

The aggregated measure of corporate governance presents the overall results for the region in terms of the ranking of companies according to the five components of the framework. The index is highly correlated with high levels of labor productivity and tariffs and low distributional losses. Positive correlations are also evident in service coverage. The correlation results are stronger for water utilities than electricity providers. For water companies, overall corporate governance is associated with low volumes of nonrevenue water and high quality standards, coverage, labor productivity, and average tariffs. The evidence shows that aggregate corporate governance is positively correlated with continuity of service, labor productivity, metering, and sewerage coverage and negatively correlated with average tariffs.

Some of the components of the aggregate index probably behave similarly. Hence, a principal component approach (PCA) was applied in order to include six indicators, thus minimizing the loss of information.[6]

The first principal component factor accounts for 36 percent of the variance of the indexes. The other two component factors account for 23 percent and 17 percent of the variance. Together the three factors account for 76 of the total variance.[7] Appendix table G.8 presents the factor loading. Factor 1 is associated with the professional management and the performance orientation dimensions. Factor 2 reflects the board competitiveness aspects. Factor 3 is related to legal soundness and transparency and disclosure. The correlation between the aggregated index as a weighted average of these factors and the aggregated corporate governance index presented earlier is significant (0.87). The ranking of countries presents some changes in the relative position for each country, but the story told earlier still holds.

Conclusion

Governance arrangements in SOEs in water and electricity distribution present a wide spectrum of designs. In contrast to private enterprises, which are characterized by the adoption of standard corporate strategies, SOE standards vary depending on countries' institutional systems and the characteristics of the service. The variety of arrangements calls for the systematization of governance practices and the identification of successful experiences. SOE performance is directly or indirectly related to the overall governance of countries or provinces.

This chapter emphasizes the need for a corporate structure that prevents political intervention, rewards performance, and is subject to public scrutiny. It focuses on the qualifications of the staff of the enterprises. Although it tries to capture as many variables from state enterprises as possible, the focus is on the design, not the effectiveness, of governance procedures.

As in a private enterprise, the organizational structure and decision making of an SOE reflects the interests and involvement of its shareholders and, hence, their strengths and weaknesses. Because these enterprises are part of the public administration and thus subject to its governance schemes and leadership, they can benefit (or suffer) from the performance of its bureaucracy. SOEs remain a complex and unique organizational mode, caught between the norms of public sector governance and corporate governance (Whincop 2005). Hence, although mimicking private enterprise arrangements might improve SOE management, it could also contribute to the consolidation of corruption and the lack of accountability in enterprises with few controls and few governing stakeholders with vested interests.

The focus on five components of design highlights the major pitfalls related to performance orientation and the selection and composition of the board of directors. SOEs plan their strategies, but it is not clear how they set objectives or monitor and enforce them. Generally, SOEs are subject to influences of different authorities, particularly during their planning process.

The major difference in staff selection in private companies and SOEs is the way in which managers are selected. From low-level employees to members of the board of directors, a significant percentage of managers are hired internally or with limited competition. Hiring from within is common among private enterprises; SOEs, however, provide more room for collusion between stakeholders. Measures need to be taken to prevent low levels of professionalism and political appointees.

Management of SOEs presents government bureaucrats with unique challenges. First—and most important—SOEs face conflicting goals, which affect their business strategy. Several departments usually compete to move their agenda to the top of the company's priorities. Interference in the companies' business is often done informally, preventing the company from making the costs of interference explicit. Second, the lack of profit orientation prevents SOEs from identifying ways to improve efficiency and performance. Because low revenues can be compensated for by government subsidies, making the company sustainable is not the top priority. Third, poor accountability systems (at the regulatory or management levels) prevent the development of an ownership structure that incentivizes senior management to behave in ways that promote efficiency.

Although it is too early to formulate policy recommendations, some potential actions emerge from both the literature and practices in the region. Considering public enterprises as private companies can in some cases lead to wrong diagnoses and, hence, inappropriate reforms. Some, if not the majority of, SOEs in water and electricity distribution are not profit driven, which makes the corporate incentives on which private enterprises are based questionable. As Whincop (2005) notes, it makes sense to design governance appropriate to the form rather than to emulate the incentive structure of alternatives. Doing so calls for the identification of governance schemes that focus on the factors that may spur efficiency, reducing the space for corruption and capture by vested interests.

It is in this context that accountability emerges as the main governance aspect of SOEs. At utilities with high levels of corruption and inefficiency, accountability systems should be put in place that prevent discretional management (both from management and political authorities) and create incentives for good performance. Regulation and performance-based management are complementary ways of achieving these goals, although care needs to be taken in creating checks and balances, such as parliamentary oversight and state auditing.

A governance design reflecting the incentives of private enterprises seems more appropriate for utilities with partial rather than full state ownership, particularly companies with significant private sector participation. For companies with significant gaps in both performance and management, transparent accountability mechanisms should be considered. At companies that are fully state owned and characterized by good performance, management need to strike a balance between private sector orientation and public accountability. Governance design needs to take into consideration sector differences. Technology and sector dynamics also determine management.

This assessment is the first of its kind. The results suggest that good corporate governance is associated with better performance and higher growth rates. As expected, performance orientation and professional management characteristics seem to be the most important contributors to performance; all the other characteristics are associated with some performance indicators. Results are stronger in the water sector than the electricity sector, presumably because of the larger number of utilities included in the sample. Further analysis should include more disaggregated data and a larger sample. It is also important to explore political economy approaches that address issues of causality, sequencing, and complex interaction effects that contribute to SOE governance and to complement the analysis with detailed case studies to improve the knowledge of the internal mechanisms affecting performance.

Notes

1. In Argentina, the ownership policies of Aguas Rionegrinas S.A. are determined by the Secretary of Management and Control of SOEs of the government of Rio Negro. In Paraguay, some SOEs are subject to the Oversight Council of SOEs, which is also in charge of signing and enforcing performance contracts with SOEs.

2. FONFAE, in Peru, developed guidelines regulating the appointment, payment, and obligations of directors of companies in which the state has any ownership. Its directive asserts that only directors with a university degree and five years of professional experience can be appointed. They are not employees of the enterprise but hired under a professional services contract (*locación de servicios*). The regulation also establishes their obligations and responsibilities. Empresas Públicas de Medellín (EPM), in Colombia, has a corporate governance code that addresses, among other issues, the criteria for appointing directors to the board. Board members must have a university degree and relevant professional experience, and five of the nine directors must be independent from the government. EPM is one of the few state enterprises in LAC that requires independence as a criterion for appointment.

3. The survey defines operational workers in the following way: Operational "qualified" workers are employees (permanent and nonpermanent) that do not have a university degree but perform tasks that require a special knowledge and practice. Operational "nonqualified" workers are employees (permanent and nonpermanent) that do not have a university degree and perform tasks that do not require special knowledge or practices.

4. ElectroSureste (Peru), SABESP, and EPM have well-designed websites with useful information for consumers, investors, and the general public. ElectroSureste's website includes an e-procurement system that provides bidding guidelines, deadlines, and results. It also publishes the projected time, responsible authorities, and purpose of the different types of claims users can pursue. It provides consumers with a virtual office to answer their questions and address their concerns.

5. State-owned electrical utilities in the Dominican Republic are under the authority of the DR Corporation of Electricity Companies. ELECTROSUR, a Dominican

SOE, for instance, discusses objectives related to coverage and quality of service with the government. It discusses efficiency and revenues issues with the holding company and issues related to work-related accidents, environment protection, and so forth within the company. A different approach to the setting of objectives is used in Colombia, where the control agency (Superintendencia de Servicios Publicos Domiciliarios) requires utilities to prepare plans based on preselected criteria and indicators. The evaluation of financial and nonfinancial performance of SOEs takes place through an independent audit by a private firm. The assessment focuses on corporate and social aspects. The first evaluation is related to financial indicators; the second is related to administrative and technical parameters and quality standards. Another set of companies coordinates policy goals and objectives through performance agreements. Some companies in Brazil and Paraguay sign performance contracts with government authorities through which they set objective and monitoring strategies. In Paraguay, ANDE signs a performance agreement with the line minister and the ownership unit (Consejo Supervisor de Empresas del Estado). The agreement is enforced by the ownership unit through periodical reports stating the level of achievement of targets. Grupo CEEE and CAESB in Brazil sign performance contracts with policy formulation authorities. Other state utilities establish objectives that are linked to development plans. Together with the sector minister, SOEs in Costa Rica set development goals, which are monitored in the context of the national evaluation system. Some utilities (ANDE in Paraguay, ERSSA and CentroSur in Peru) use scorecard methodologies.

6. The principal component approach was used to jointly take into account the information provided by the six main governance indicators ratios (appendix table G.8) and generate orthogonal indexes to measure corporate governance. Factor scores were then calculated for each of the utilities. As a first step, the number of factors in the analysis was determined. Appendix table G.7 reports the estimated factors and their eigenvalues. Only factors accounting for more than 10 percent of the variance (eigenvalues >1) were kept in the analysis (the first three factors).

7. These factors allow a factor score coefficient matrix to be computed. The varimax factor rotation method was used to reduce the number of variables that have high loadings on a factor. This method makes it the most likely to identify each variable with a single factor. This approach greatly enhances the ability to make substantive interpretation of the main factors. Appendix table G.8 presents the factor loadings; variables with large loadings ($N > 0.4$) for a given factor are highlighted in bold.

References

Andrés, L. A., J. L. Guasch, and S. L. Azumendi. 2011. "Governance in State-Owned Enterprises Revisited: The Cases of Water and Electricity in Latin America and the Caribbean." Policy Research Working Paper 5747, World Bank, Washington, DC.

OECD (Organisation for Economic Co-operation and Development). 2005. *Guidelines of Corporate Governance in SOEs.* Paris: OECD.

Schwartz, K. 2006. *Managing Public Water Utilities: An Assessment of Bureaucratic and New Public Management Models in the Water Supply and Sanitation Sectors in Low- and Middle-Income Countries.* UNESCO–IHE Institute for Water Education, Delft, the Netherlands.

Vagliasindi, M. 2008. *Governance Arrangements for State-Owned Enterprises.* London: European Bank for Reconstruction and Development.

————. 2009. *The Links between Internal and External Governance and the Performance of Infrastructure Service Providers.* World Bank, Washington, DC.

Whincop, M. J. 2005. *Corporate Governance in Government Corporations.* Aldershot, U.K.: Ashgate.

World Bank. 2009. LAC SOE Governance Database. Washington, DC.

CHAPTER 6

Other Determinants of Sector Performance

This chapter briefly summarizes a number of additional factors that may affect sector performance and examines the interaction of some of them. It reviews and summarizes the results of previous empirical analyses of factors that affect utilities' decision-making process. These decisions have an impact that can be measured through the indicators proposed in this study.

Researchers have modeled and empirically tested the impact of such issues as corruption, market structure, economies of scope and density, renegotiation, and reputation. Some have proposed that other issues—such as subsidy mechanisms, cost recovery, and the political economy and social accountability of the sector— also affect performance. Few econometric studies exist on this connection; most analyses rely on comprehensive analytical case studies.

Corruption

Corruption can have a destructive effect on sector performance. As previous research suggests, it affects the pace and nature of private sector participation in infrastructure service, affecting competitive bidding and resulting in unequal allocation of bids that can lead to monopoly rents instead of efficiency gains (Andrés, Diop, and Guasch 2008).

Corruption directly affects sector performance through multiple transmission mechanisms. Various studies have linked corruption not only with lower levels of investments but also with types of investments, service quality, access, and prices.[1] Dal Bó and Rossi (2007) show that corruption diverts managerial effort away from the productive process, forcing firms to use a different (suboptimal) combination of inputs to meet their service obligations. Their model shows that more corrupt countries have less efficient (lower labor productivity) firms.

By measuring the impact of corruption on performance and the interaction between reforms (introducing private participation, an independent regulatory agency, or both) and corruption, Estache, Goicoechea, and Trujillo (2009) test the extent to which "reform policies have managed to reinforce or offset the impacts of corruption and, vice versa, the extent to which corruption reinforces or offsets the impacts of the policies" (p. 194). Their results show that in electricity distribution, corruption offsets the impact of reforms. An increase in the corruption index results in a decrease in energy use. In countries with state-owned enterprises, an increase in corruption is associated with lower residential prices and deterioration of access and quality. For water, the model is less conclusive, possibly because of the poor quality of the data.

In the electricity and telecommunications sectors, the negative interaction between corruption and the introduction of an independent regulatory agency suggests that the presence of these agencies offsets the effects of corruption. Clarke and Xu (2004) provide evidence for the effects of petty corruption at the utility level and the impact on service provision and sector performance.[2] They show that corruption increases the constraints on utility capacity and reduces competition among utilities.

Cost Recovery

Cost recovery is considered the most significant policy aspect explaining water policy performance. Among the seven policy aspects Saleth and Dinar (1999) consider, cost recovery ranks as the most significant in explaining water policy performance.[3] They evaluate the overall performance of water institutions and their ultimate impact on performance by studying the linkages between institutions and performance. For example, better water sector performance in China, Mexico, and other countries suggests that macroeconomic policies condition the effectiveness of water policy. Traditionally, utilities have charged tariffs that are far below cost-recovery levels; failure to recover costs was one of the fundamental reasons for promoting private sector participation in fixed telecommunications, electricity distribution, and water distribution during the 1990s in Latin America and the Caribbean (LAC). Low tariffs led to lack of network expansion, low coverage rates, and poor service quality. As poor customers could not (and cannot) afford service at higher prices, subsidy mechanisms were (and remain) part of the price structure in electricity and water. Some studies suggest a link between the type of subsidy mechanism and sector performance, as the mechanism creates incentives for particular behavior from customers that hinders the utility's ability to maximize its profits and perform efficiently (Komives and others 2005).

Role of Civil Society

The voice of users is often ignored. The lack of a mechanism for incorporating users' priorities and preferences into the decision-making processes of the service provider may lead to service deterioration and client estrangement. Muller, Simpson, and van Ginneken (2008) explore innovative approaches to public management that hold service providers more directly accountable to their users for the outcomes of their work. Accountability in this context is about directly channeling users to service providers.

A study by the Asian Development Bank (2004) looks at the role of civil society in water provider accountability in 18 Asian cities. It explores priority areas for both users and service providers, such as improving governance and reducing corruption, and suggests that this overlap of priorities may be a powerful determinant of improved sector performance.

Contract Arrangements

Investment levels and contract arrangements are significant determinants of effective and equitable public services. Various studies have assessed the challenges, opportunities, and options for public-private partnerships and their impact on sector performance. According to Ogunbiyi (2004), several schemes have had a "negative impact on the poorest of the poor by restricting their access to clean supplies because of high tariffs" (p. 4). Ogunbiyi asserts that public-private partnership schemes involving management contracts—which combine public finance and private management of technical and commercial operations—could be the best type of contractual arrangement for water supply and sanitation in Africa. In Senegal, for example, the choice of an *affermage* contract, which was enhanced by the addition of strong financial incentives to reduce leakage and improve billing and collection efficiency, was innovative.[4] The contract addressed the needs of the government, kept the assets in the government's hands, and clearly defined operations and maintenance functions. The nature of the contract fostered a partnership between the government and the private operator.

Private Sector Participation and Renegotiation

Although renegotiation may be the inevitable consequence of contract incompleteness—and sometimes the solution to some of the inefficiencies caused by it—several authors have identified negative practical consequences. Engel, Fischer, and Galetovic (1997) study the effects of government guarantees and renegotiation on the efficiency of the public-private partnership contracts. They find that renegotiations increase the discretion of the government, reduce the incentives for efficiency, and encourage firms to lowball their bids for the projects, especially if they have experience lobbying. Guasch (2004) notes that lowball strategies in the bidding process undermine the efficiency of the allocation—and as a consequence reduce consumer welfare and sector performance.

The most relevant research on the relation between renegotiation and lowballing bidding strategies is by Guasch, Kartasheva, and Quesada (2001); Estache and Quesada (2001); Guasch (2004); and others who develop theoretical models in which lowballing is an equilibrium strategy for rational bidders. Guasch and others (2001) provide a quantitative measure of the lowballing effect of the expectations of future renegotiation over bidding strategies. They conclude that renegotiation expectations appear to significantly affect the competitive bidding of public-private partnership infrastructure projects. Disaggregating by the party requesting the renegotiation, they find evidence of a positive effect if the requesting party is the winning firm; the evidence is slightly less clear if the government is the requesting party.

Private Sector Participation and Reputation

Bajari, Houghton, and Tadelis (2011) develop a structural auction model in which they use data on characteristics of a project to construct highways in California, including the size of ex post adjustments to the original construction budgets, as a measure of the expected extra revenues the firm may obtain after requesting contract renegotiation. As the extra revenues affect the bids at the auction stage less than proportionally, the authors conclude that there is a sizable transaction cost from the renegotiation process.

To measure ex ante expectations, Andrés, Diaz, and Guasch (2009) consider the ex post outcome (the occurrence of renegotiation). They model the expectations of renegotiation using ex post occurrences of renegotiation for a given country. Their framework allows them to use more information and eliminate possible bias from the estimation. The results suggest that bidders (especially bidders with the highest valuations for the project) adjust their investment offer upward when renegotiation is a plausible outcome after the concession is awarded.

Economies of Scope, Scale, and Density

Research to determine the optimal size of utilities focuses on estimating cost or production functions in which firms either minimize costs or maximize profits. Through the use of these types of models, a number of studies have been able to establish the optimal size of a given utility firm and determine the existence or nonexistence of economies of scale and scope in different sectors.[5]

Additional research has focused on trying to measure the existence of economies of density in electricity and water. Using frontier analysis estimation methods, a number of studies have examined the factors that affect productivity and efficiency at individual firms. These models consider structural variables to account for the potential existence of economies of scale and density. In some cases, the results suggest that settlement density; urban versus rural location (Cullmann, Crespo, and Plagnet 2008); and consumer structure affect the productivity of utilities (von Hirschhausen and Kappeler 2004). By estimating cost functions, several studies show the existence of economies of density and economies of scale for small and medium-size electric utilities. As smaller utilities do not operate at an optimal service level, costs can be reduced by merging and increasing their service area (Filippini 1998; Filippini and Wild 2001). Performance can suffer in low population density service areas, where it is difficult to exploit economies of scale in management and physical plants (Gómez-Ibáñez 2007). Using total factor productivity analysis for a set of utilities in Southern Africa, Estache, Tovar, and Trujillo (2007) find a correlation between performance on the one hand and market structure, the existence of a private actor, dependence on the water source, the degree of vertical integration, and the existence of an independent regulator on the other.

Under certain conditions, economies or diseconomies of scale and density exist. Models show that there are diseconomies of scale for residential service and economies of scale for nonresidential service. Economies of scale achieved in water treatment are largely lost in the distribution of water; however, utilities experience economies of scope associated with joint production of water and sanitation (Kim and Clark 1988). In a study of four developing countries, Nauges and Van den Berg (2008) show that there are economies of scope in areas where utilities provide both water and sewerage services.

Competition in the Telecommunication Sector

During the 1990s, both privatization and the introduction of competition in the telecommunications sector were recommended in Latin America. There is broad agreement among academics and practitioners that competition is the most effective method of promoting investments in the telecom sector. A monopoly provider, whether a state-owned enterprise or a private operator, faces fewer incentives to improve service and reduce prices than enterprises operating in a competitive environment (Wallsten 2001). In most countries, liberalization of the long-distance market took place a few years after privatization (Andrés Diop, and Guasch 2008).

To identify the effects of competition on performance, the literature uses two proxies for competition: liberalization of long-distance fixed-line telephone service and the existence and coverage of cellular phone providers (as a competitive threat to fixed-line operators). Petrazzini and Clark (1996) find that service coverage is higher in competitive markets. Wallsten (2001) finds that competition is associated with deeper mainline penetration, a larger number of pay phones, greater connectivity capacity, and lower prices for local calls. Andrés, Diop, and Guasch (2008) find that the main driver for sector performance in these markets is private sector participation. When a control variable for private sector participation is included in their model, introducing competition in the market is associated with a reduction in prices.

Conclusion

This chapter attempts to understand sector performance by examining the performance of individual utilities in Latin American and the Caribbean. By themselves, the factors studied—corruption; cost recovery; civil society; contracts arrangements and their renegotiation; reputation; economies of scope, scale, and density; and competition—may not affect the performance indicators examined in this volume. But direct links (such as subsidy mechanisms that result in tariffs that are below cost-recovery levels, restricting the utility's financial ability to expand coverage and provide adequate service quality) and indirect links (such as improving social accountability by introducing a mechanism that can hold service providers more directly accountable to users for the outcomes of their work) interact to create the incentive framework utilities use to make management and operation decisions. The objective of this chapter was not to fully explain sector performance but to recognize and acknowledge issues that may affect utility behavior and the type of incentives they have to perform efficiently.

Notes

1. For a comprehensive review of recent studies on corruption and infrastructure, see Estache (2008).

2. Clarke and Xu (2004) use a unique dataset for 21 Eastern European countries that includes information about bribes paid to utilities for service provision.

3. These policy aspects are the project selection criteria, the cost-recovery status, the effectiveness of interregional/sectoral water transfer policy, the extent of the impact of government policy toward private sector and user participation, the effects of other economic policies on water policy, and the extent of linkage between water law and water policy.

4. In an *affermage* contract, the private utility operates a publicly owned system and collects revenues that it then shares with the public owner, who remains in charge of investment.

5. For water supply, Kim and Clark (1988) study the effects of economies of scale and scope in a multiproduct utility, using a translog multiproduct joint cost function. For electricity, Hjalmarsson and Veiderpass (1992) use data envelope analysis to examine productivity growth and the effects of economies of density in retail electricity distribution in Sweden.

References

ADB (Asian Development Bank). 2004. *Water in Asian Cities: Utilities Performance and Civil Society Views.* Water for All Series No. 10, Manila: ADB.

Andrés, L., J. G. Diaz, and J. L. Guasch. 2009. *An Empirical Study of the Effects of Renegotiations over the Auctioning of PPP Concessions.* World Bank, Washington, DC.

Andrés, L., M. Diop, and J. L. Guasch. 2008. "Achievements and Challenges of Private Participation in Infrastructure in Latin America: Evaluation and Future Prospects." In *Euromoney Infrastructure Financing,* edited by H. Davis. Oxford, U.K.: Oxford University Press.

Bajari, P., S. Houghton, and S. Tadelis. 2011. "Bidding for Incomplete Contracts: An Empirical Analysis of Adaptation Costs." Working Paper, University of Minnesota, Minneapolis.

Clarke, G. R. G., and L. C. Xu. 2004. "Privatization, Competition, and Corruption: How Characteristics of Bribe Takers and Payers Affect Bribes to Utilities." *Journal of Public Economics* 88: 2067–2097.

Cullmann, A., H. Crespo, and M. Plagnet. 2008. "International Benchmarking in Electricity Distribution: A Comparison of French and German Utilities." DIW Discussion Paper 830, German Institute for Economic Research, Berlin.

Dal Bó, E., and M. A. Rossi. 2007. "Corruption and Inefficiency: Theory and Evidence from Electric Utilities." *Journal of Public Economics* 91 (5–6): 939–62.

Engel, E., R. Fischer, and A. Galetovic. 1997. "Infrastructure Franchising and Government Guarantees." In *Dealing with Public Risk in Private Infrastructure*, edited by T. Irwin, M. Klein, G. Perry, and M. Thobani, 89–118. Washington, DC: World Bank.

Estache, A. 2008. "Infrastructure and Development: A Survey of Recent and Upcoming Issues." In *Rethinking Infrastructure for Development: Annual World Bank Conference on Development Economics*, edited by F. Bourguignon and B. Pleskovic, 47–82. Washington, DC: World Bank.

Estache, A., A. Goicoechea, and L. Trujillo. 2009. "Utilities Reforms and Corruption in Developing Countries." *Utilities Policy* 17 (2): 191–202.

Estache, A., and L. Quesada. 2001. "Concession Contract Renegotiations: Some Efficiency versus Equity Dilemmas." Policy Research Working Paper 2705, World Bank, Washington, DC.

Estache A., B. Tovar, and L. Trujillo. 2007. "Are African Electricity Distribution Companies Efficient? Evidence of Southern African Countries." Discussion Paper, Department of Economics, City University, London.

Filippini, M. 1998. "Are Municipal Electricity Distribution Utilities Natural Monopolies?" *Annals of Public and Cooperative Economics* 69 (2): 157–74.

Filippini, M., and J. Wild. 2001. "Regional Differences in Electricity Distribution Costs and Their Consequences for Yardstick Regulation of Access Prices." *Energy Economics* 23 (4): 477–88.

Gómez-Ibáñez, A. J. 2007. "Private Infrastructure in Developing Countries: Lessons from Recent Experience." Paper presented to the Commission on Growth and Development, "Workshop on Global Trends and Challenges," Yale Center for the Study of Globalization, New Haven, CT, September 28–29.

Guasch, J. L. 2004. *Granting and Renegotiating Infrastructure Concessions: Doing it Right.* Washington, DC: World Bank.

Guasch, J. L., A. Kartasheva, and L. Quesada. 2001. "Concession Contracts in Latin America and Caribbean Region: An Economic Analysis and Empirical Evidence." Working Paper, World Bank, Washington, DC.

Hjalmarsson, L., and A. Veiderpass. 1992. "Productivity in Swedish Electricity Retail Distribution." *Scandinavian Journal of Economics* 94 (Supplement): 193–205.

Kim, H. Y., and M. R. Clark. 1988. "Economies of Scale and Scope in Water Supply." *Regional Science and Urban Economics* 18 (4): 479–502.

Komives, K., V. Foster, J. Halpern, and Q. Wodon. 2005. *Water, Electricity and the Poor: Who Benefits from Utility Subsidies?* Directions in Development. Washington, DC: World Bank.

Muller, M., R. Simpson, and M. van Ginneken. 2008. "Ways to Improve Water Services by Making Utilities More Accountable to Their Users: A Review." Water Working Notes, World Bank, Washington, DC.

Nauges, C., and C. van den Berg. 2008. "Economies of Density, Scale and Scope in the Water Supply and Sewerage Sector: A Study of Four Developing and Transition Economies." *Journal of Regulatory Economics* 34: 144–63.

Ogunbiyi, C. 2004. "PPPs: Fad or Good for SADC?" SADC PPP Pathway, SADC Banking Association PPP Capacity Building Programme, Newsletter No. 1, July.

Petrazzini, B. A., and T. H. Clark. 1996. "Costs and Benefits of Telecommunications Liberalization in Developing Countries." Paper presented at Institute for International Economics, "Liberalizing Telecommunications," Washington, DC, January 29.

Saleth, R. M., and A. Dinar. 1999. "Evaluating Water Institutions and Water Sector Performance." Technical Paper 447, World Bank, Washington, DC.

von Hirschhausen, C., and A. Kappeler. 2004. "Productivity Analysis of German Electricity Distribution Utilities." DIW Discussion Paper 418, German Institute for Economic Research, Berlin.

Wallsten, S. 2001. *Reverse Auctions and Universal Telecommunications Service: Lessons from Global Experience.* Technology Policy Institute, Stanford University, Stanford, CA.

CHAPTER 7

Conclusions

As a result of reforms, Latin America and the Caribbean (LAC) witnessed significant improvements in the performance of the electricity distribution, water and sanitation, and fixed telecommunications sectors. In the early 2000s, however, public and private investment declined significantly, dissatisfaction with some of the policies implemented during the 1990s rose, and poor people found it difficult to secure access to affordable services.

Against this backdrop, the analysis examined several determinants that affected sector performance between 1990 and 2006. By analyzing trends in sector performance and several of its determinants, this analysis provides the empirical knowledge and foundation necessary for meeting the infrastructure challenges the region currently faces. Understanding the various interventions and conditions that explain sector performance is critical to reducing the region's infrastructure gap.

The results of this book can be summarized in three main messages:[1]

1. *Performance in all three sectors improved significantly, but there is still much room for improvement.* Between 1990 and 2006, coverage, service quality, and labor productivity in all three sectors improved.

   - Coverage for the utilities covered in the databases increased to 95 percent in electricity, 97 percent in water, and 62 percent in fixed telecommunications by 2005.
   - The quality of service also improved: the frequency of electricity interruptions fell nearly by half, the continuity of water service increased 8 percent, and the number of annual telephone faults declined from 23 to 8.
   - Private sector participation had a positive effect on labor productivity, efficiency, and quality.
   - Introducing Independent Regulatory Agencies in the electricity and water sectors promoted gradual improvements in performance.
   - Service provision improved in both private and public companies. Although the average top private performer outperformed the top public utility, some top public utilities outperformed average private utilities.
   - Smaller companies outperformed larger companies.

- Some countries were top performers in electricity, others in water.
- The differences in performance across utilities suggest that different approaches and variables contribute to good performance. The results usually depend on initial conditions and implementation mechanisms. Part of the heterogeneity in performance is explained by regulatory governance arrangements, the degree of private sector participation, and the governance design of state-owned enterprises (SOEs).

2. *Both the government (as a regulator and a service provider) and the private sector (as a service provider) can play active roles in enhancing sector performance.* Introducing private sector participation alone was not the answer to better sector performance. Although the government continues to be at the heart of infrastructure service delivery, private sector participation was an important partner in improving sector performance. However, the manner in which private sector participation was developed determined the extent of its impact on performance. By promoting transparent and accountable regulatory governance design, the government can make positive contributions to sector performance. An independent regulatory agency free of political interference and accountable for its decisions significantly improves utility performance, even for SOEs. SOEs that have a corporate governance structure that reduces political interference, rewards performance, and opens decisions to public scrutiny perform better than SOEs that allow politics to influence decision making.

3. *Improving sector performance requires a holistic and case-based approach that goes beyond conducting a comprehensive assessment of a key determinant and proposing specific designs that address issues related to that determinant.* It entails an approach that integrates policies that address a wide range of issues. By acknowledging and determining the differences among service providers and the environments in which they operate, policy makers can design comprehensive solutions to complex problems in infrastructure service provision.

This book describes and benchmarks the region's good and poor utility performers. It calls on further analytical work to explain how the various determinants interact and affect specific performance indicators and why there are such large differences across countries and utilities. An in-depth analysis of the facts presented here would allow additional conclusions to be drawn about the trends and changes that characterize the region.

A thorough understanding of how and why regional, country, and utility performance improved or worsened will allow countries to share their experiences and learn from one another by assessing what has worked and what has not. By doing so, stakeholders can work together to establish the strongest possible foundation for efficient and reliable sectors in the future. Future analytical work can target potential audiences, such as the private sector, utility managers, political decision makers, policy makers, and regulators, among others, providing potential users with the knowledge and tools to move ahead and providing policy makers with the impetus for future reform.

To move ahead, it is also important to maintain, update, and improve the quality of the data on infrastructure, so that they remain an ongoing resource for the World Bank and the community at large. Efforts to continue data collection and analysis are crucial if the Bank is to provide a resource that remains useful for LAC and other regions.

Utility sector performance encompasses a variety of dimensions. Impacts on each of these dimensions are not necessarily straightforward, with differences determined by sector and internal and external environments. Policy makers considering sector reforms should first prioritize their performance objectives. Once the objectives are identified, the detailed results presented by the analysis can be mined to determine the circumstances in which the objectives can be achieved. For instance, if a utility prioritizes quality and efficiency over retaining employees, private sector participation would be an attractive option. If reducing distributional losses in an SOE is a key objective, a sound design of the enterprise's corporate governance with well-designed performance orientation rules could be considered.

The results presented in this book highlight pitfalls in sector reform programs. Identifying in advance problems associated with poor design and faulty implementation—problems that explain many of the shortcomings in reform processes—can help policy makers design proactive counter measures. Consider the case of an electricity distribution policy maker who has prioritized improving quality and reducing distributional losses—and hence decided to move ahead with private sector participation. By drawing lessons from the experience detailed in this analysis, policy makers could design a public relations campaign emphasizing expected benefits and warning consumers of potential price increases and reductions in sector employment. The analysis in this book can help policy makers make informed decisions and well-designed change strategies, allowing them to maximize both technical and political objectives.

The analysis indicates that programs and reforms could have been implemented better. Overall results were quite positive, but perceptions appear quite negative. To achieve greater benefits and higher popular approval, in some countries the process of introducing private sector participation could have been better prepared and communicated. The context in which the programs of private sector participation were developed in the region was one of excessive optimism, a belief in quick positive profits, too many promises, a lack of realism, poor handling of expectations, and a constant breach in contractual agreements by both parties. Social distribution and lack of transparency throughout the process appear as common denominators.

By creating an environment that maximizes the benefits of reform and promotes a broad consensus, reform programs in the infrastructure sectors can be successfully implemented. In moving forward, the lessons from the past need to be accounted for and corrected. The ultimate objective is to improve sector performance and long-term efficiency; reduce poverty, through better concession design and regulation; and foster compliance with the terms agreed to by both the government and the operator. To ensure that these objectives are met, concession laws and contracts should focus on securing long-term sector efficiency and proper risk assignments and mitigation, as well as discouraging opportunistic bidding and renegotiation; be embedded in regulations that foster transparency and predictability, support incentives for efficient behavior, impede opportunistic renegotiation, and force contract compliance; address social concerns and focus on poverty; and promote accountability as the main governance aspect of SOEs.

Governments remain at the heart of infrastructure service delivery. SOEs that have a corporate governance structure that reduces political interference, rewards performance, and opens decisions to public scrutiny perform better than SOEs that have a structure that allows politics to influence decision making. Furthermore, even with private sector participation, there may be a need for public involvement. Governments need to regulate infrastructure provision as well as contribute a significant share of investment. They must leverage their resources to attract complementary financing. They are also responsible for setting distributional objectives and ensuring that resources and policies are available to increase access for the poor.

Infrastructure service provision requires well-performing SOEs and private companies that can disseminate good practices and, with the government, finance capital investments. Raising private sector participation to previous levels requires addressing past problems and building on lessons learned. Under the current environment, in which infrastructure competes with other investments for financial resources, increasing transparency and improving the risk profile for projects rise as necessary conditions for further development. Regulatory risk must fall, and better risk mitigation mechanisms need to be developed for private participation in infrastructure. In some countries, very negative public perceptions of private participation in infrastructure represent a serious constraint on further participation that needs to be addressed. Changing these perceptions requires greater transparency, improved transaction design and oversight to reduce renegotiations and poor performance, and better management of providers that stand to lose out.

Making new reforms sustainable requires that not only the technical and financial aspects but also the social aspects most responsible for the backlash be addressed. Better communication is critical to create popular support. It is essential to promote programs' infrastructure improvements, publicize initiatives, explain the impact of failing to improve the status quo, and realistically present the program's cost-benefit tradeoff. The communication strategy must not only justify programs but also periodically inform on their progress as well as any changes or problems. It is not enough that reforms be successful: their success must be communicated.

Experiences in the region show that the key elements of a successful program must include the following:

- *Improved institutional context.* Projects generally should be selected by the sectoral ministry, based on the country's strategic planning program and objectives. An interministerial group should be led by the finance minister to evaluate and approve the projects (accompanied by the appropriate economic and financial analysis) identified by the sectors.

- *Improved contract and concession design.* Concession contracts should be awarded competitively—rather than through direct adjudication or bilateral negotiation—and designed to avoid ambiguities as much as possible. Contracts should be carefully designed and reviewed, and the qualifications of bidders should be screened. Outcome targets (regulation by objectives or service levels) rather than investment obligations (regulation by means) should be the norm. Contracts should clearly define the treatment of assets, evaluation of investments, outcome indicators, procedures and guidelines to adjust and review tariffs, and criteria and penalties for early termination of concessions and procedures for resolution of conflicts. The sanctity of the bid is essential. For private sector participation to be successful and achieve the desired objectives, contracts and regulations need to be designed and enforced appropriately. The key objective should be to ensure that the contracting parties comply with the agreed conditions.

- *Stronger regulatory framework.* An appropriate regulatory framework and agency should be in place, with sufficient autonomy and implementation capacity to ensure high-quality enforcement and deter political opportunism. In addition, the tradeoffs between types of regulation—price cap and rate of return—should be well understood, including their different allocations of risk and implications for renegotiation. Technical regulation should fit information requirements and existing risks, and regulation should be by objectives, not by means. Performance objectives should be used instead of investment obligations.

- *Proper regulatory instruments.* Proper regulatory accounting of all assets and liabilities should be in place to avoid any ambiguity about the valuation of assets and liabilities and the regulatory treatment and allocation of cost, investments, the asset base, revenues, transactions with related parties, management fees, and operational and financial variables. Cost and financial models of the regulated utility should be standard regulatory instruments to assess performance, with emphasis on the evaluation of the cost of capital. Extensive use of benchmarking should be common best practice of regulatory agencies; it is critical to assess the efficiency of operations and conduct ordinary five-year tariff reviews.

- *Better corporate governance.* Accountability emerges as the main governance aspect of SOEs. In companies with high levels of corruption and inefficiency, accountability systems should prevent discretional management (both from management and political authorities) and create incentives for good performance. Regulation and performance-based management could be considered complementary ways of achieving these goals, although care needs to be taken in creating checks and balances such as parliamentary oversight and state auditing. An important observation is related to the importance of tailoring governance strategies to companies' realities. For utilities with partial state ownership, particularly utilities with significant private sector participation, a governance design reflecting the incentives of private enterprises seems appropriate. For companies with significant gaps in performance and management, transparent accountability mechanisms should be considered. Fully state-owned utilities characterized by good sector performance and management need to strike a balance between private sector orientation and public accountability. Governance design needs to take sector differences into consideration. Technology and sector dynamics also determine management.

- *Inclusion of social tariffs.* Social tariffs should be a standard component of all programs. Programs that subsidize access for the poor should be a part of all relevant projects, and programs and policies should be implemented to support adversely affected workers. Involving affected communities from the start, at least in a consultative process, should be an integral part of any reform. Initiatives should be launched and supported from the bottom up in areas and locations where the benefits and costs will be incurred.

- *Greater transparency and better communications.* Communication serves as a safeguard against corruption at all levels and as a tool for garnering popular support. Better communication is also essential to promote the program's infrastructure improvements, publicize the initiative, explain the likely impact and the consequences of maintaining the status quo, and realistically describe the program's cost-benefit tradeoff. The communication must not only justify the programs, it must also periodically inform on the program's progress, as well as any changes or problems. The success of reforms must be communicated. Greater transparency in the overall process, financing, and use of funds is critical to safeguard against corruption at all levels and obtain greater popular support.

- *Evaluation and monitoring.* It is essential to periodically evaluate the accomplishments to improve efficiency and achieve the expected results, and broadly communicate advances and pitfalls.

Sector performance should play a major role in defining sectoral reforms. Modalities of private sector participation beyond strict privatization and proper corporate governance design for SOEs offer significant potential for improving sector performance. In particular, chances of success will be increased for programs that comply with the above-listed elements.

Improvements in infrastructure for growth and poverty cannot be delayed. There are significant threats and opportunities. Most countries, including in LAC, are at a crossroads on how to improve sector performance. Success may require some form of private sector involvement and financing. If obstacles such as poor perception of private sector participation are not removed, the significant gains and the very necessary modernization of the sector might fail, and private financing will prove costly if not difficult. Conversely, opportunity exists to refine the model, by attacking the problems and deficiencies of the past, through second-generation reforms that are constructive and broadly participatory. New reform processes that incorporate lessons learned with the clear participation of all stakeholders and a key role for the public sector are crucial.

Note

1. Other determinants also affect sector performance, but their interactions have not yet been thoroughly evaluated. These factors include corruption, market structure, the potential for contract renegotiation and reputation, the type of contract arrangements for service provision, and the existence of social accountability mechanisms. Because the main objective of this book is to provide a factual description of changes and policies that could be empirically tested and analyzed, its scope was restricted to some of the potential policies that could be developed within the sectors.

Empirical Approach

We will follow a similar approach to econometric method proposed by Andrés and others (2008). The main difference is that we will build dummies for each characteristic and we will interact them with the ownership dummies both methodologies.

In order to identify the effects of the characteristics we will modify (1') and (2') as follows:

$$\ln(y_{ijt}) = \delta^T DUM\_TRAN_{ijt} * X_{ijt} + \delta^P DUM\_POST_{ijt} * X_{ijt}$$
$$+ \sum_{ij} \phi_{ij} D_{ij} + v_{ijt} \tag{1''}$$

$$\ln(y_{ijt}) = \delta^T DUM\_TRAN_{ijt} * X_{ijt} + \delta^P DUM\_POST_{ijt} * X_{ijt}$$
$$+ \sum_{ij} \phi_{ij} D_{ij} + \sum_{ij} \theta_{ij} t_{ij} + v_{ijt} \tag{2''}$$

where

$$DUM\_TRAN_{ijt} \begin{cases} 1 & \text{if } s_{ijt} \geq -1 \\ 0 & \text{otherwise} \end{cases}$$

and

$$DUM\_POST_{ijt} \begin{cases} 1 & \text{if } s_{ijt} \geq 2 \\ 0 & \text{otherwise} \end{cases}$$

where s_{ijt} is a time trend that has a value equal to zero for the past year when the company had a public owner. Now, δ^T, that was a scalar number in our previous specifications, became a vector with the coefficients for each characteristic of the vector X_{ijt} than is of the form $(1, x_{ijt}^1, ..., x_{ijt}^N)$ with N as the total number of characteristics evaluated. Note that the specifications used by

Andrés and others (2008) were a particular case when we use a vector X_{ijt} equal to (1,0,...,0). In this case, the first coefficient will identify the average effect of change in ownership during the transitional period on a given indicator. As soon as we use the specification proposed in this appendix, the first coefficient of the vector δ^T will become the average effect of change in ownership during the transitional period on a given indicator for a firm without the characteristics evaluated in the other elements of the vector X_{ijt}.

Equivalently, the vector δ^P will contain the coefficients for the different characteristics of vector X_{ijt}, but for the posttransitional years.

As suggested by Andrés and others (2008), there are some indicators that present time trends. For this reason, firm-specific time trend analysis, as shown in equation (2") is a better indicator. Again, this relies on the assumption that trends between the three periods of analysis are the same. In order to relax this assumption, we run a second set of equations (1") but using the (log) annual growth in each indicator. In this case, it will identify average changes in growth between the periods.

Given the fact that we are using a semilogarithmic functional form of these models for each of the indicators, when interpreting the coefficient estimates of the dummy, it should be remembered that the percentage impact in each indicator is given by $e^\delta - 1$ (Halvorsen and Palmquist 1980).

In order to correct for potential nonspherical errors, a Generalized Least Square (GLS) approach will be more adequate. But, the GLS estimation requires the knowledge of the unconditional variance matrix of v_{ijt}, Ω, up to scale. Hence, we must be able to write $\Omega = \sigma^2 C$, where C is a known G×G positive definite matrix. But, in our case, as this matrix is not known, our second set of estimators will be a Feasible GLS (FGLS) that replaces the unknown matrix Ω with a consistent estimator.

References

Andrés, L., J. L. Guasch, T. Haven, and V. Foster. 2008. *The Impact of Private Sector Participation in Infrastructure: Lights, Shadows, and the Road Ahead.* Washington, DC: World Bank.

Halvorsen, R., and R. Palmquist. 1980. "The Interpretation of Dummy Variables in Semilogarithmic Equations." *American Economic Review* 70: 474–75.

Data Sets

Seven data sets were used and merged to provide a comprehensive analysis in this analysis. The performance indicators data set developed for this analysis is unique because of the comprehensiveness of the indicators and sectoral coverage. The data also have a relatively long time span, starting in 1995 and continuing until 2005–07, depending on the sector. Data were collected from a variety of sources and was cross-checked, when possible. A particular effort was made in corroborating the company data with several public sources and with data of the firms provided by different government offices. In addition, the research was particularly cautious about the consistency and comparability of the data. In order to ensure high data quality and consistency, appropriate calculations and approximations were made to construct missing data points. For example, through the method of interpolation, data were constructed for the earlier years of certain variables, such as number of connections, number of employees, and so on. However, interpolation and other means of constructing data were the exception, and when used, were based on already concrete data and time trends. Specific methodologies were designed according to the variables at hand to ensure their comparability and consistency across time and utilities.[1]

The data sets are the following:

Performance Indicators Data Set

The performance indicators data set developed for Andrés and others (2008) is unique because of the comprehensiveness of the indicators and sectoral coverage. It covers 181 infrastructure firms in Latin America that changed from public to private ownership during the 1990s. Many studies look only at the financial performance of privatized companies, which is just part of the story; this analysis considers changes in output, labor, efficiency, labor productivity, quality, coverage, and prices. In terms of sectors, the analysis includes the often-neglected water and electricity distribution sectors, in addition to fixed telecommunications. The analysis focuses on these sectors because of data availability and because they present similar characteristics (in the sense that they all have monopolistic features and are networking markets, allowing for similar interpretations of such indicators as labor productivity, coverage, and distributional losses), a feature that allows for cross-sectoral comparison. For these reasons, other sectors, such as transport, mobile telecommunications, and generation and transmission of electricity, among others, were excluded from the analysis.

The data also have a relatively long time span, starting five years before the change in ownership and continuing five years after that. The time span allows for the separation of short-run or transitional effects from long-run results. How short- and long-run effects are separated is discussed in the following methodology sections. The database targeted utilities privatized mainly in the period from 1990 to 2003—the main private sector participation wave in the region. The database also includes a few companies changed ownership during the 1980s (in cases in which data from the period before private sector participation were available).

Data were gathered from a variety of sources and was cross-checked, when possible. This research required the construction of an unbalanced panel data set of key indicators for utilities in Latin America and the Caribbean (LAC). For this, official data reported to investors by the firms and statistical reports of the regulatory agencies of each country was used. Information was requested from each of the companies, as well as from each regulatory office. Furthermore, additional sources were used, such as ITU (International Telecommunication Union) and OLADE (*Organización Latinoamericana de Energía*, Latin American Organization of Energy). A particular effort was made in corroborating the company data with several public sources and with data of the firms provided by different government offices. In addition, the research was particularly cautious about the consistency and comparability of the data across time and across countries.[2]

The analysis focused on several indicators of outcomes, employment, labor productivity, efficiency, quality, coverage, and prices. Some of these variables have been used by other authors in other samples, such as Ros (1999), who used equivalent indicators for *coverage, labor productivity, quality*, and *prices*, but did so for the telecommunications sector. Ramamurti (1996) used analogous indicators in *output, coverage*, and *labor productivity* for the four Latin American telecommunications firms of his study. Saal and Parker (2001) used similar indicators for *output, employment, quality*, and *prices*, but did so for water and sewerage companies of England and Wales.

The countries analyzed in electricity distribution were Argentina, Bolivia, Brazil, Chile, Colombia, El Salvador, Guatemala, Nicaragua, Panama, and Peru. The sample consists of unbalanced panel data that includes 116 firms and 1,103 firm-year observations. Each of the firms included in the sample contains at least one year of data from the period before private sector participation. In fact, 98 of the 116 firms have information for at least the previous three years.

For water and sewerage, the paper reviewed companies in Argentina, Bolivia, Brazil, Chile, Colombia, Mexico, and Trinidad and Tobago. The sample consists of unbalanced panel data that includes 49 firms and 515 firm-year observations. Each of the firms included in the sample contains at least one year of data from the period before private sector participation, and 35 of the 49 firms have information for at least the previous two years.

The countries studied for the telecommunication sector were Argentina, Bolivia, Brazil, Chile, El Salvador, Guatemala, Guyana, Jamaica, Mexico, Nicaragua, Panama, Peru, Trinidad and Tobago, and República Bolivariana de Venezuela. The sample consists of unbalanced panel data that includes 16 firms and 267 firm-year observations. Each of the firms included in the sample contains at least four years of data from the period before private sector participation, and 17 out of the 18 firms have information for at least the previous four years.

Table 2.1 presents the definitions of the variables used in the present analysis.

LAC Electricity Distribution Benchmarking Database

The LAC electricity distribution benchmarking database was built by the World Bank (Andrés and Dragoiu 2008) and contains annual information of 250 private and state-owned utilities using 26 variables indicating coverage, output, input, labor productivity, operating performance, quality and customer services, and prices. The time frame covers data from as early as 1990, but the main focus is the period from 1995 to 2005. Data availability and data sources vary by country, often times depending on their ownership and means of regulation. Although the benchmarking study uses a homogenous set of variables to collect data and measure performance, each country represents a special case and therefore efforts were made to ensure consistency of the data across time and utility. This database is representative of 89 percent of the electrification in the region (see table B.1). Furthermore, we argue that there is no significant self-selection in this database due the high data coverage. More precisely, most of the countries in the region were covered with at least 75 percent of the electricity connections in the country. The only countries not covered were Cuba, Guyana, Haiti, Trinidad and Tobago, and some other islands in the Caribbean.

The primary means of conducting research was field data collection and in-house data collection. A standard template and set of variables were used by both field and in-house consultants. Field consultants collected data to complement the information in some of the countries. Because of limited information available on the Web for these countries, local consultants were the most resourceful. For these selected countries and utilities, a preliminary feasibility screening was conducted to determine which countries would be likely to provide information. Although field workers had direct access to the respective utility and government, the process of data collection was often hindered by unexpected factors, such as political affairs, bureaucracy, un-systematized data, and confidentiality issues, among other elements.

The main sources for the in-house data collection were the World Wide Web, information collected by World Bank staff for other projects, and the internal World Bank databases (Development Data Platform, Integrated Records and Information System [IRIS], and so on). The main sources of information on the Internet were the utilities' Web sites. For some countries, the following sources proved to be useful: regulators, ministries, partnerships, central banks, online financial journals, papers, loan reports, financial reports, annual reports, monthly

Table B.1 Electricity Coverage and Data Coverage (Base Year = 2005)

	Electricity coverage (census data; several sources)			Population (source: WDI & ITU)			Households with power connection (own calculation)	LAC Electricity Benchmarking Database	
	% Urban	% Rural	% Total	Total	% Urban	Total HH		Residential CXs	% Total CXs
Argentina		70	95.4	38,747,148	9140.0	10,530,123	10,045,737	9,252,165	92
Bolivia	85	28	64.4	9,182,015	6420.0	2,135,003	1,374,942	942,805	69
Brazil			96.5	186,830,759	8420.0	54,223,593	52,325,767	49,600,000	95
Chile		90	98.6	16,295,102	8760.0	4,791,755	4,724,670	4,486,053	95
Colombia	93	55	86.1	42,889,000	7360.0	9,028,323	7,773,386	7,773,386	100
Costa Rica	100	87	98.5	4,327,228	6170.0	1,006,053	990,962	990,962	100
Cuba				11,259,905	7560.0	3,188,425	–		
Dominican Republic		40	82.5	9,469,601	6680.0	2,704,434	2,231,158	844,613	38
Ecuador	96	54	90.3	13,060,993	6360.0	2,902,443	2,620,906	2,620,906	100
El Salvador	97	72	79.5	6,668,356	5980.0	1,531,173	1,217,283	1,191,459	98
Guatemala			78.6	12,709,564	4720.0	2,955,713	2,323,190	1,583,268	68
Guyana				739,472	2820.0	198,842	–		
Haiti		45	36.0	9,296,291	4270.0	2,067,902	744,445	–	0
Honduras	94	45	69.0	6,834,110	4650.0	1,558,640	1,075,462	809,843	75
Jamaica			92.0	2,650,400	5270.0	764,827	703,641	491,452	70
Mexico	100	95	96.0	103,089,133	7630.0	24,703,635	23,715,490	23,715,490	100
Nicaragua	90	40	69.3	5,462,539	5590.0	974,652	675,434	534,886	79
Panama			85.2	3,231,502	7080.0	787,808	671,213	606,127	90
Paraguay			85.8	5,898,651	5850.0	1,453,110	1,246,769	871,717	70
Trinidad and Tobago				1,323,722	1220.0	351,709	–		
Uruguay			95.4	3,305,723	9200.0	1,322,289	1,261,464	1,091,523	87
Venezuela, RB			98.6	26,577,000	9230.0	5,945,522	5,862,285	4,802,261	82
Others[a]			90	6,303,557	83.6	1,969,846	1,772,861	230,707	
LAC			91.6	553,426,037	77.1	143,019,699	131,006,044	116,036,948	89

a. Antigua and Barbuda, Aruba, The Bahamas, Barbados, Belize, Cayman Islands, Dominica, Grenada, the Netherlands Antilles, Puerto Rico, St. Kitts and Nevis, St. Lucia, St. Vincent and the Grenadines, Suriname, and Virgin Islands (U.S.).

bulletins, statistics offices, and contacts with the companies and regulators. In addition, the following associations and organizations provided valuable statistics for the region: ARIAE (*Asociación Iberoamericana de Entidades Reguladores de Energía*), ECLAC (*Economic Commission for Latin America and the Caribbean*), IEA (*International Energy Agency*), and CIER (*Comisión de Integración Energética Regional*). Because regulators, international organizations, and commissions often cover the electricity distribution of the entire region, most of the information provided was aggregated at the country level and not disaggregated by utility. One of the challenges of data collection was the inconsistency between the data provided by utilities or regulators in annual and financial reports.

To best describe the efficiency of the distribution sector of LAC, indicators were selected to determine utility-level performance. The utility-level indicators reflect relevant and feasible measurements in depicting the distribution segment of the electricity sector. The utility-level indicators were computed to measure such factors as technical efficiency, operating efficiency, cost-efficiency, quality of service, and so on. Technical efficiency is defined as the capacity of the utility to achieve maximum output from a given set of inputs. To compute the technical efficiency of a utility, output and input indicators reflecting operating- and cost-efficiency were aggregated.

Table B.2 is a statistics summary for the datasets used in this analysis. We have calculated the number of observations, mean, standard deviation, minimum, and maximum, for the main indicators. The statistics show the heterogeneity and comprehensiveness of the data.

The LAC Electricity benchmarking dataset includes information for 250 utilities in 26 countries. The size of the utilities varies between over 17 million connections and as little as 289 connections. The dataset includes the information

Table B.2 LAC Electricity Distribution Benchmarking Database—Summary Statistics

Electricity	Observations	Mean	Standard deviation	Minimum	Maximum
Number of utilities	250				
Total connections (millions)	247	432,697	1,308,686	289	17,900,000
Total residential connections	247	377,889	1,147,699	251	15,800,000
Total energy sold (GWh)	248	2,605.0	8,997.4	4.1	111,000.0
Employees	235	1,244	3,062	13	36,942
Distribution losses (%)	221	16.1	8.6	1.6	49.8
Average duration of interruptions per subscriber	149	26.1	33.2	0.5	209.2
Frequency of interruptions per subscriber	137	27.6	47.7	1.0	285.2
Coverage (%)	151	78.8	17.0	28.1	100.0
Residential connection per worker	231	392.9	273.5	58.3	2,694.1
Average GWh sold per worker	230	1.8	1.4	0.14	11.8

Note: Each observation in this table corresponds to the simple average (across all the years with available information) for each utility.

for most of the largest companies in the region, and some of the smaller companies. Evidence of this also is the difference in the energy sold yearly by each
company. The utility with the lowest total energy sold sells 4.1 GWh a year,
while the utility with the largest total energy sold sells 111,000 GWh a year.
Distributional losses range between 1.6 and almost 50 percent of the energy
produced. In terms of quality, the indicators that show the differences among
the observations in the sample are average duration of interruptions per subscriber, and frequency of interruptions per subscriber. The minimum and maximum for these indicators are respectively 0.5 and 209 minutes and 1.0 and
285.2 times. Labor productivity varies between 58.3 and 2,694 connections per
employee, and 0.14 and 11.8 GWh sold per employee. Average number of
employees varies between 13 and 36,942.

LAC Water and Sanitation Benchmarking Database

The LAC Water and Sanitation benchmarking database was built by the
World Bank (World Bank 2009) and contains annual information for 1,700 private
and state-owned utilities using 34 variables indicating coverage, output, input,
labor productivity, operating performance, quality and customer services, and
prices. The time frame covers data as early as 1990, but the main focus is the
period from 1995 to 2006. Data availability and data sources vary by country,
often times depending on their ownership and means of regulation. Although the
benchmarking study uses a homogenous set of variables to collect data and measure performance, each country represents a special case and therefore efforts
were made to ensure consistency of the data across time and utility. This database is representative of 59 percent of the water connections in the region
(see table B.3). Furthermore, most of the main utilities in the region covering
urban areas were included in this database. The only countries not covered were
Cuba, the Dominican Republic, Guatemala, Guyana, Haiti, Jamaica, República
Bolivariana de Venezuela, and some other islands in the Caribbean.

The primary means of conducting research was in-house and direct data
collection. A standard template and set of variables were used to collect the
information. Because of limited information available on the Web for these countries, where feasible the information was requested directly from regulatory and
sectoral agencies. In some cases, the utilities provided the information directly by
completing the template.

The main sources for the in-house data collection were the World Wide Web,
information collected by World Bank staff for other projects, and the internal
World Bank databases (Development Data Platform, IRIS, and so on). The main
sources of information on the Internet were the utilities' Web sites. For some
countries, the following sources proved to be useful: regulators, ministries, partnerships, journals, papers, loan reports, financial reports, annual reports, monthly
bulletins, statistics offices, and contacts with the companies and regulators. In
addition, the following associations and organizations provided valuable statistics
for the region: ADERASA (*Asociación de Entes Reguladores de Agua Potable y*

Table B.3 Water Coverage and Data Coverage (Base Year = 2004)

	Water coverage (source: JMP)			Population (source: WDI & ITU)			Households with water connection (own calculation)	LAC Water Benchmarking Database	
	% Urban	% Rural	% Total	Total	% Urban	Total HH		Residential CXs	% Total CXs
Argentina	83	45	79.6	38,371,527	91.1	10,419,503	8,297,383	4,669,379	56
Bolivia	90	44	73.3	9,009,045	63.7	2,086,000	1,529,272	1,227,044	80
Brazil	91	17	78.9	184,317,696	83.6	51,939,168	40,961,306	37,100,000	91
Chile	99	38	91.2	16,123,815	87.3	4,741,622	4,325,715	3,555,960	82
Colombia	96	51	84.0	42,306,000	73.3	8,733,700	7,334,998	4,344,921	59
Costa Rica	99	81	92.0	4,253,037	61.2	989,172	910,125	397,902	44
Cuba	82	49	73.9	11,246,670	75.6	3,181,522	2,352,672	–	0
Dominican Republic	92	62	81.8	9,324,633	65.9	2,663,357	2,177,986	–	0
Ecuador	82	45	68.3	12,917,362	62.9	2,870,525	1,960,218	617,605	32
El Salvador	81	38	63.6	6,576,008	59.5	1,542,091	980,671	545,223	56
Guatemala	89	65	76.2	12,396,581	46.8	2,817,405	2,147,629	–	0
Guyana	66	45	50.9	738,992	28.3	197,004	100,351	–	0
Haiti	24	3	11.7	9,149,270	41.3	2,008,392	234,355	–	0
Honduras	91	62	75.4	6,702,291	46.1	1,532,907	1,155,248	301,916	26
Jamaica	92	46	70.2	2,638,100	52.5	750,222	526,350	–	0
Mexico	96	72	90.2	102,049,758	76.0	24,626,697	22,221,949	8,241,126	37
Nicaragua	84	27	58.7	5,393,597	55.7	964,143	566,205	566,205	100
Panama	96	72	88.8	3,175,354	69.8	777,133	689,721	409,673	59
Paraguay	82	25	58.0	5,788,088	57.9	1,422,496	824,766	237,847	29
Peru	82	39	69.5	26,958,549	71.0	6,068,751	4,220,125	2,354,301	56
Trinidad and Tobago	80	67	68.5	1,319,139	11.9	350,223	240,076	240,076	100
Uruguay	97	84	95.9	3,301,732	91.9	1,303,720	1,250,813	715,563	57
Venezuela, RB	84	61	82.1	26,127,000	91.8	5,743,930	4,716,306	–	0
Others[a]	n.a.	n.a.	n.a.	6,255,641	83.2	1,955,934			
LAC	90	42	79.2	546,439,884	77.1	139,392,648	110,336,799	65,524,741	59

a. Antigua and Barbuda, Aruba, The Bahamas, Barbados, Belize, Cayman Islands, Dominica, Grenada, the Netherlands Antilles, Puerto Rico, St. Kitts and Nevis, St. Lucia, St. Vincent and the Grenadines, Suriname, and Virgin Islands (U.S.).

Saneamiento de las Américas) and IBNET (*International Benchmarking Network for Water and Sanitation Utilities*). The information collected is for specific utility companies. In some cases, the existing data were at the municipal level. For those cases, we considered that the data for the municipality were that of the utility operator.[3] In cases where the data were at the Municipal level and we were able to establish that the same operator serviced several municipalities, the data were aggregated at the utility level. One of the challenges of data collection was the inconsistency between the data provided by utilities or regulators and the annual and financial reports. Considering this, appropriate calculations and approximations were made to construct missing data points. For example, through the method of interpolation, data were constructed for the earlier years of certain variables, such as number of connections, number of employees, and so on. Interpolation and other means of constructing data were the exception based on already concrete data and time trends. Specific methodologies were designed according to the variables at hand to ensure their comparability and consistency across time and utilities.

To best describe the efficiency of the distribution sector of LAC, indicators were selected to determine utility-level performance. The utility-level indicators reflect relevant and feasible measurements in depicting the distribution segment of the water and sanitation sector. The utility-level indicators were computed to measure such factors as technical efficiency, operating efficiency, cost-efficiency, quality of service, and so on. Technical efficiency is defined as the capacity of the utility to achieve maximum output from a given set of inputs. To compute the technical efficiency of a utility, output and input indicators reflecting operating- and cost-efficiency were aggregated.

Table B.4 summarizes the statistics for the datasets used in this analysis. As we presented for the LAC Electricity Distribution Benchmarking Database, we have calculated the number of observations, mean, standard deviation, minimum, and maximum, for the main indicators.

The LAC Water and Sanitation Benchmarking dataset includes information for 1,708 utilities in 16 countries. The size of the utilities varies between over 6 million connections and as little as 110 connections. Coverage in the service area of the utilities in the sample varies between less than 10 and 100 percent. The dataset includes the information for most of the largest companies in the region, and some of the smaller companies. Evidence of this also is the difference in the volume of water produced by each utility. The utility with the lowest total volume of water produced 20,000 cubic meters a year, while the utility with the largest total volume of water produced 2.6 billion cubic meters a year. For sewerage collection, the wastewater collection varies between 0 and 420 million cubic meters. In terms of efficiency of service provision, the utility with the lowest collection rates, collect 16.4 percent of what they bill yearly, while the best collect 100 percent. Metered connections vary between those that have no meters, and those that have all connection with meters. Labor productivity, measured as number of connections per employee ranges between 38 and over 1,700 connections per employee.

Table B.4 LAC Water and Sanitation Benchmarking Database—Summary Statistics

Water	Observations	Mean	Standard deviation	Minimum	Maximum
Number of utilities	1,708				
Total water connections	927	75,109	329,216	110	6,843,391
Total residential water connections	927	68,652	300,203	100	6,247,583
Total sewerage connections	612	67,769	271,620	10	5,271,316
Total residential sewerage connections	612	61,638	246,481	10	4,783,496
Total volume of water produced (millions cubic meter)	1,200	24.5	122.0	0.00002	2,610.0
Total volume of water sold (millions cubic meter)	859	19.2	86.6	0.00021	1,720.0
Total volume of wastewater collected (millions cubic meter)	722	6.3	31.6	0.0	420.0
Number of employees	938	258	950	1	18,291
Unaccounted for water (%)	803	35.4	17.3	0.0	99.9
Collection rate (%)	1,006	89.5	15.0	16.4	100.0
Continuity of service (hrs)	523	22.7	3.7	1.9	24.0
Potability (%)	621	95.2	9.5	16.1	100.0
Water coverage (%)	1,214	92.5	13.1	2.4	100.0
Sewerage coverage (%)	1,073	79.3	25.9	1.2	100.0
Number of customer complaints	778	8,362	42,622	1	1,017,398
Labor productivity (connections per employee)	869	262.5	162.2	37.8	1,787.9
Metered (%)	699	72.2	31.7	0.0	100.0

Note: Each observation in this table corresponds to the simple average (across all the years with available information) for each utility.

ITU World Telecommunication/ICT Indicators Database

This database contains annual time series from 1975–2007 for about 100 sets of telecommunication statistics covering telephone network size and dimension, mobile services, quality of service, traffic, staff, tariffs, revenue, and investment. Data for over 200 economies are available. The data is collected through an annual questionnaire sent out by the Telecommunication Development Bureau (BDT) of the ITU. The questionnaire is sent to the government agency in charge of the telecommunications sector, usually a line ministry or the regulator. The ITU's Market Information and Statistics (STAT) unit verifies, harmonizes, carries out additional research, and collects missing information from government websites, and operator's annual reports, particularly for those countries that do not provide answers to the questionnaire. Market research data is used to cross-check the data and complement missing values. In some cases, estimates are made by the ITU staff.

For telecom, the ITU data includes information of 32 countries in LAC for most indicators. The sample includes small and large countries, as seen through the minimum and maximum statistics for telecom penetration and coverage. Furthermore, full-time staff varies between 188 and 90,576 employees. Quality also varies among the countries in the sample, from countries with 3.4 to 133

Table B.5 ITU Database—Summary Statistics (for LAC)

Telecommunications	Observations	Mean	Standard deviation	Minimum	Maximum
Main (fixed) lines in operation (millions)	32	2.0	4.9	0.2	24.9
Main (fixed) telephone lines per 100 inhabitants	32	16.7	15.3	1.0	79.6
Mobile cellular telephone subscribers per 100 inhabitants	32	30.0	22.3	2.2	109.4
% Households with a main line	27	41.4	26.0	4.3	90.0
% Residential main lines	32	73.2	5.7	59.3	85.0
% Digital main lines	32	83.5	16.3	38.3	100.0
Number of local (fixed) telephone calls (billions of calls)	17	1.9	2.9	0.0005	9.5
Number of local (fixed) telephone minutes (billions of minutes)	24	12.1	30.5	0.0009	133.0
% of telephone faults cleared by next working day	29	58.2	20.7	19.7	95.0
Faults per 100 main (fixed) lines a year	29	42.9	30.9	3.4	133.2
Residential telephone connection charge (US$)	32	8.02	5.21	1.11	24.50
Price of a 3-minute fixed telephone local call (off-peak US$)	29	0.06	0.04	0.00	0.19
Price of a 3-minute fixed telephone local call (peak-US$)	30	0.10	0.11	0.00	0.64
Staff (full-time telecommunications)	32	10,960	20,037	188	90,576
Waiting list for main (fixed) lines	30	146,816	242,245	615	980,262

Note: Each observation in this table corresponds to the simple average (across all the years with available information) for each utility.

faults per 100 main (fixed) lines a year. Also, the percentage of telephone faults cleared by the next working day varies from 20 to 95 percent. Table B.5 gives the reader a better idea of the diversity of countries in the data.

Contract and Regulatory Characteristics Data Set

The performance indicators data set was matched to a novel data set built by the World Bank that describes the characteristics of nearly 1,000 infrastructure projects awarded in Latin American and Caribbean countries from 1989 to 2002 (see Guasch 2004). The data set provides details on the private sector participation process, including how many bidders participated, the contract process,[4] the award criterion,[5] and the type of concession.[6] The data set covers the regulatory framework, including how the legal framework was established,[7] how tariffs are regulated,[8] if there was a possibility of renegotiation of the contract, and if so, who might be the initiator of the renegotiation (table B.6).[9]

The data set captures additional private sector participation contract details, including information about termination clauses, the arbitration process, claim-solving institutions, universal service obligations, contract duration, contract renewal, government guarantees, government subsidies, frequency of tariff review, and how the exchange and commercial risk were borne. If the contract was

Table B.6 Contract and Regulatory Variables

Variable	Description
Private sector participation process	
Auction	Dummy with value 1 if the concession was awarded through an auction process.
Award: highest price	Dummy with value 1 if the concession was awarded according to the highest price.
Award: best investment plan	Dummy with value 1 if the concession was awarded according to the best investment plan.
Regulatory board	
Full autonomy	Dummy with value 1 if the regulatory board was fully autonomous.
Partial autonomy	Dummy with value 1 if the regulatory board was partially autonomous.
Duration	Dummy with value 1 if the duration of appointments to the regulatory board was five or more years.
Investors	
Investors: foreign	Dummy with value 1 if the investors were foreign.
Investors: mixed	Dummy with value 1 if some of the investors were foreign.
Tariff regulation	
Tariffs: rate of return	Dummy with value 1 if the tariffs were regulated according to the rate of return.
Tariffs: price cap	Dummy with value 1 if the tariffs were regulated according to price cap.

Source: Andrés and others 2008c.

renegotiated, the reason given and the renegotiation outcome are also known. Characteristics of the regulator—such as an index of the regulator's autonomy, its budget source, the duration of the regulatory board member mandate, and the year of the regulatory board's inceptions—are captured in the data set.

For this book's analysis, not all of the aforementioned variables could be used because of data constraints. Only the variables that had sufficient variation across firms were employed, making it possible to measure the effect of different contract and regulatory characteristics on performance outcomes.

This database contains annual time series from 1975–2007 for about 100 sets of telecommunication statistics covering telephone network size and dimension, mobile services, quality of service, traffic, staff, tariffs, revenue, and investment.

Regulatory Governance

In order to assess the governance of electricity regulators in LAC, we designed a survey that was distributed to all electricity regulatory agencies in the region, including not only national but also provincial or state regulators (particularly in the cases of Argentina and Brazil). All LAC countries that are members of the World Bank Group and have an electricity or water regulatory agency were included.

The database comprises data from 43 electricity and 28 water regulatory agencies, whose coverage in terms of consumers exceeds 90 percent of the region. Each country was represented by its own regulatory agency, with the exception of Colombia and Chile, for which we assigned unique values since they each have two different entities with regulatory functions.

In both Colombia and Chile, for instance, regulatory responsibilities are shared between a National Energy Commission in charge of the main regulatory aspects (tariffs, approval of contracts) and an Oversight Electricity Agency (in the case of Chile, the *Superintendencia de Electricidad y Combustibles* and in the case of Colombia, the *Superintendencia de Servicios Públicos*) in charge of the sector's oversight (service quality, sanctions' enforcing, consumer complaints). Considering that both agencies perform different tasks that in other countries are undertaken by only one regulator, the database "merged" both administrative bodies and assigned a unique value for the country. For those institutional aspects that should be reflected in both agencies, such as the independence of their decision-making (for example. the appointment of directors) or the transparency of their management (for example account audits), the data assigned the country an average score calculated from both agencies' scores on the same question. For instance, if the *Comisión Nacional de Energía* of Chile was assigned 0 for not auditing its accounts and the *Superintendencia de Electricidad y Combustibles* was assigned 1 for auditing its accounts, then Chile would obtain 0.5 for that question. In those aspects where the agencies had separate responsibilities (for example the regulation of tariffs by the *Comisión Reguladora de la Energía* of Colombia and the reception of consumers' claims by the *Superintendencia de Servicios Públicos*), the data assigned the country the score achieved by the agency with responsibility in that issue, regardless of the score obtained by the other agency for the same issue.

The questionnaire is composed of 97 questions (for the full version of the survey, see Andrés and others 2007) reflecting the four variables of agencies' governance and both formal and informal aspects of their functioning. The data also included a general section aimed at capturing characteristics of electricity markets such as the methodology for tariff calculation, the degree of market liberalization, and social tariffs.

Corporate Governance of State-Owned Enterprises

These data were collected through surveys sent to 110 different utilities of the region in both the electricity distribution and water sectors. Final respondents were 45 SOEs. The initiative included both public companies with full state ownership and companies where, even though there is private investment, state ownership is at least 51 percent of total shares (only a few in this category).

This database compresses detailed information on the governance of SOEs in infrastructure through six indexes. The Corporate Governance Index (CGI) is the main index and is the result of the aggregation of the other five. Other indexes include: the Legal Soundness Index, the Board Competitiveness Index, the Professional Management Index, the Performance-Oriented Index, and the Transparency and Disclosure Index. Indexes are composed of different variables representing various aspects of the management of SOEs. Questions were valued between 0 (worst) and 1 (best).

In selecting the questions and in giving values, the data uses as a main benchmark a public enterprise that is corporatized and subject to the same conditions, in terms of access to finance and auditing, than any other private enterprise. The data adjusted the benchmark to sector specificities such as the mechanisms to appoint the Board of Directors, economic regulation, and performance-based orientation. Different from other approaches to the governance of SOEs, it also included the study of the selection, appointment, salary, and educational levels of the staff. Previous approaches have only emphasized the role of the Board and its relationship with the shareholder/s. The data considered that in the infrastructure sector, the role of the staff of a state enterprise is a vital aspect of good management. Because most of these enterprises are not profit-oriented, we were not able to focus on revenues as parameters of good performance, and also because a good bureaucracy is a good filter to political intervention, we believe that an index that reflects the professionalism (given by educational levels, hiring criteria, and rewards) of the staff might give us a good proxy of the performance of the enterprise.

Notes

1. This is the case, for instance, of the variable that measures number of employees in the case of utilities that were formerly vertically integrated. We compare the total number of employees of the different vertically disintegrated units and we compare with the total number of employees before the change. We assumed that this change was proportionally similar to all the new units and then we use the growth rates for the previous years.

2. As quality indexes vary across countries, the most similar indexes were collected to compare their evolution across time, rather than absolute quality levels.

3. For Mexico, the data submitted by the *Consejo Nacional de Agua* was at the municipal level. According to their description, the data for each Municipality corresponds to the data of the utility operator in the municipality area. For the few private operators, in Mexico, we were able to get data directly from the operator.

4. Bid, direct adjudication, invitation, petition, or request.

5. Highest cannon, highest price, tariff, lowest government subsidy, investment plan, shorter duration of the concession, or multiple criteria.

6. Operation, BOT, BOO, privatization, and so on.

7. Law, decree, contract, or license.

8. Revenue cap, price cap, rate of return, or no regulation.

9. The government, the concessionaire, both, or nobody.

References

Andrés, L., and G. Dragoiu. 2008. "Benchmarking Electricity distribution Report 1995–2005." World Bank, Washington, DC.

Andrés, L., J. L. Guasch, M. Diop, and S. L. Azumendi. 2007. "Assessing the Governance of Electricity Regulatory Agencies in the Latin American and the Caribbean Region: A Benchmarking Analysis." Policy Research Working Paper 4380, World Bank, Washington, DC.

Andrés, L., J. L. Guasch, T. Haven, and V. Foster. 2008. *The Impact of Private Sector Participation in Infrastructure: Lights, Shadows, and the Road Ahead.* Washington, DC: World Bank.

Guasch, J. L. 2004. *Granting and Renegotiating Infrastructure Concessions: Doing it Right.* Washington, DC: World Bank.

Ramamurti, R. 1996. *Privatizing Monopolies: Lessons from the Telecommunications and Transport Sector in Latin America.* Baltimore, MD: The Hopkins University Press.

Ros, A. 1999. "Does Ownership or Competition Matter? The Effects of Telecommunications Reform on the Network Expansion and Efficiency." *Journal of Regulatory Economics* 15 (1): 65–92.

Saal, D. S., and D. Parker. 2001. "Productivity and Price Performance in the Privatized Water and Sewerage Companies of England and Wales." *Journal of Regulatory Economics* 20 (1): 61–90.

World Bank. 2009, "Understanding Sector Performance: The Case of Utilities in Latin America and the Caribbean." Sustainable Development Department, Economics Unit, Latin America and the Caribbean Region, World Bank, Washington, DC. June.

Benchmarking Analysis

Electricity Distribution

Regional Benchmarking Assessment

Figure C.1 Regional Benchmarking—Electricity Distribution: Output, Coverage, and Labor Productivity

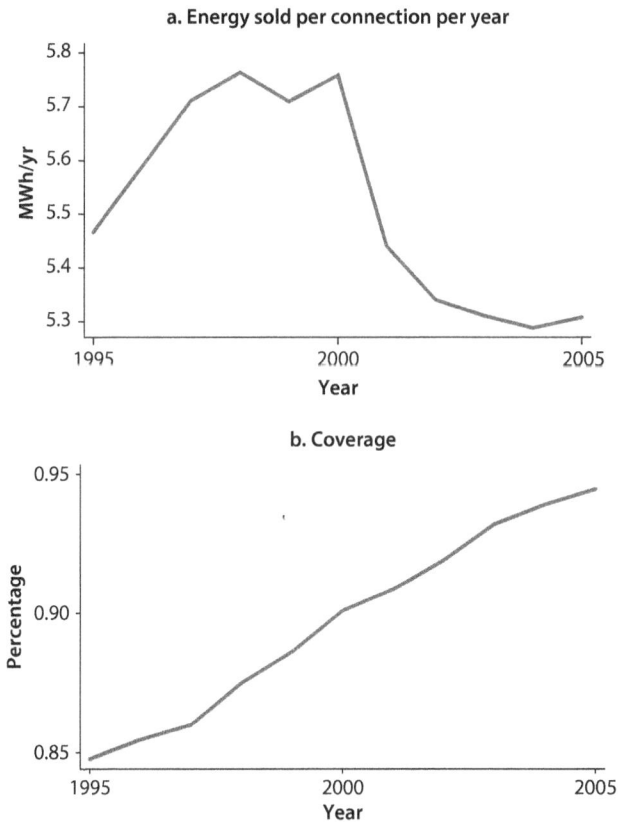

a. Energy sold per connection per year

(y-axis: MWh/yr, ranging 5.3 to 5.8; x-axis: Year, 1995 to 2005)

b. Coverage

(y-axis: Percentage, ranging 0.85 to 0.95; x-axis: Year, 1995 to 2005)

figure continues next page

Figure C.1 Regional Benchmarking—Electricity Distribution: Output, Coverage, and Labor Productivity *(continued)*

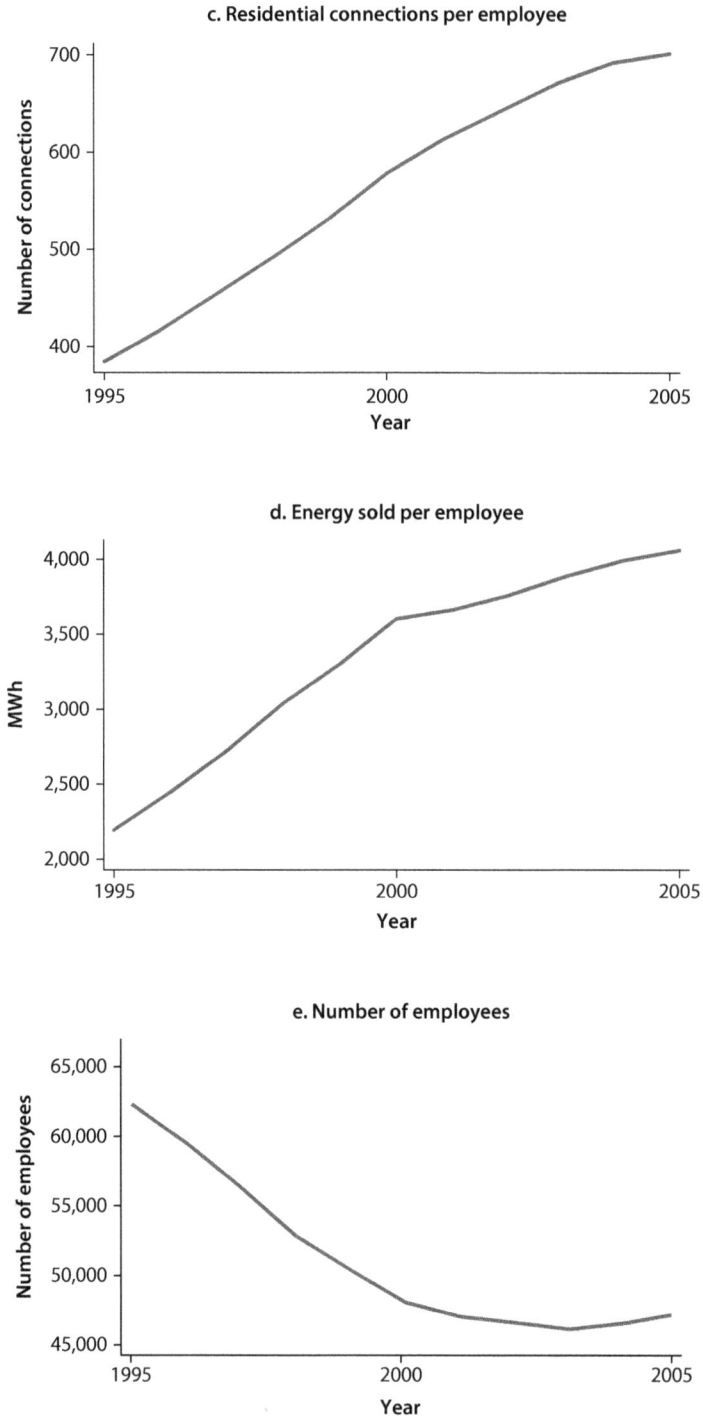

c. Residential connections per employee

d. Energy sold per employee

e. Number of employees

figure continues next page

Figure C.1 Regional Benchmarking—Electricity Distribution: Output, Coverage, and Labor Productivity *(continued)*

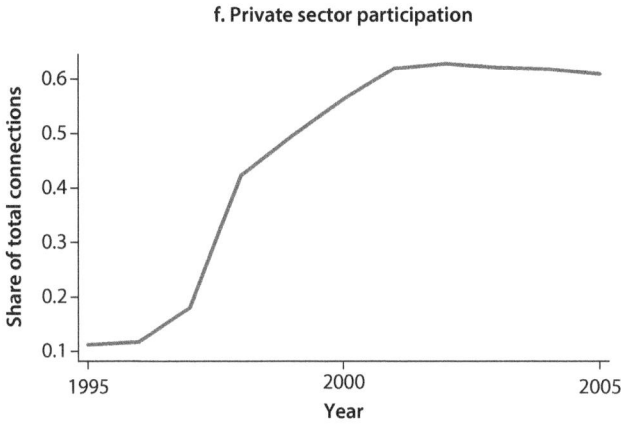

f. Private sector participation

Source: LAC Electricity Benchmarking Database, World Bank, 2007.

Figure C.2 Regional Benchmarking—Electricity Distribution: Distributional Losses and Quality of the Service

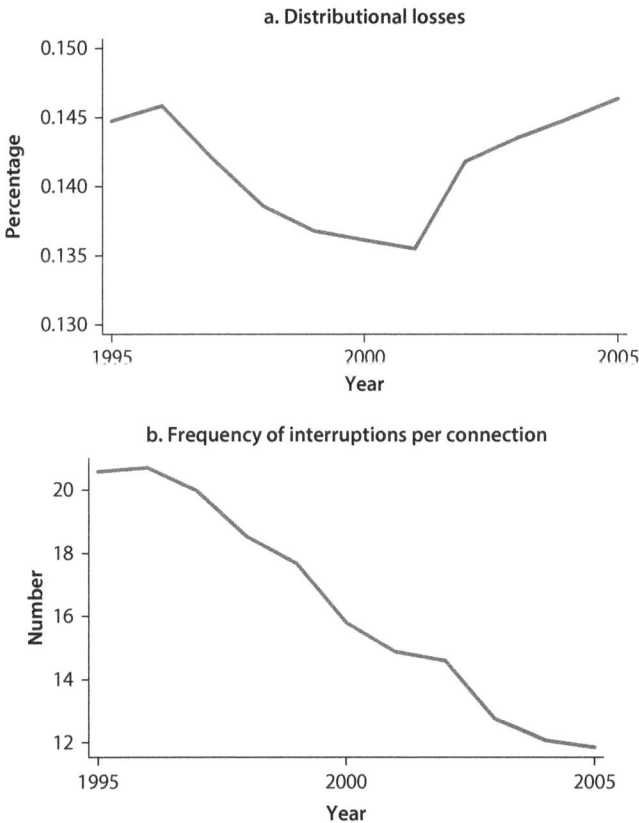

a. Distributional losses

b. Frequency of interruptions per connection

figure continues next page

Figure C.2 Regional Benchmarking—Electricity Distribution: Distributional Losses and Quality of the Service *(continued)*

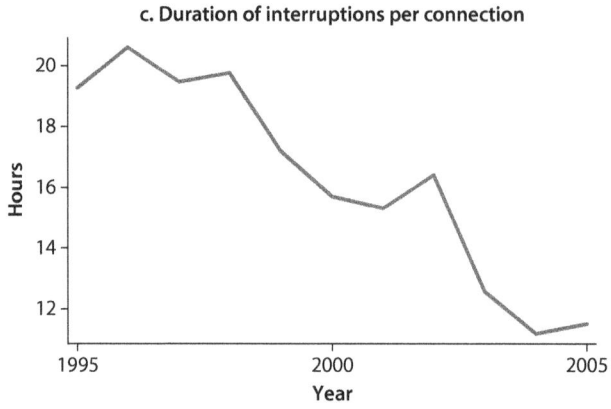

c. Duration of interruptions per connection

Source: LAC Electricity Benchmarking Database, World Bank, 2007.

Figure C.3 Regional Benchmarking—Electricity Distribution: Tariffs and Expenses

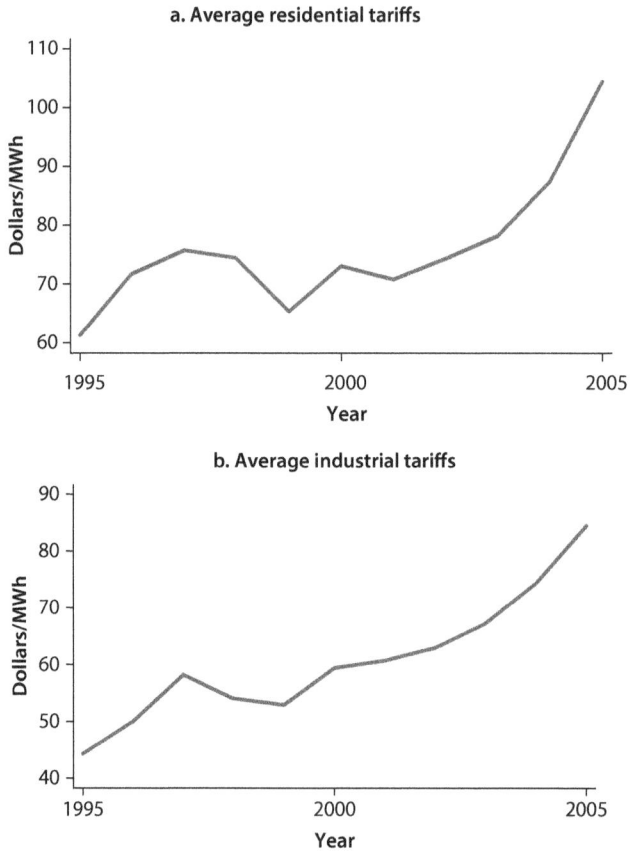

a. Average residential tariffs

b. Average industrial tariffs

figure continues next page

Figure C.3 Regional Benchmarking—Electricity Distribution: Tariffs and Expenses *(continued)*

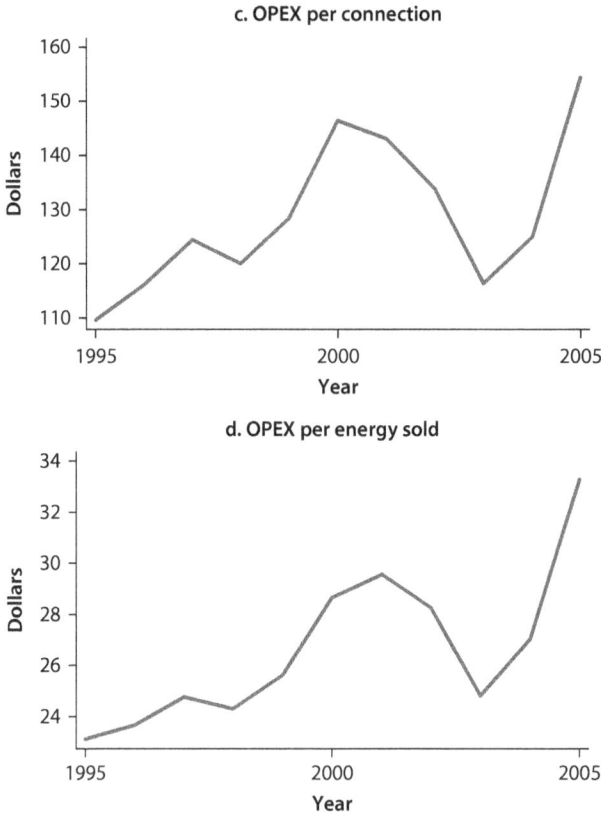

c. OPEX per connection

d. OPEX per energy sold

Source: LAC Electricity Benchmarking Database, World Bank, 2007.

Utility-Level Benchmarking Assessment

Figure C.4 Utility Level Benchmarking—Electricity Distribution: Coverage, Output, and Labor Productivity

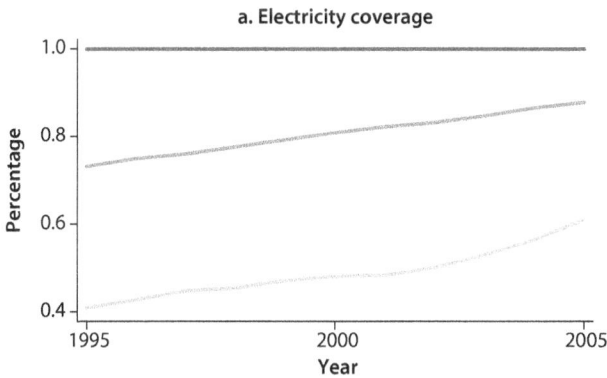

a. Electricity coverage

figure continues next page

Figure C.4   Utility Level Benchmarking—Electricity Distribution: Coverage, Output, and Labor Productivity *(continued)*

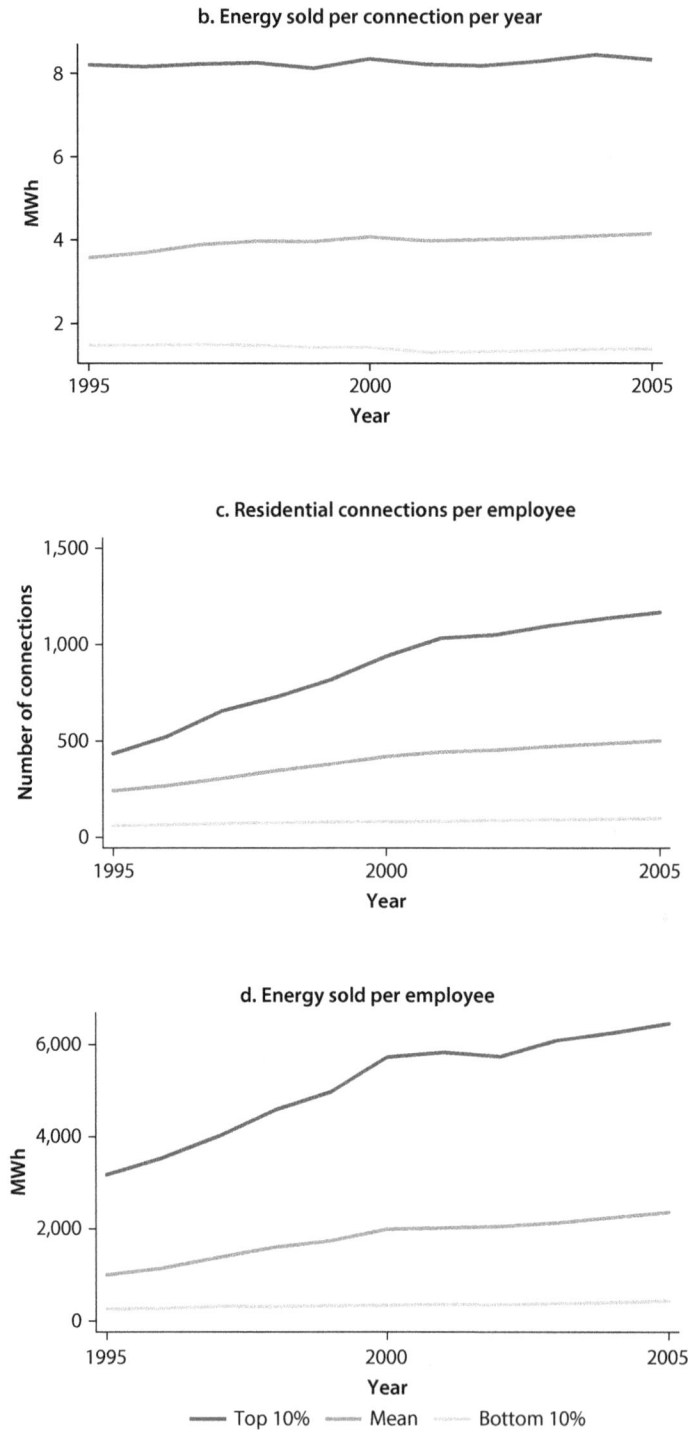

b. Energy sold per connection per year

c. Residential connections per employee

d. Energy sold per employee

Top 10%   Mean   Bottom 10%

Source: LAC Electricity Benchmarking Database, World Bank, 2007.

Figure C.5 Utility Level Benchmarking—Electricity Distribution: Distributional Losses and Quality of the Service

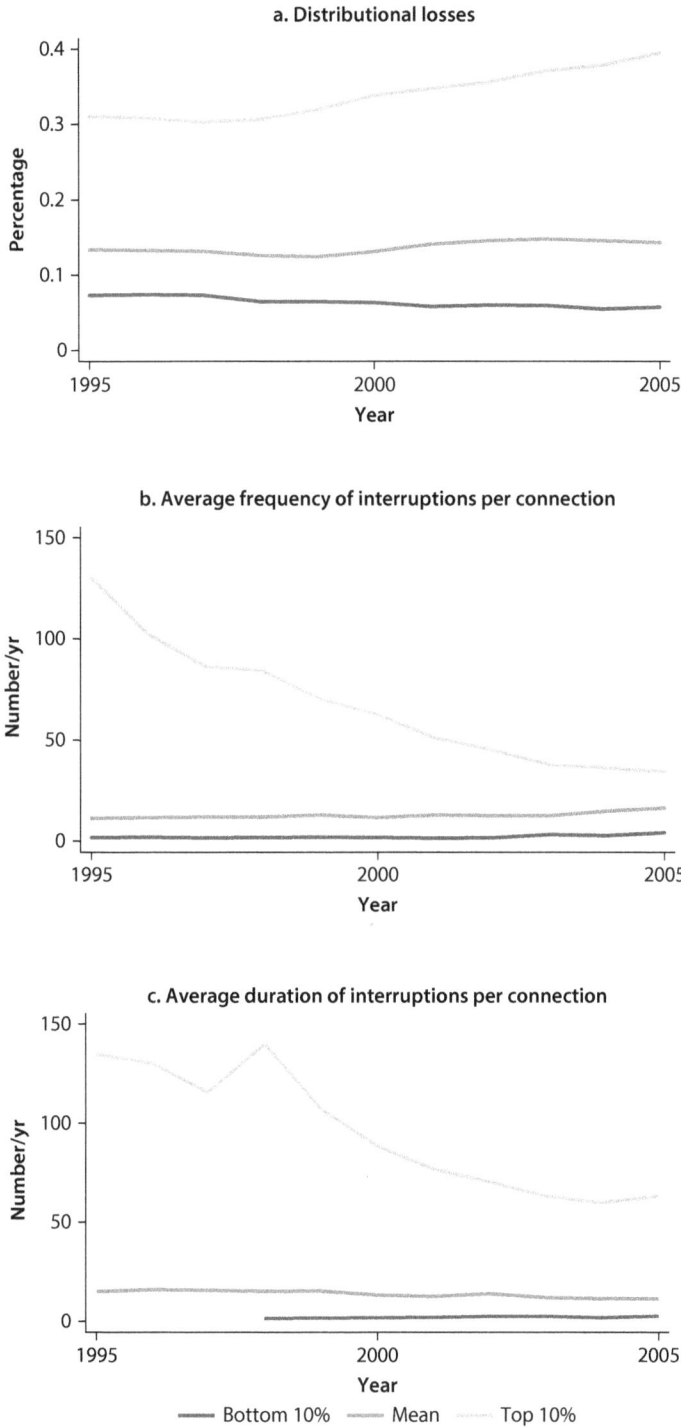

a. Distributional losses

b. Average frequency of interruptions per connection

c. Average duration of interruptions per connection

Bottom 10% ――― Mean ········· Top 10%

Source: LAC Electricity Benchmarking Database, World Bank, 2007.

Uncovering the Drivers of Utility Performance • http://dx.doi.org/10.1596/978-0-8213-9660-5

Figure C.6 Utility Level Benchmarking—Electricity Distribution: Tariffs and Expenses

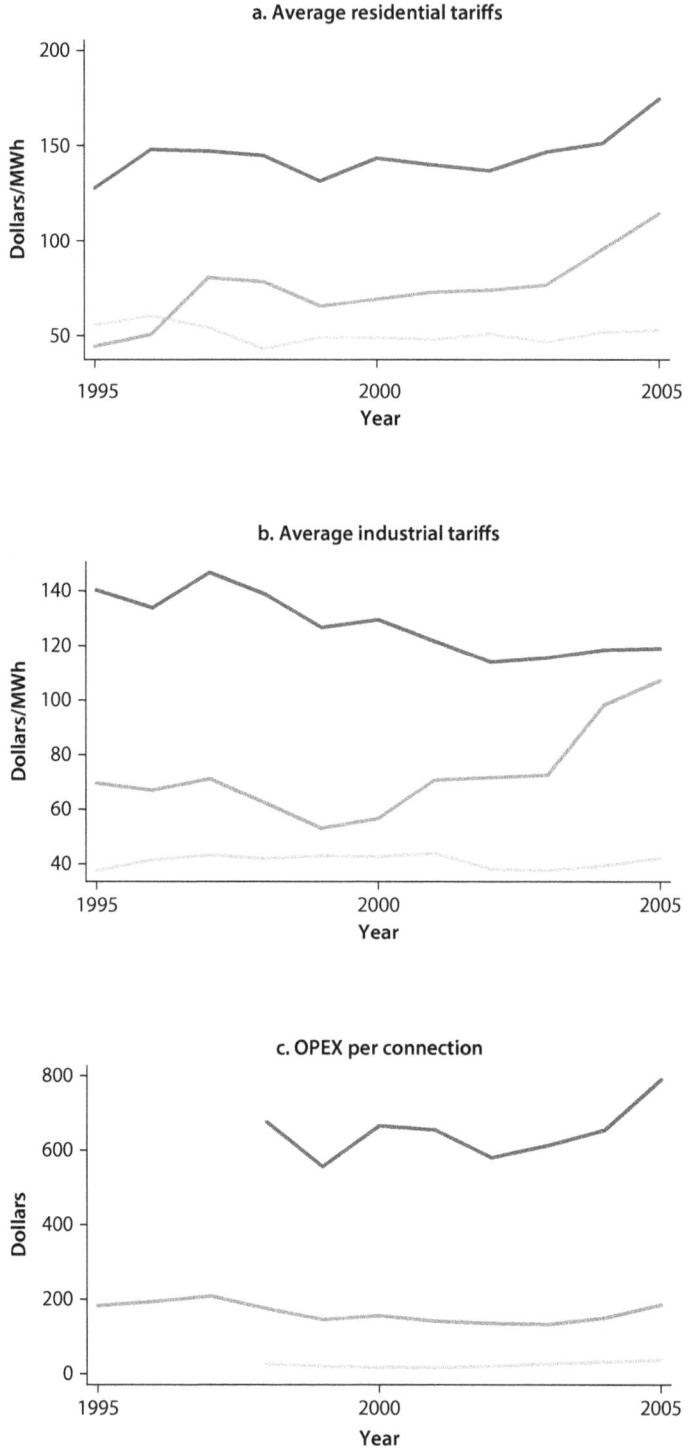

a. Average residential tariffs

b. Average industrial tariffs

c. OPEX per connection

figure continues next page

Figure C.6 Utility Level Benchmarking—Electricity Distribution: Tariffs and Expenses *(continued)*

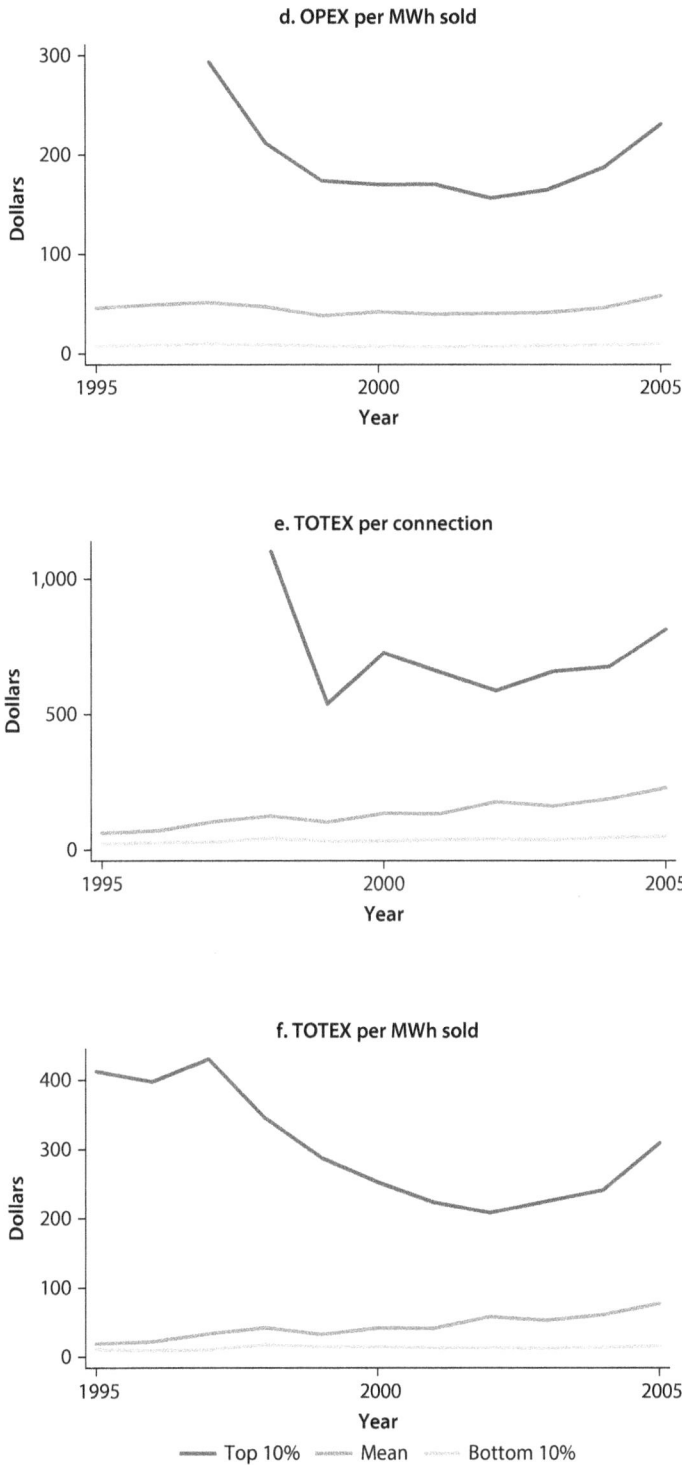

d. OPEX per MWh sold

e. TOTEX per connection

f. TOTEX per MWh sold

Top 10% — Mean — Bottom 10%

Source: LAC Electricity Benchmarking Database, World Bank, 2007.

Water and Sanitation Sector

Regional-Level Benchmarking Assessment

Figure C.7 Regional Benchmarking—Water and Sanitation: Coverage, Output, and Labor Productivity

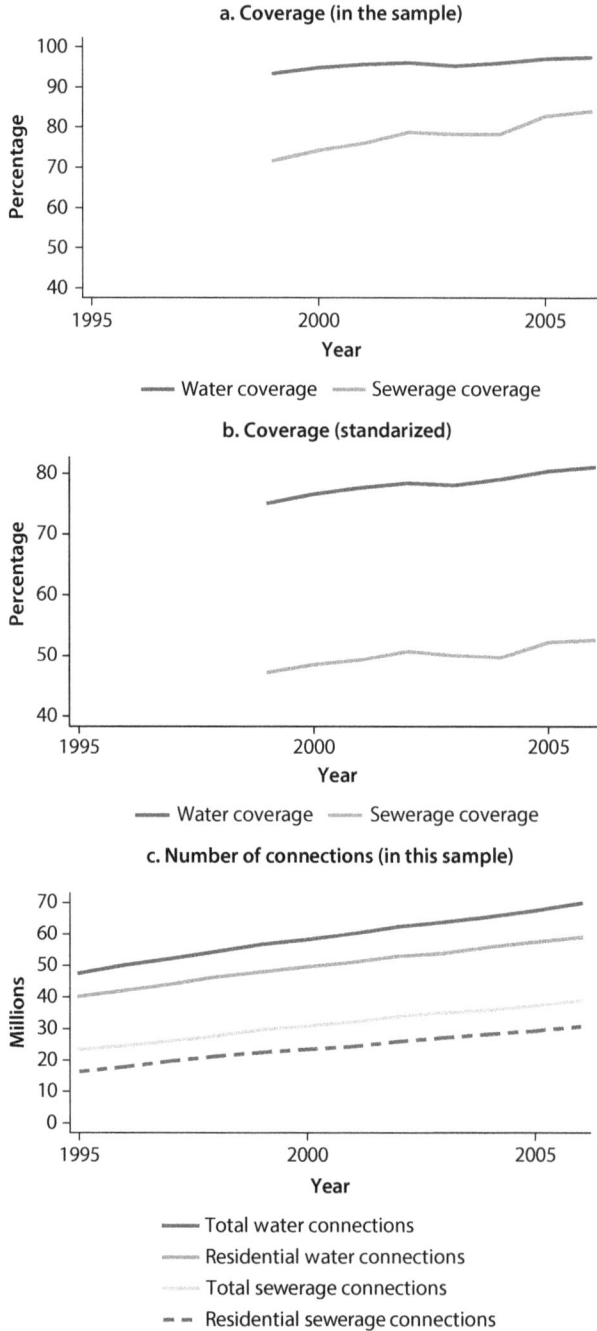

a. Coverage (in the sample)

Water coverage — Sewerage coverage

b. Coverage (standarized)

Water coverage — Sewerage coverage

c. Number of connections (in this sample)

Total water connections
Residential water connections
Total sewerage connections
Residential sewerage connections

figure continues next page

Figure C.7 Regional Benchmarking—Water and Sanitation: Coverage, Output, and Labor Productivity *(continued)*

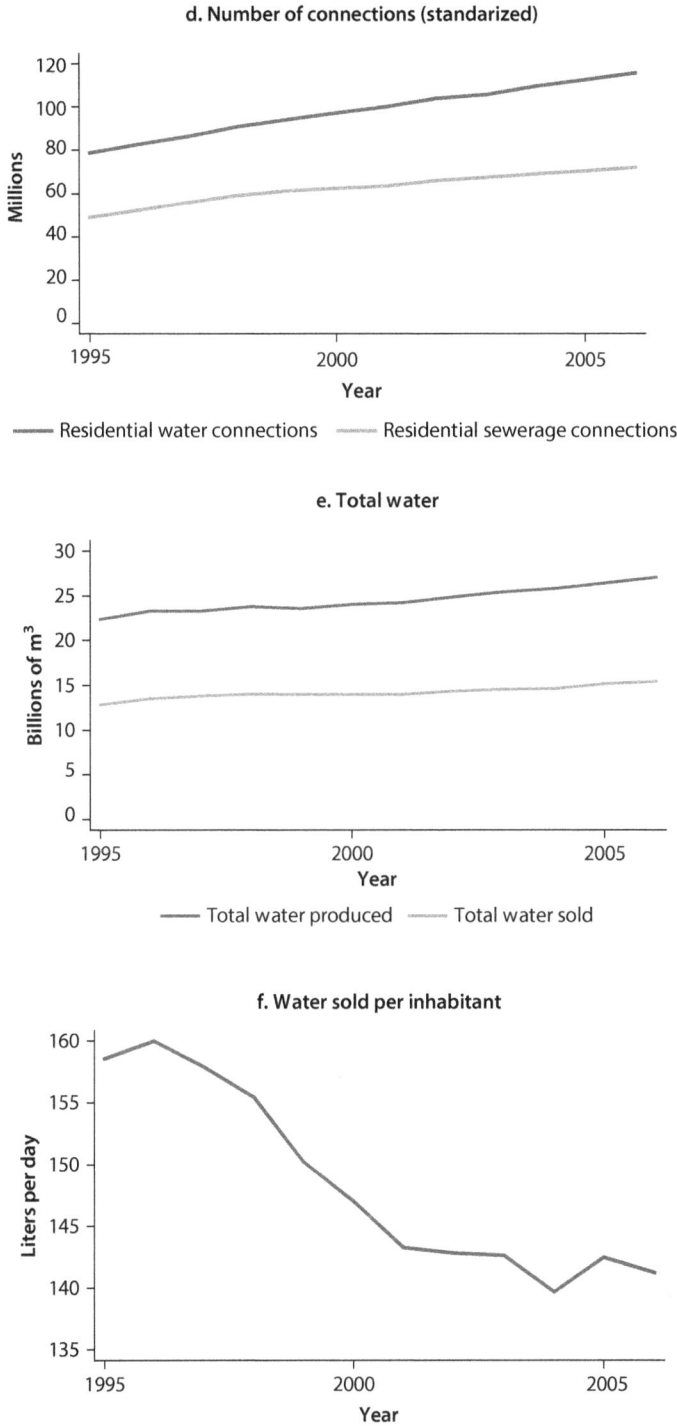

d. Number of connections (standarized)

Residential water connections   Residential sewerage connections

e. Total water

Total water produced   Total water sold

f. Water sold per inhabitant

Source: LAC Water Benchmarking Database, World Bank, 2009.

Uncovering the Drivers of Utility Performance • http://dx.doi.org/10.1596/978-0-8213-9660-5

Figure C.8 Regional Benchmarking—Water and Sanitation: Efficiency, Labor Productivity, and Quality of the Service

a. Efficiency indicators (within this sample)

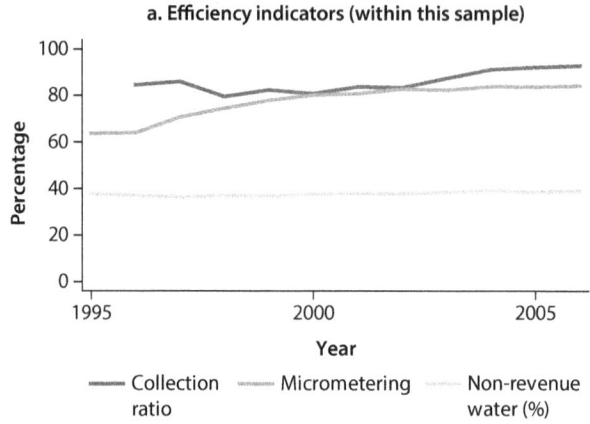

b. Total water connections per employee

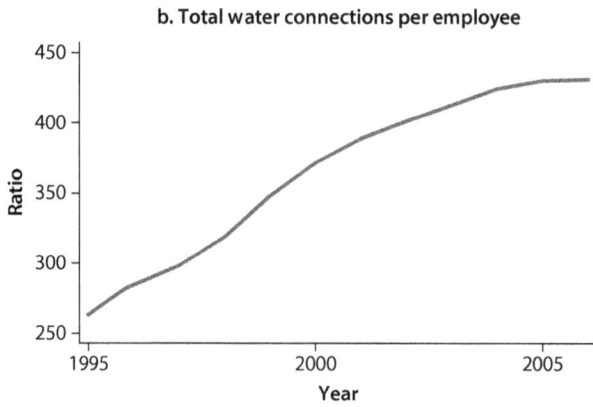

c. Continuity of the service

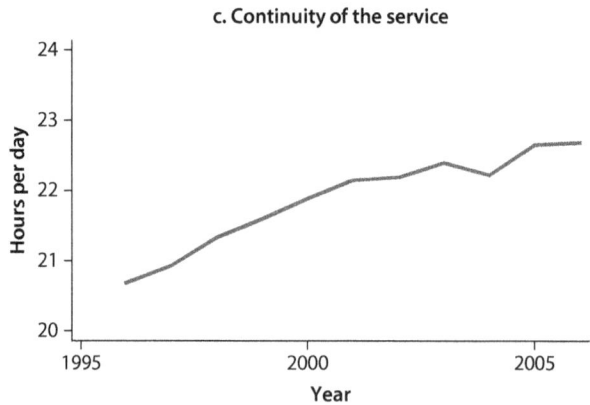

figure continues next page

Figure C.8 Regional Benchmarking—Water and Sanitation: Efficiency, Labor Productivity, and Quality of the Service (continued)

d. Potability

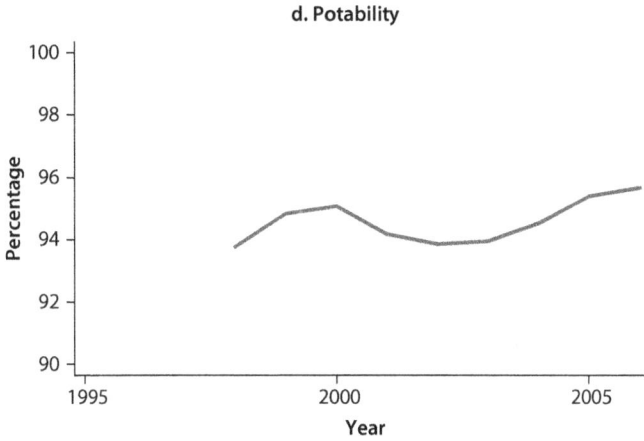

Source: LAC Water Benchmarking Database, World Bank, 2009.

Figure C.9 Regional Benchmarking—Water and Sanitation: Tariffs and Expenses

a. Average residential tariff

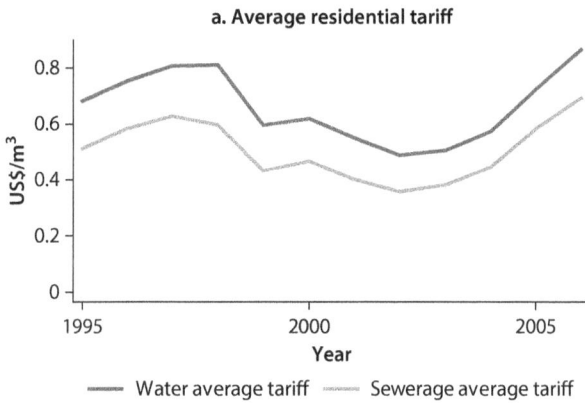

Water average tariff   Sewerage average tariff

b. Expenditures per cubic meter sold

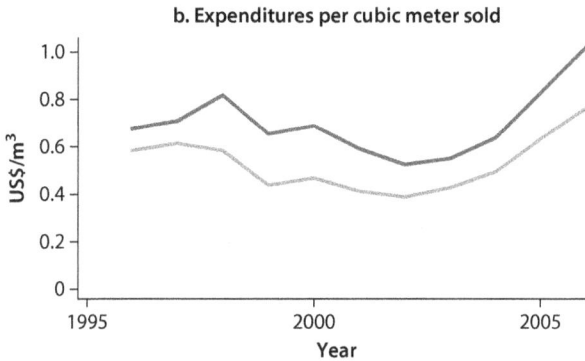

figure continues next page

Figure C.9 Regional Benchmarking—Water and Sanitation: Tariffs and Expenses *(continued)*

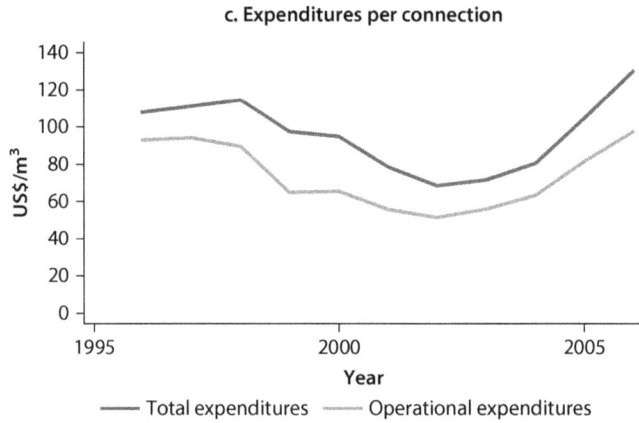

c. Expenditures per connection

Source: LAC Water Benchmarking Database, World Bank, 2009.

Utility-Level Benchmarking Assessment

Figure C.10 Utility Level Benchmarking—Water and Sanitation: Coverage and Output

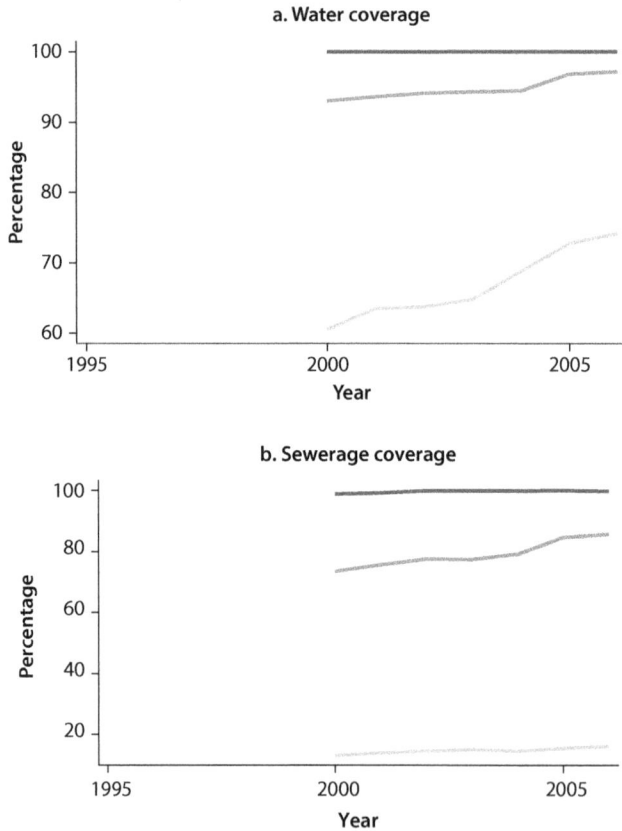

a. Water coverage

b. Sewerage coverage

figure continues next page

Figure C.10 Utility Level Benchmarking—Water and Sanitation: Coverage and Output (continued)

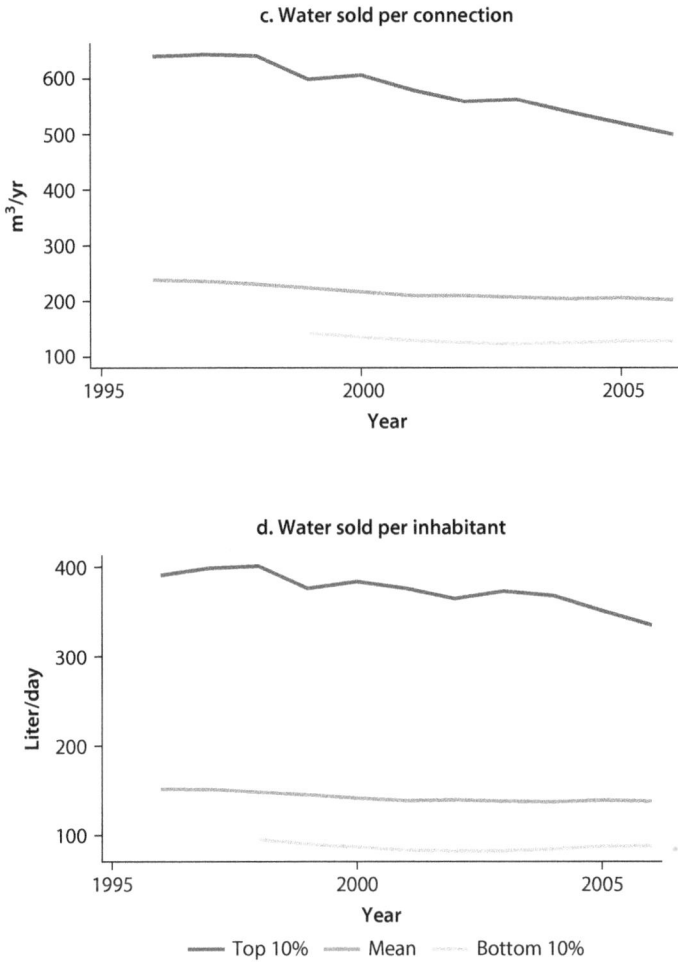

c. Water sold per connection

d. Water sold per inhabitant

Top 10%   Mean   Bottom 10%

Source: LAC Water Benchmarking Database, World Bank, 2009.

Figure C.11 Utility Level Benchmarking—Water and Sanitation: Labor Productivity, Efficiency, and Quality of the Service

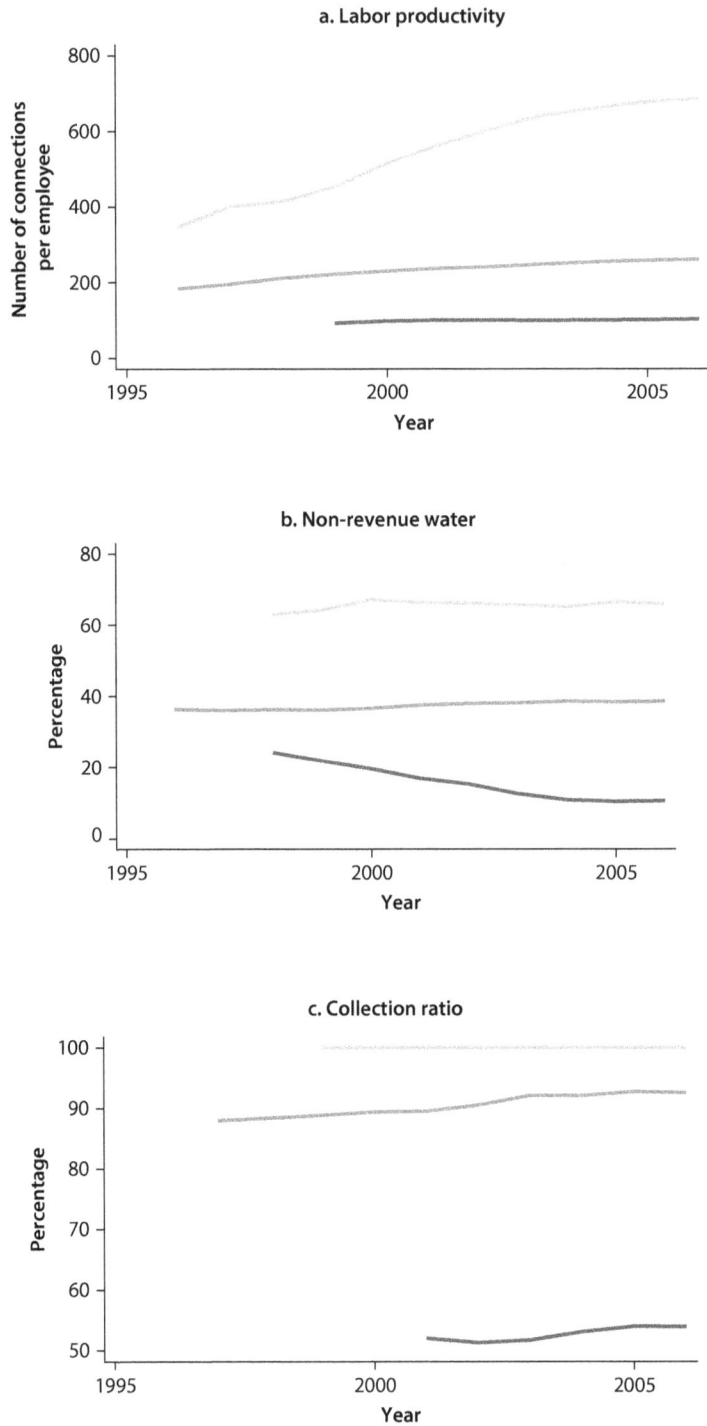

a. Labor productivity

b. Non-revenue water

c. Collection ratio

figure continues next page

Figure C.11 Utility Level Benchmarking—Water and Sanitation: Labor Productivity, Efficiency, and Quality of the Service *(continued)*

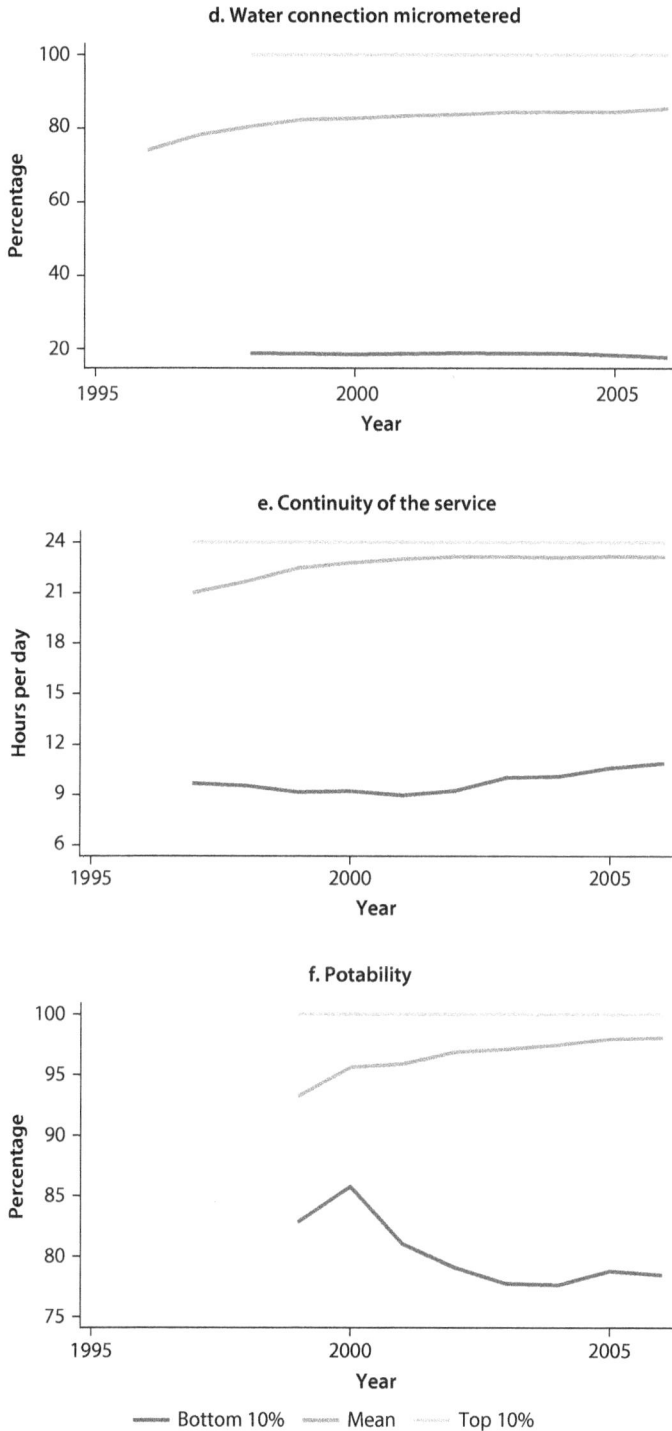

d. Water connection micrometered

e. Continuity of the service

f. Potability

——— Bottom 10%   ⸻ Mean   ········· Top 10%

Source: LAC Water Benchmarking Database, World Bank, 2009.

Uncovering the Drivers of Utility Performance • http://dx.doi.org/10.1596/978-0-8213-9660-5

Figure C.12 Utility Level Benchmarking—Water and Sanitation: Tariffs and Expenses

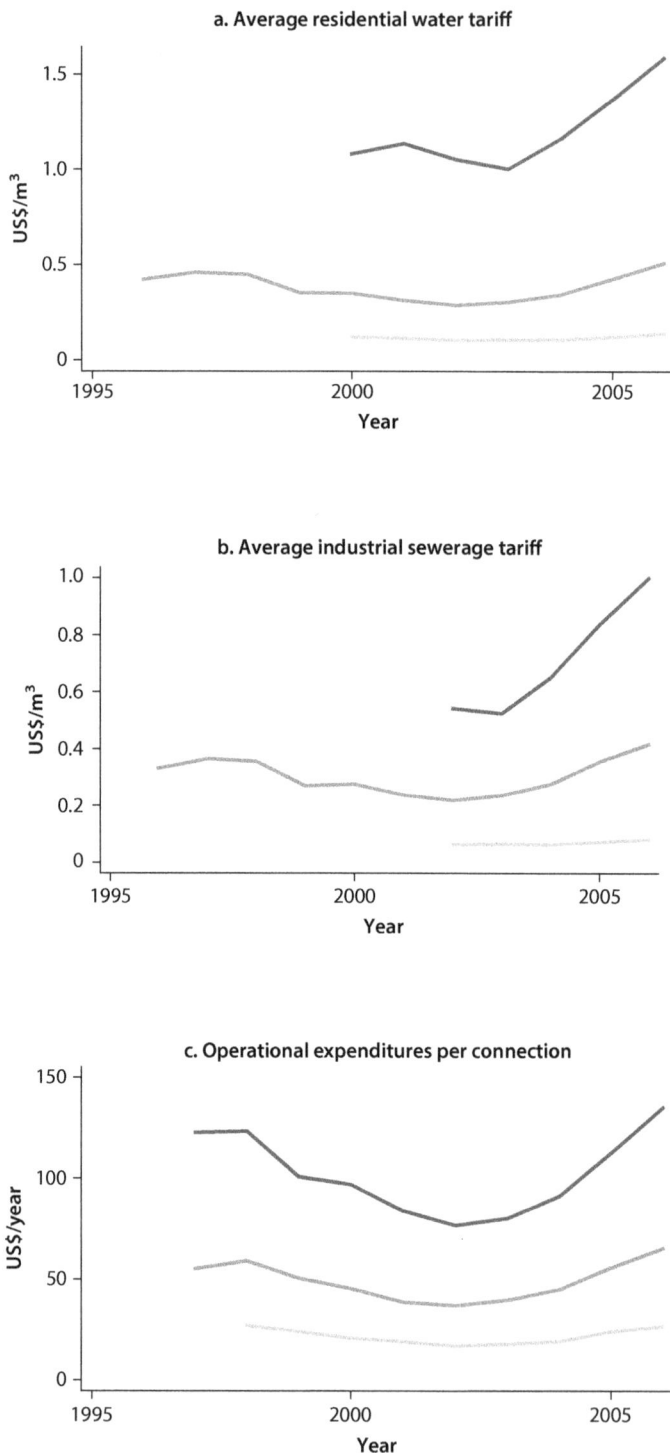

a. Average residential water tariff

b. Average industrial sewerage tariff

c. Operational expenditures per connection

figure continues next page

Figure C.12 Utility Level Benchmarking—Water and Sanitation: Tariffs and Expenses *(continued)*

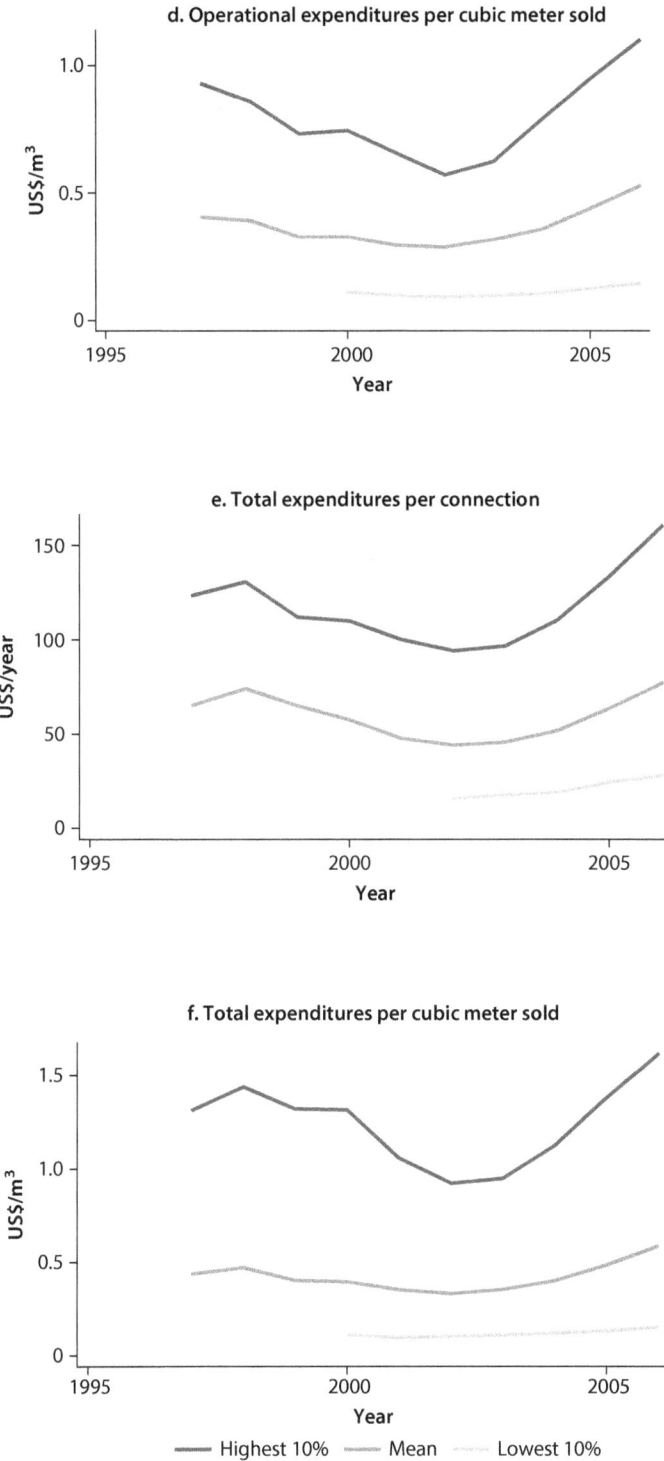

d. Operational expenditures per cubic meter sold

e. Total expenditures per connection

f. Total expenditures per cubic meter sold

Highest 10% — Mean — Lowest 10%

Source: LAC Water Benchmarking Database, World Bank, 2009.

Telecommunications Sector

Figure C.13 Fixed Telecommunications Sector

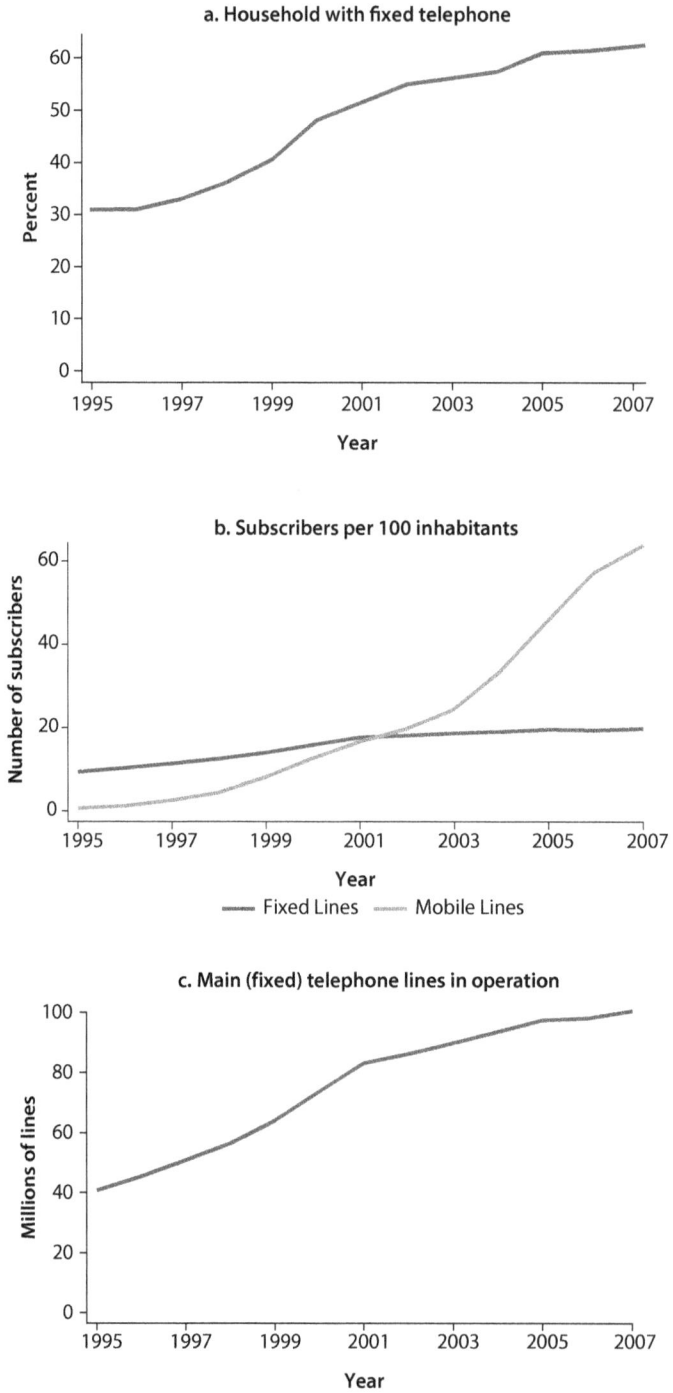

a. Household with fixed telephone

b. Subscribers per 100 inhabitants

Fixed Lines ———   Mobile Lines ·········

c. Main (fixed) telephone lines in operation

figure continues next page

Figure C.13 Fixed Telecommunications Sector *(continued)*

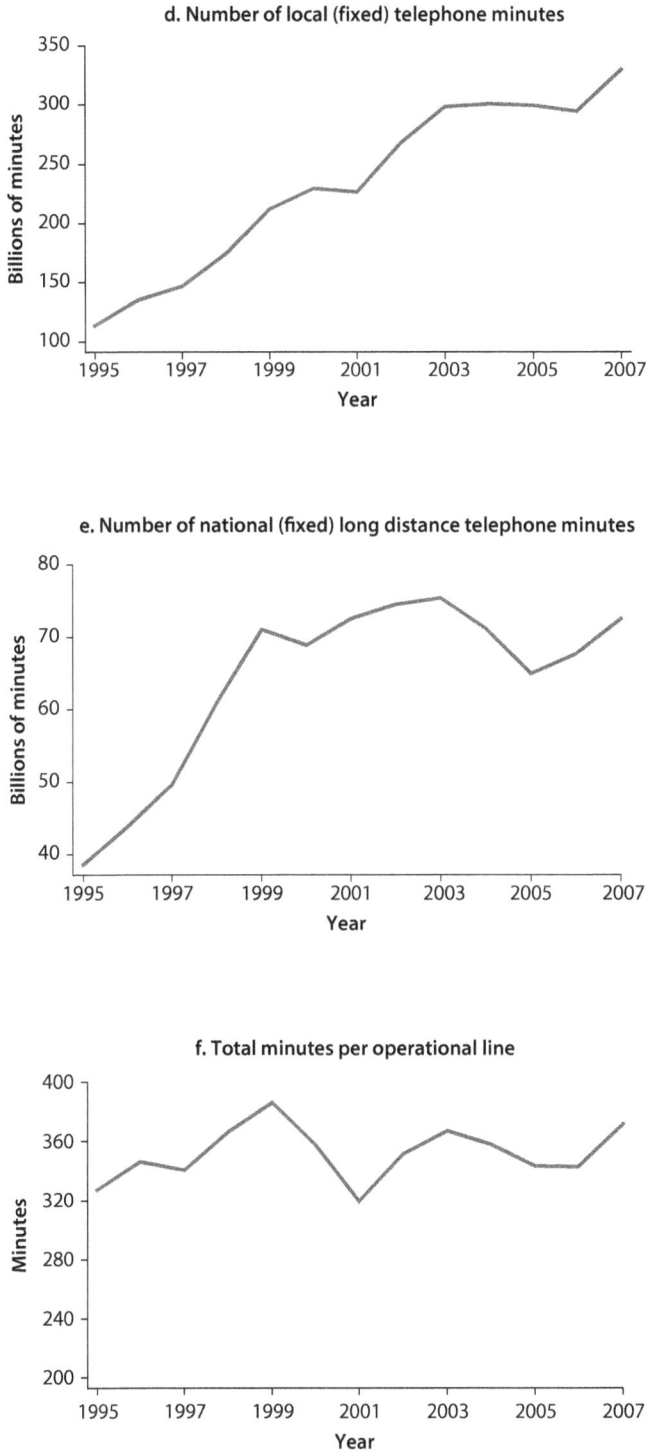

d. Number of local (fixed) telephone minutes

e. Number of national (fixed) long distance telephone minutes

f. Total minutes per operational line

figure continues next page

Figure C.13 Fixed Telecommunications Sector *(continued)*

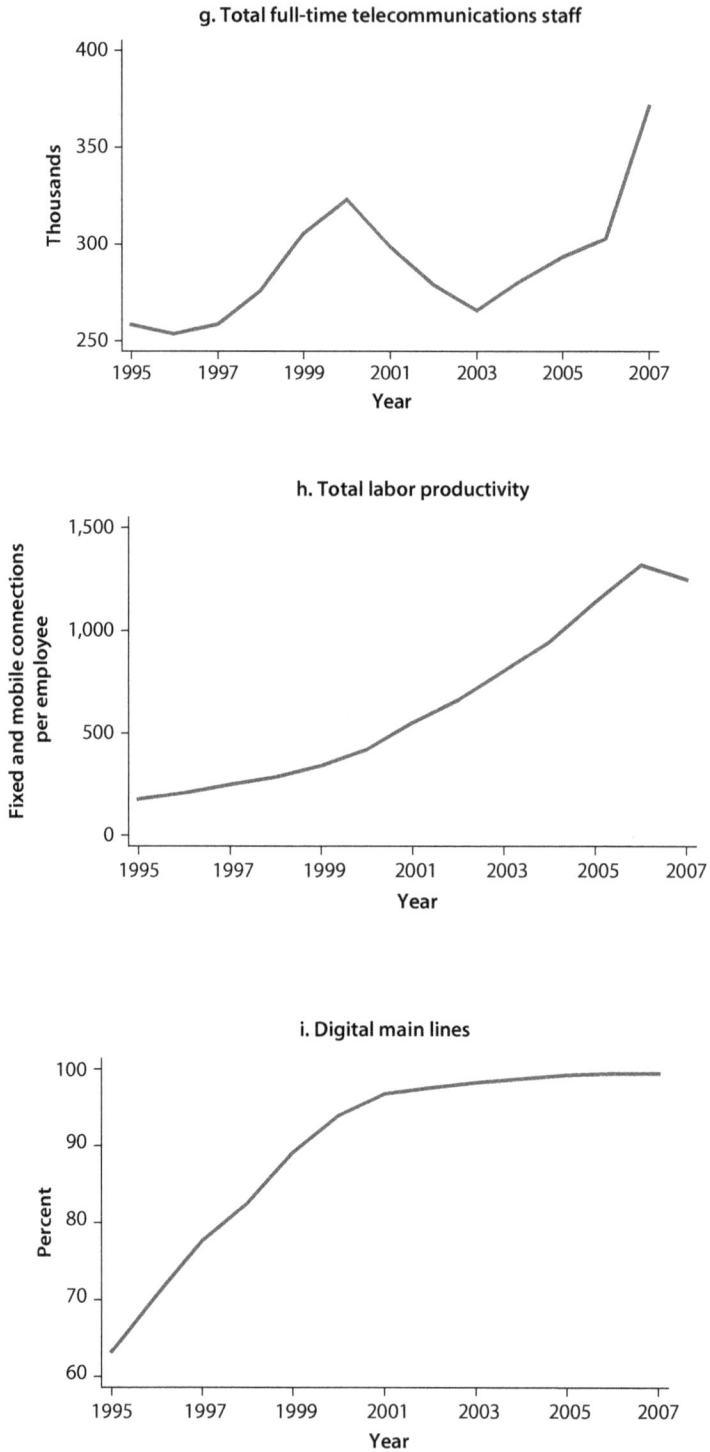

g. Total full-time telecommunications staff

h. Total labor productivity

i. Digital main lines

figure continues next page

Uncovering the Drivers of Utility Performance • http://dx.doi.org/10.1596/978-0-8213-9660-5

Figure C.13 Fixed Telecommunications Sector *(continued)*

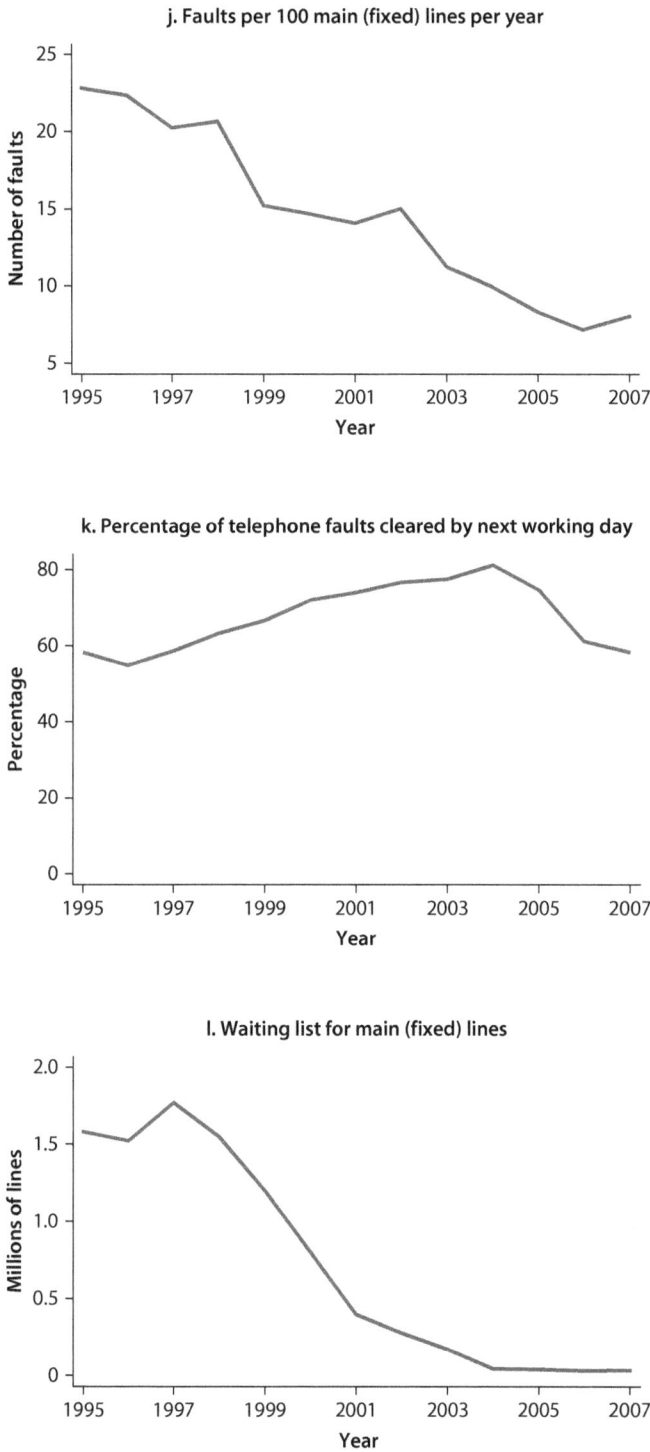

j. Faults per 100 main (fixed) lines per year

k. Percentage of telephone faults cleared by next working day

l. Waiting list for main (fixed) lines

figure continues next page

Figure C.13 Fixed Telecommunications Sector *(continued)*

m. Price of 3-minute local call (off-peak US$)

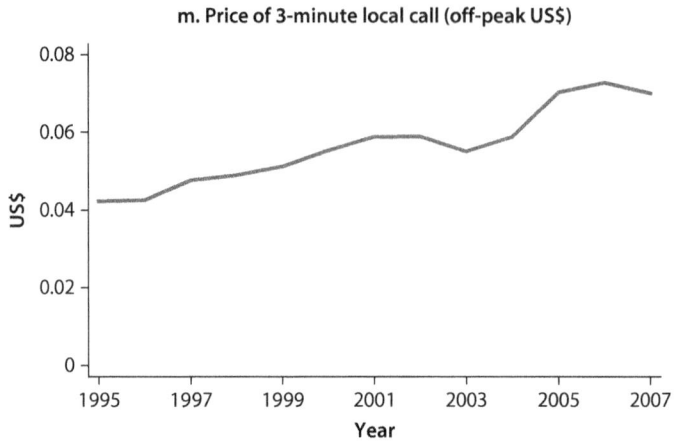

n. Price of 3-minute local call (peak US$)

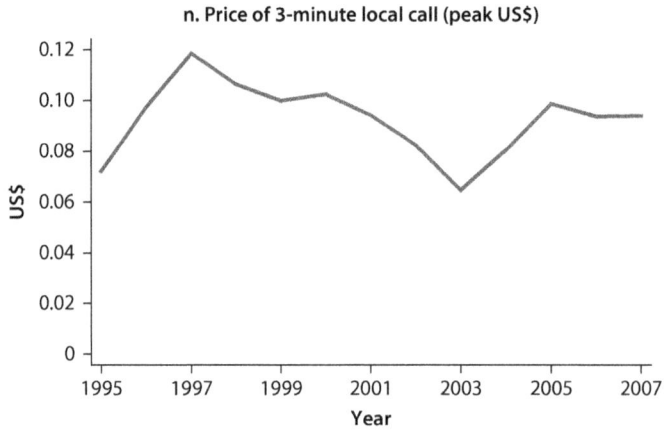

o. Residential monthly telephone subscription

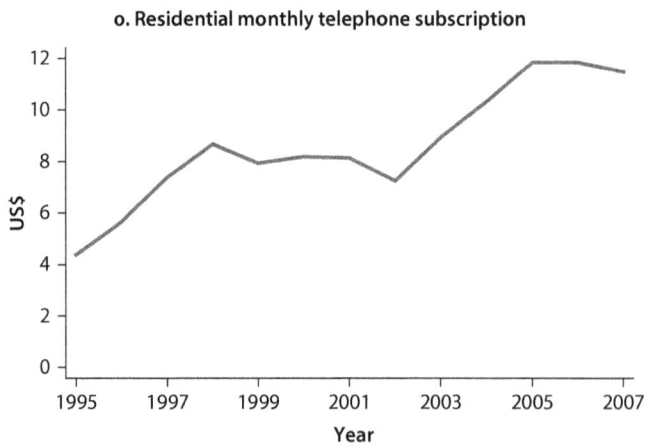

figure continues next page

Figure C.13 Fixed Telecommunications Sector *(continued)*

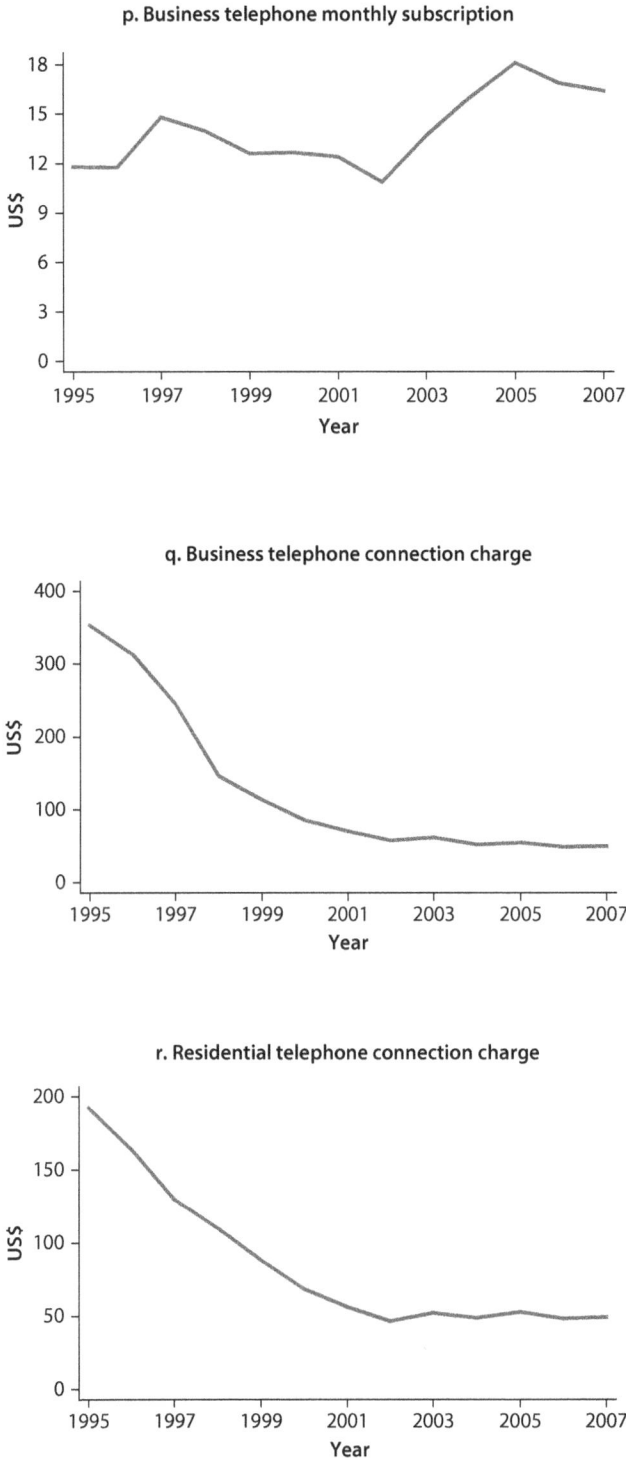

p. Business telephone monthly subscription

q. Business telephone connection charge

r. Residential telephone connection charge

Source: International Telecommunication Union 2008.

Uncovering the Drivers of Utility Performance • http://dx.doi.org/10.1596/978-0-8213-9660-5

Public versus Private Benchmarking Assessment

Figure C.14 Public versus Private Benchmarking Assessment

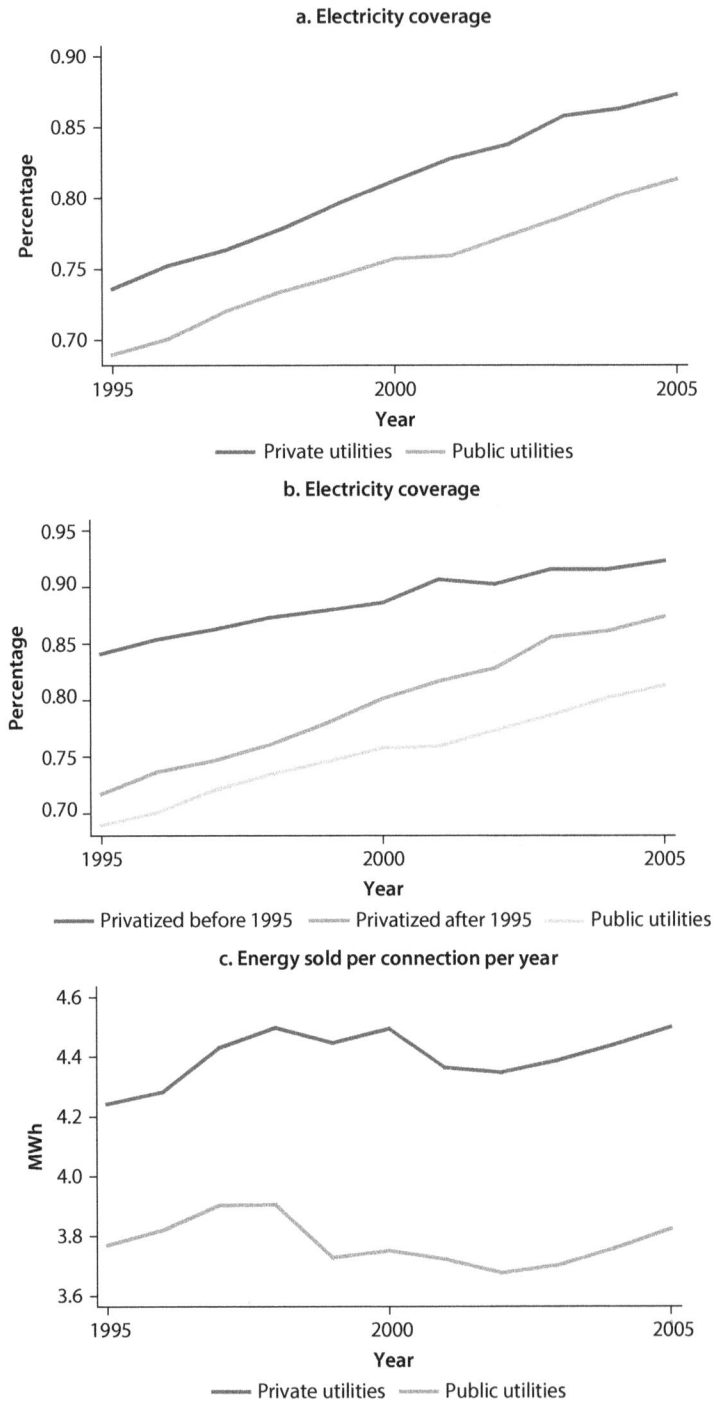

a. Electricity coverage

b. Electricity coverage

c. Energy sold per connection per year

figure continues next page

Figure C.14 Public versus Private Benchmarking Assessment *(continued)*

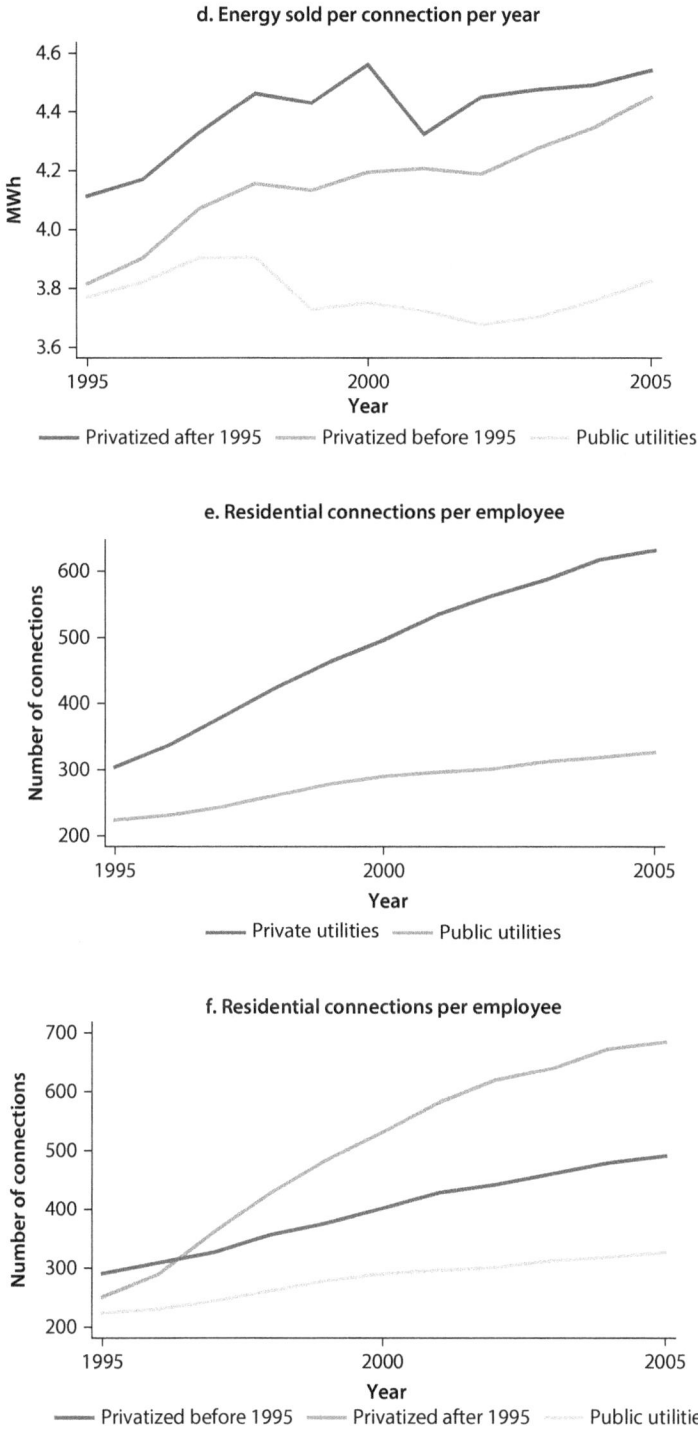

d. Energy sold per connection per year

Privatized after 1995 ——— Privatized before 1995 ……… Public utilities

e. Residential connections per employee

Private utilities ——— Public utilities

f. Residential connections per employee

Privatized before 1995 ——— Privatized after 1995 ……… Public utilities

figure continues next page

Figure C.14 Public versus Private Benchmarking Assessment *(continued)*

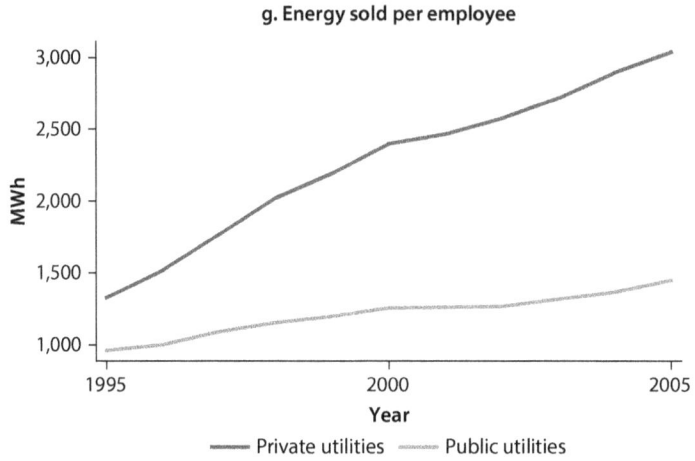

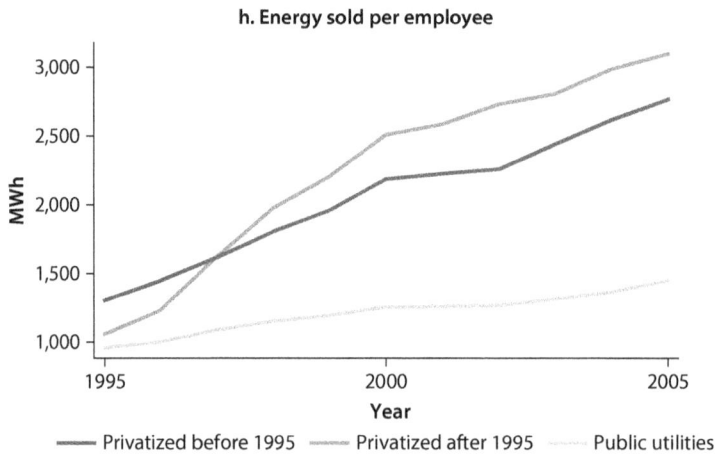

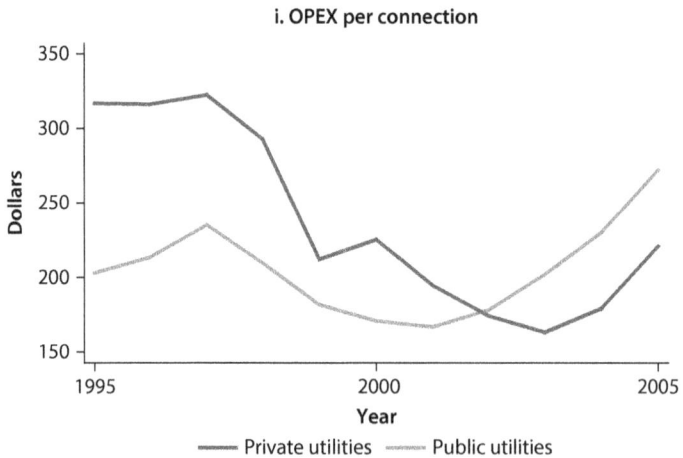

g. Energy sold per employee

h. Energy sold per employee

i. OPEX per connection

figure continues next page

Figure C.14 Public versus Private Benchmarking Assessment *(continued)*

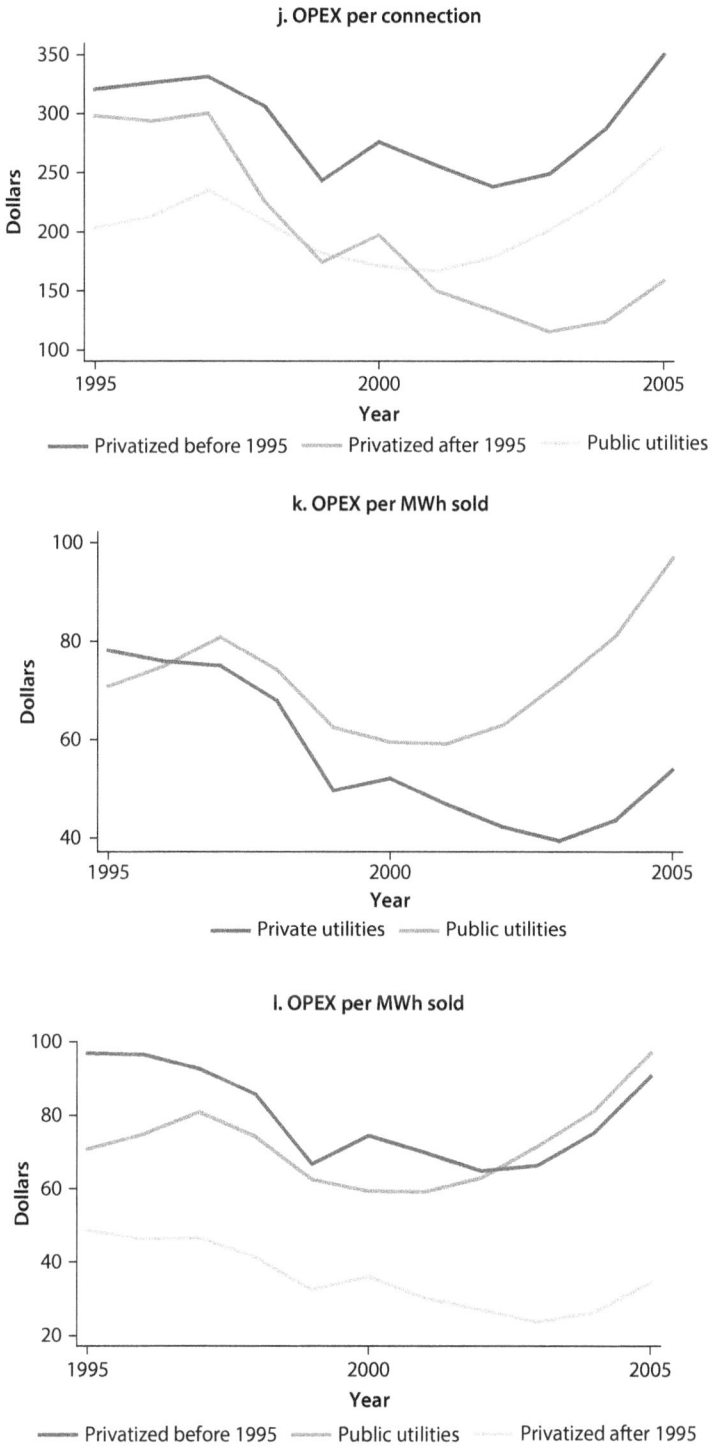

j. OPEX per connection

Legend: —— Privatized before 1995 —— Privatized after 1995 ⋯⋯ Public utilities

k. OPEX per MWh sold

Legend: —— Private utilities ⋯⋯ Public utilities

l. OPEX per MWh sold

Legend: —— Privatized before 1995 —— Public utilities ⋯⋯ Privatized after 1995

figure continues next page

Figure C.14 Public versus Private Benchmarking Assessment *(continued)*

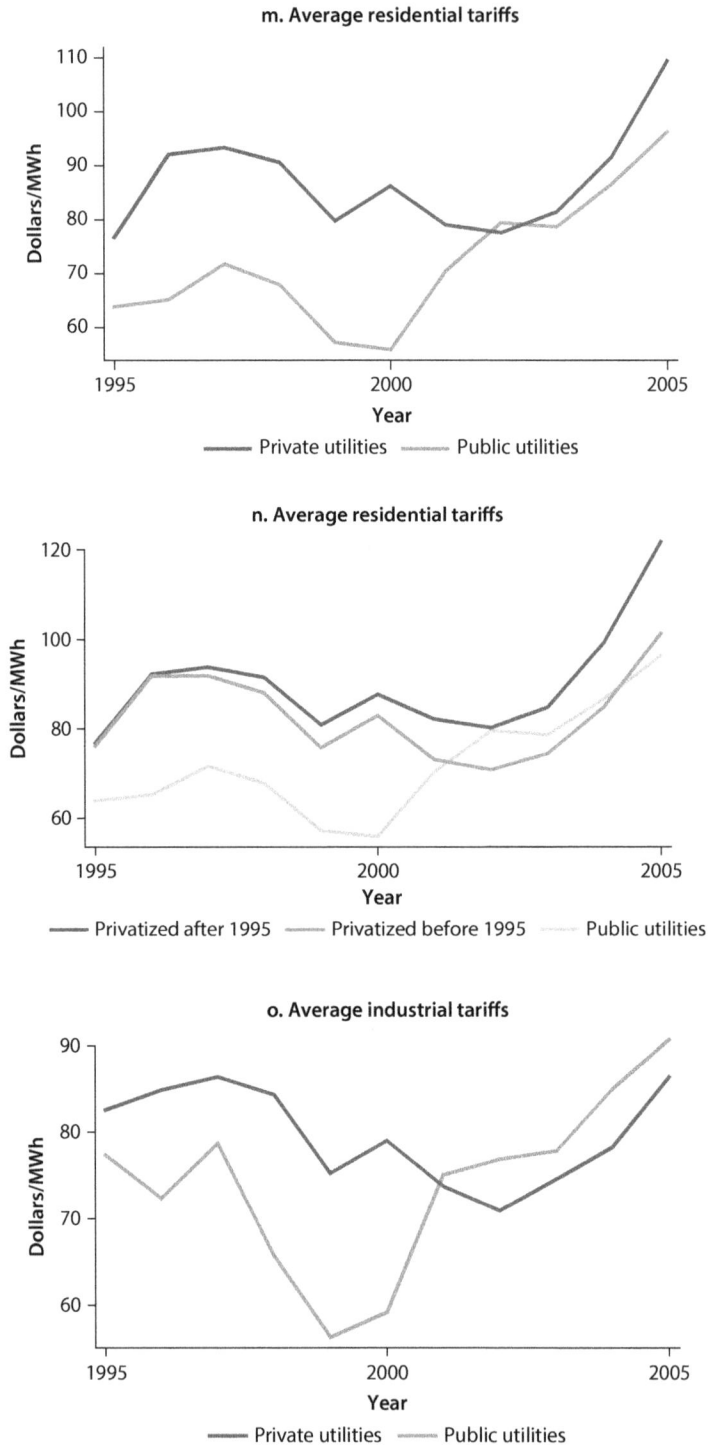

m. Average residential tariffs

Private utilities — Public utilities

n. Average residential tariffs

Privatized after 1995 — Privatized before 1995 — Public utilities

o. Average industrial tariffs

Private utilities — Public utilities

figure continues next page

Figure C.14 Public versus Private Benchmarking Assessment *(continued)*

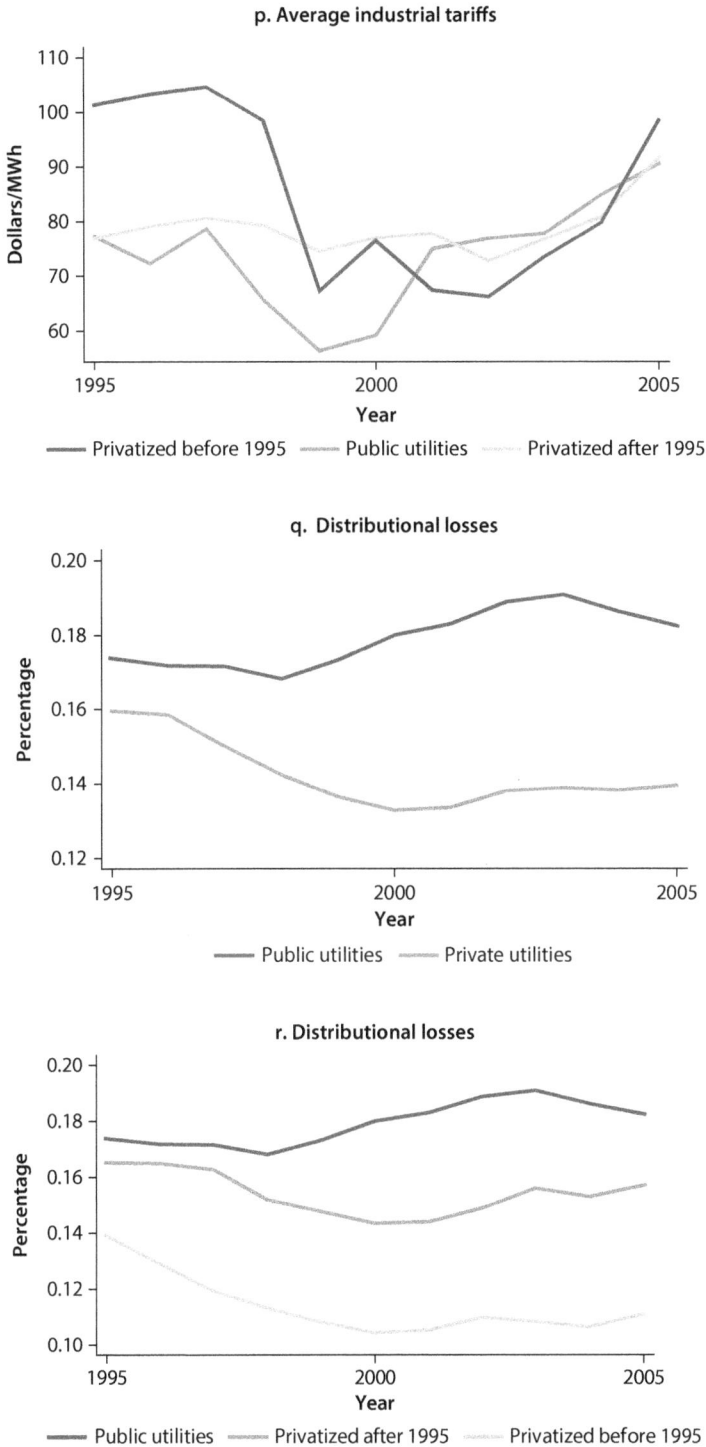

p. Average industrial tariffs

——— Privatized before 1995   ——— Public utilities   ········ Privatized after 1995

q. Distributional losses

——— Public utilities   ——— Private utilities

r. Distributional losses

——— Public utilities   ——— Privatized after 1995   ········ Privatized before 1995

figure continues next page

Figure C.14 Public versus Private Benchmarking Assessment *(continued)*

s. Average frequency of interruptions per connection

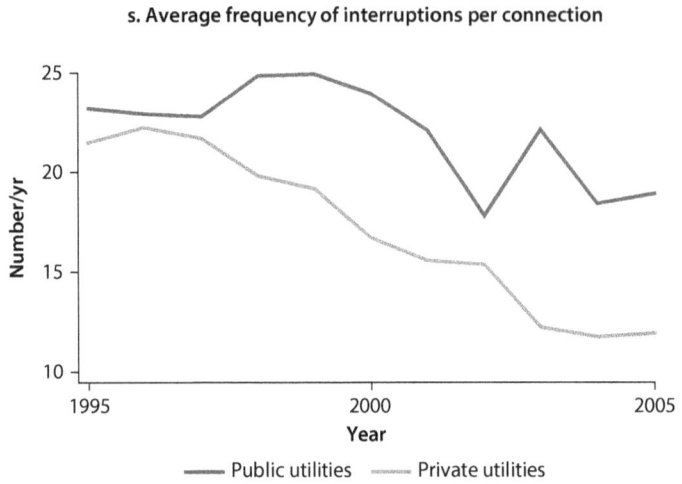

Public utilities — Private utilities

t. Average frequency of interruptions per connection

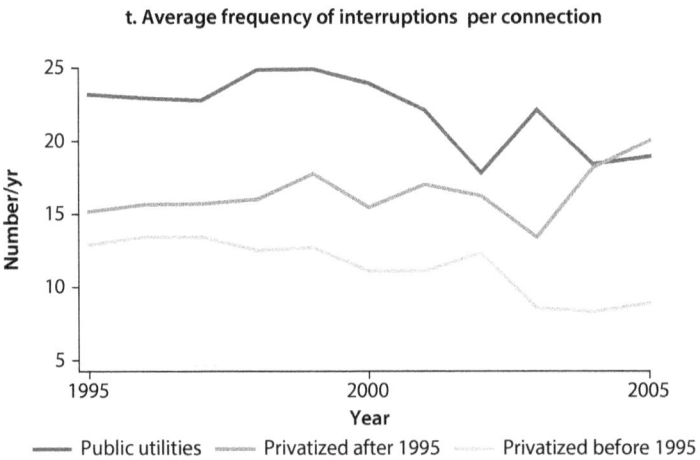

Public utilities — Privatized after 1995 — Privatized before 1995

u. Average duration of interruptions per connection

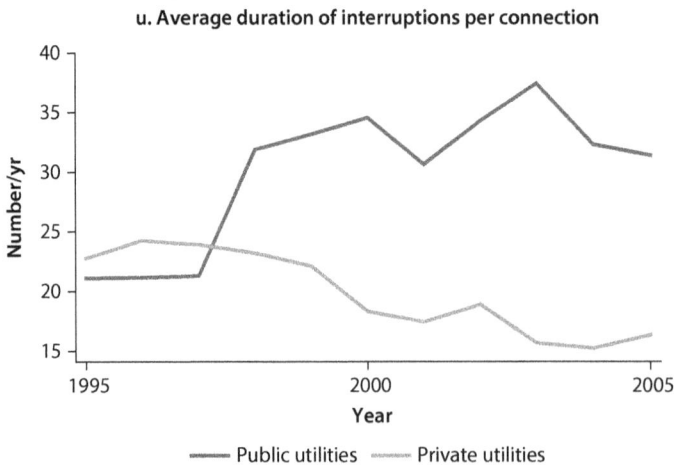

Public utilities — Private utilities

figure continues next page

Figure C.14 Public versus Private Benchmarking Assessment *(continued)*

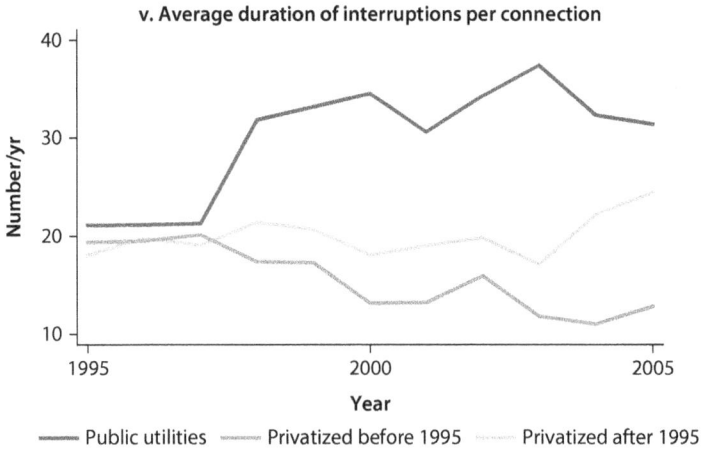

v. Average duration of interruptions per connection

——— Public utilities ——— Privatized before 1995 ········· Privatized after 1995

Source: LAC Electricity Benchmarking Database, World Bank, 2007.

Figure C.15 Top Ten and Bottom Ten Percent Performers

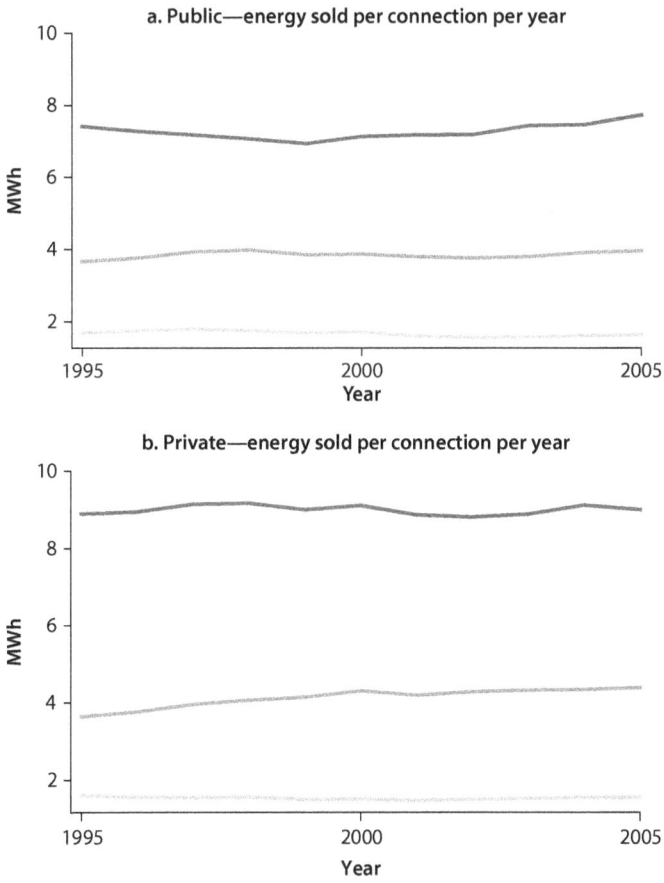

a. Public—energy sold per connection per year

b. Private—energy sold per connection per year

figure continues next page

Figure C.15 Top Ten and Bottom Ten Percent Performers *(continued)*

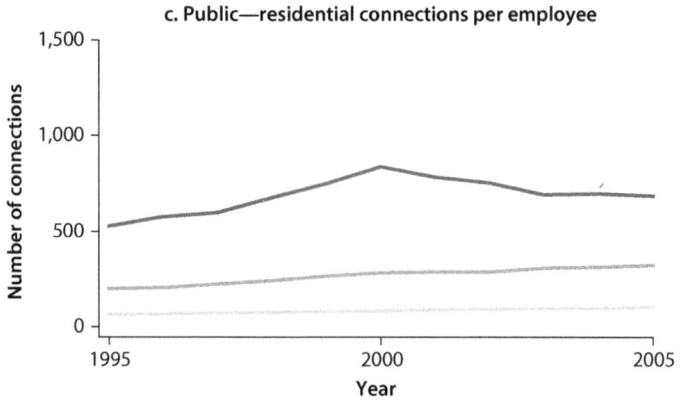

c. Public—residential connections per employee

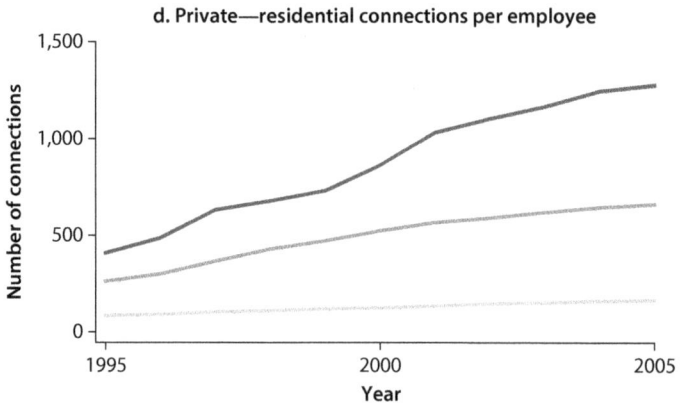

d. Private—residential connections per employee

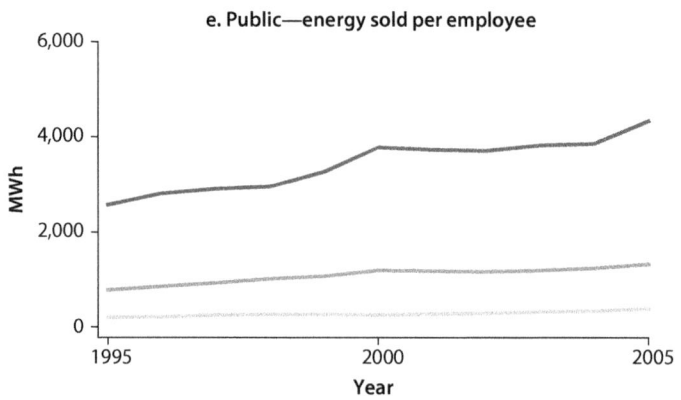

e. Public—energy sold per employee

figure continues next page

Figure C.15 Top Ten and Bottom Ten Percent Performers *(continued)*

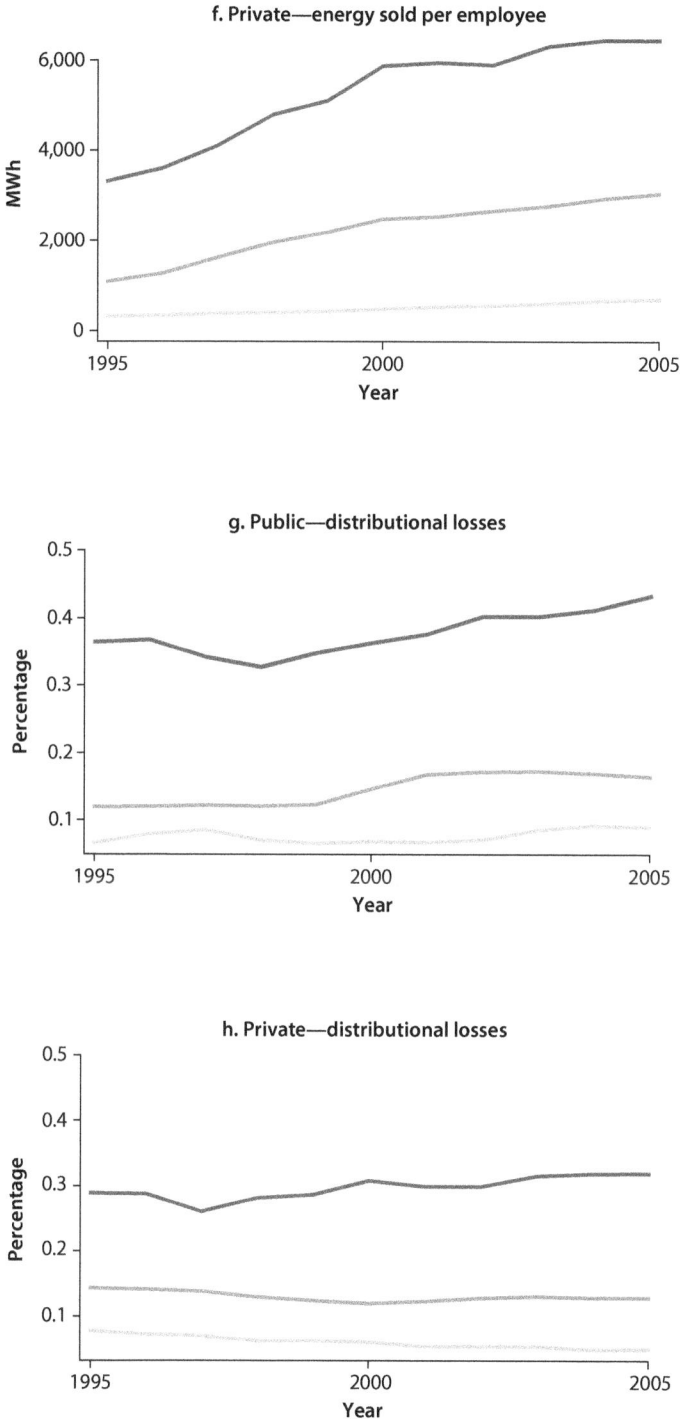

f. Private—energy sold per employee

g. Public—distributional losses

h. Private—distributional losses

figure continues next page

Figure C.15 Top Ten and Bottom Ten Percent Performers *(continued)*

i. Public—average frequency of interruptions per connection

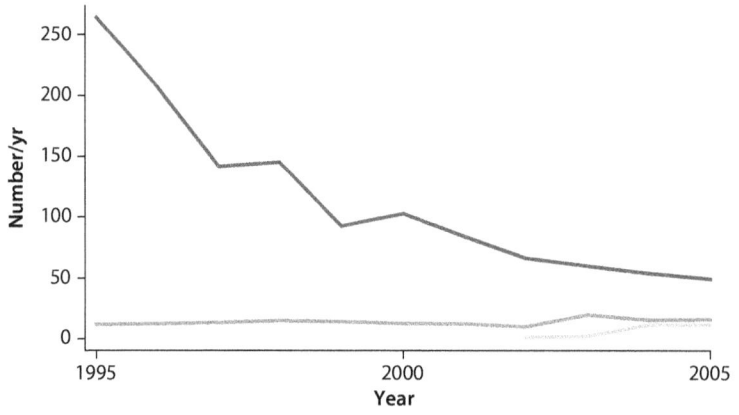

j. Private—average frequency of
interruptions per connection

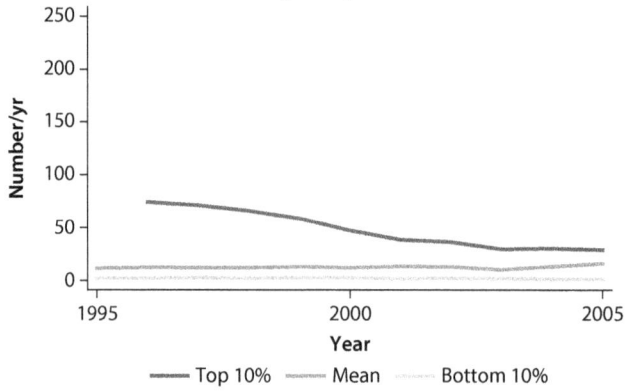

Top 10% ——— Mean ——— Bottom 10%

Source: LAC Electricity Benchmarking Database, World Bank, 2007.

Detailed Results of the Empirical Analysis

Table D.1 Means and Medians Analysis in Levels—Electricity Distribution

Variable	Statistics	Mean			Difference in levels			T-statistics (Z-statistics) for difference in means (medians) in levels		
		Pre-private	Transition	Post-private	(2)–(1)	(3)–(2)	(3)–(1)	(2)–(1)	(3)–(2)	(3)–(1)
		(1)	(2)	(3)	(4)	(5)	(6)	(7)	(8)	(9)
Outputs										
Residential connections	mean	85.83	102.26	120.48	17.32	17.11	35.16	−16.209***	−17.493***	−16.809***
	p50	85.94	102.00	119.59	17.11	16.55	34.33	−7.843***	−7.306***	−7.459***
	sd	9.20	2.53	10.04	9.68	8.76	16.94			
	N	82	116	74	82	74	71			
MWh sold per year	mean	82.29	102.67	119.22	20.82	15.60	36.74	−13.119***	−11.882***	−7.554***
	p50	82.59	101.20	117.13	19.88	15.17	34.60	−7.399***	−6.945***	−6.128***
	sd	14.11	6.44	21.12	14.28	17.77	25.69			
	N	81	116	74	81	74	69			
Inputs										
Number of employees	mean	162.71	100.65	86.59	−61.37	−14.27	−78.19	8.949***	8.678***	5.432***
	p50	147.46	100.00	86.17	−48.38	−14.76	−63.63	6.252***	5.903***	5.057***
	sd	54.42	6.76	23.63	52.22	20.18	63.71			
	N	58	116	59	58	59	50			
Efficiency										
Connections per employee	mean	60.24	103.33	147.42	45.38	40.83	88.62	14.738***	13.344***	9.334***
	p50	59.90	100.00	135.26	44.65	32.10	88.86	−6.543***	−6.093***	−6.438***
	sd	18.65	9.86	42.10	23.25	33.31	46.49			
	N	57	116	58	57	58	49			

table continues next page

Table D.1 Means and Medians Analysis in Levels—Electricity Distribution *(continued)*

Variable	Statistics	Mean			Difference in levels			T-statistics (Z-statistics) for difference in means (medians) in levels		
		Pre-private	Transition	Post-private	(2)–(1)	(3)–(2)	(3)–(1)	(2)–(1)	(3)–(2)	(3)–(1)
		(1)	(2)	(3)	(4)	(5)	(6)	(7)	(8)	(9)
GWh per employee	mean	58.56	103.97	145.09	47.50	37.64	86.27	−17.097***	−11.362***	−6.901***
	p50	59.68	100.00	129.76	46.04	26.76	71.15	−6.567***	−6.093***	−6.182***
	sd	18.58	11.98	53.86	20.98	41.54	53.15			
	N	57	116	58	57	58	49			
Distributional losses	mean	112.19	98.73	87.78	−12.92	−9.75	−25.14	3.658***	4.657***	3.515***
	p50	104.37	100.00	85.34	−6.13	−11.06	−19.93	3.268***	4.272***	3.341***
	sd	26.96	7.33	26.03	27.14	21.12	37.79			
	N	59	116	58	59	58	49			
Quality										
Duration of interruptions per year per consumer	mean	134.49	100.34	72.42	−30.61	−25.32	−41.34	3.250***	2.687***	3.782***
	p50	123.37	100.00	65.42	−24.11	−30.41	−34.37	3.477***	3.143***	4.019***
	sd	67.57	20.00	42.58	57.28	41.80	75.35			
	N	37	116	39	37	39	24			
Frequency of interruptions per year per consumer	mean	132.59	98.63	82.71	−34.90	−13.65	−31.66	4.256***	1.300	1.078
	p50	119.54	100.00	67.96	−21.20	−29.20	−32.86	3.809***	3.571***	4.326***
	sd	57.83	13.77	93.00	49.88	79.05	119.29			
	N	37	116	39	37	39	24			

table continues next page

Table D.1 Means and Medians Analysis in Levels—Electricity Distribution *(continued)*

Variable	Statistics	Mean			Difference in levels			T-statistics (Z-statistics) for difference in means (medians) in levels		
		Pre-private (1)	Transition (2)	Post-private (3)	(2)–(1) (4)	(3)–(2) (5)	(3)–(1) (6)	(2)–(1) (7)	(3)–(2) (8)	(3)–(1) (9)
Coverage										
Residential connections per 100 HHs	mean	94.93	101.17	110.66	6.93	8.67	16.46	−6.886***	−8.162***	−8.333***
	p50	95.35	100.00	108.92	5.60	7.62	14.16	−6.016***	−6.110***	−6.323***
	sd	7.91	2.22	10.09	8.42	8.26	15.09			
	N	70	116	63	70	63	56			
Prices										
Average tariff per residential GWh (in dollars)	mean	106.24	98.48	94.87	−9.49	−2.88	−9.91	3.305***	2.808***	1.313*
	p50	97.85	100.00	95.61	−0.09	−1.38	−16.37	2.437**	2.690***	1.702*
	sd	23.68	7.52	24.63	23.85	18.73	26.18			
	N	69	116	73	69	73	55			
Average tariff per residential GWh (in real local currency)	mean	91.77	100.81	109.61	9.21	8.46	17.90	−5.164***	−5.143***	−5.067***
	p50	88.27	100.00	107.07	15.25	4.64	24.26	−4.774***	−4.181***	−4.643***
	sd	12.83	4.97	18.59	14.81	14.27	25.81			
	N	69	116	73	69	73	55			

Source: Andrés and others 2008.

Note: GWh = gigawatt hours; HH = household; MWh = megawatt hours.

* significant at 10 percent; ** significant at 5 percent; *** significant at 1 percent.

Table D.2 Means and Medians Analysis in Growth—Electricity Distribution

Variable	Statistics	Average annual growth			Annual difference in growth			T-statistics (Z-statistics) for difference in means (medians) in growth		
		Preprivate	Transition	Postprivate	(2)–(1)	(3)–(2)	(3)–(1)	(2)–(1)	(3)–(2)	(3)–(1)
		(1)	(2)	(3)	(4)	(5)	(6)	(7)	(8)	(9)
Outputs										
Residential connections	mean	4.3%	5.5%	3.4%	1.3%	−2.8%	−0.8%	−1.787**	3.590***	1.976**
	p50	4.4%	4.7%	3.2%	0.4%	−1.7%	−1.0%	−1.456	5.116***	2.366**
	sd	2.6%	5.5%	2.0%						
	N	79	84	60	79	60	56			
MWh sold per year	mean	6.7%	6.7%	3.2%	−0.5%	−5.0%	−3.2%	0.616	3.085***	3.362***
	p50	6.6%	5.9%	2.8%	−0.7%	−2.9%	−2.7%	0.708	4.096***	3.159***
	sd	4.5%	8.7%	4.7%						
	N	74	85	57	74	57	51			
Inputs										
Number of employees	mean	−6.6%	−9.9%	−2.1%	−3.2%	9.7%	2.1%	2.056*	−5.398***	−1.519*
	p50	−6.1%	−9.0%	−1.8%	−3.8%	8.7%	4.0%	2.306**	−4.505***	−1.776*
	sd	8.1%	10.0%	4.8%						
	N	53	69	44	53	44	32			
Efficiency										
Connections per employee	mean	13.4%	18.4%	5.5%	4.2%	−16.4%	−4.2%	−1.813**	5.691***	2.183**
	p50	11.1%	14.0%	5.6%	4.5%	−10.6%	−3.5%	2.333**	4.975***	2.300**
	sd	12.6%	16.8%	5.1%						
	N	53	66	43	53	43	32			

table continues next page

Table D.2 Means and Medians Analysis in Growth—Electricity Distribution *(continued)*

Variable	Statistics	Average annual growth			Annual difference in growth			T-statistics (Z-statistics) for difference in means (medians) in growth		
		Preprivate	Transition	Postprivate	(2)–(1)	(3)–(2)	(3)–(1)	(2)–(1)	(3)–(2)	(3)–(1)
		(1)	(2)	(3)	(4)	(5)	(6)	(7)	(8)	(9)
GWh per employee	mean	15.1%	20.3%	5.5%	3.7%	−19.9%	−6.7%	1.426*	6.539***	2.826***
	p50	12.8%	15.0%	4.0%	3.0%	−16.4%	−6.3%	−1.624	5.084***	3.011***
	sd	13.5%	16.9%	7.6%						
	N	53	66	43	53	43	32			
Distributional losses	mean	0.6%	−5.5%	−1.3%	−4.7%	6.4%	−2.0%	3.301***	−3.474***	0.960
	p50	0.1%	−4.9%	−0.1%	−4.5%	6.5%	−1.5%	3.317***	−2.944***	0.786
	sd	7.8%	10.2%	9.6%						
	N	57	73	46	57	46	36			
Quality										
Duration of interruptions per year per consumer	mean	4.1%	−9.8%	−3.8%	−11.2%	3.4%	−10.5%	1.788*	4.476***	5.122***
	p50	−5.2%	−12.9%	−3.2%	−7.0%	8.5%	−5.1%	2.132**	−0.749	0.711
	sd	31.6%	25.7%	24.8%						
	N	32	51	26	32	26	11			
Frequency of interruptions per year per consumer	mean	2.7%	−10.6%	−11.4%	−11.1%	−2.9%	−17.8%	1.653*	0.378	3.093***
	p50	−5.0%	−10.8%	−6.6%	−2.8%	−2.4%	−14.4%	1.664*	−0.165	2.490**
	sd	29.0%	20.3%	20.5%						
	N	32	51	26	32	26	11			

table continues next page

Table D.2 Means and Medians Analysis in Growth—Electricity Distribution (continued)

Variable	Statistics	Average annual growth			Annual difference in growth			T-statistics (Z-statistics) for difference in means (medians) in growth		
		Preprivate	Transition	Postprivate	(2)–(1)	(3)–(2)	(3)–(1)	(2)–(1)	(3)–(2)	(3)–(1)
		(1)	(2)	(3)	(4)	(5)	(6)	(7)	(8)	(9)
Coverage										
Residential connections per 100 HHs	mean	2.0%	2.2%	1.9%	0.4%	–1.0%	–0.6%	–0.903	1.702**	0.780
	p50	1.5%	1.9%	1.3%	0.4%	–0.9%	–0.3%	–1.408	3.186***	0.619
	sd	3.9%	3.0%	3.6%						
	N	65	76	50	65	50	42			
Prices										
Average tariff per residential GWh (in dollars)	mean	9.3%	–3.3%	2.0%	–15.2%	4.3%	–11.4%	6.251***	–1.821**	3.172***
	p50	9.7%	–6.3%	0.1%	–15.1%	1.3%	–13.1%	5.329***	–1.442	2.785***
	sd	16.0%	5.0%	14.1%						
	N	59	86	57	59	57	35			
Average tariff per residential GWh (in real local currency)	mean	10.2%	2.0%	0.6%	–7.8%	0.2%	–12.3%	4.744***	–0.172	4.899***
	p50	5.9%	2.3%	1.8%	–5.3%	0.9%	–9.7%	4.454***	–0.734	4.063***
	sd	12.6%	7.3%	7.9%						
	N	59	86	56	59	56	35			

Source: Andrés and others 2008.

Note: GWh = gigawatt hours; HH = household; MWh = megawatt hours.

* significant at 10 percent; ** significant at 5 percent; *** significant at 1 percent.

Table D.3 Econometric Analysis—Electricity Distribution

	(1) Number of connections	(2) Energy sold per year	(3) Number of employees	(4) Connections per employee	(5) Energy per employee	(6) Distributional losses	(7) Duration of interruptions	(8) Frequency of interruptions	(9) Coverage	(10) Average price per MWh (in dollars)	(11) Average price per MWh (in real local currency)
Model 1: Log levels without firm-specific time trend											
Transition	0.150***	0.201***	−0.307***	0.442***	0.474***	−0.031**	−0.144***	−0.107***	0.053***	−0.013	0.105***
(t >= −1)	(0.005)	(0.007)	(0.016)	(0.019)	(0.021)	(0.013)	(0.028)	(0.025)	(0.004)	(0.018)	(0.008)
Post-transition	0.176***	0.169***	−0.193***	0.368***	0.346***	−0.141***	−0.344***	−0.308***	0.077***	−0.028***	0.071***
(t >= 2)	(0.005)	(0.007)	(0.016)	(0.019)	(0.021)	(0.013)	(0.026)	(0.022)	(0.004)	(0.010)	(0.007)
Observations	823	808	586	575	570	614	376	377	698	687	685
Model 2: Log levels with firm-specific time trend											
Transition	−0.002	0.040***	−0.054***	0.049***	0.086***	0.021	0.068**	0.076***	−0.007***	0.078***	0.034***
(t >= −1)	(0.002)	(0.005)	(0.013)	(0.012)	(0.017)	(0.013)	(0.033)	(0.029)	(0.002)	(0.012)	(0.008)
Post-transition	0.009***	−0.014***	0.047***	−0.037***	−0.080***	−0.040***	−0.115***	−0.120***	0.009***	0.036***	0.007
(t >= 2)	(0.002)	(0.005)	(0.013)	(0.013)	(0.017)	(0.013)	(0.031)	(0.027)	(0.002)	(0.009)	(0.007)
Observations	823	808	586	575	570	614	376	377	698	687	685
Model 3: Growth											
Transition	0.001	−0.002	−0.050***	0.048***	0.046***	−0.042***	−0.063***	−0.050**	−0.000	−0.117***	−0.082***
(t >= −1)	(0.001)	(0.003)	(0.008)	(0.008)	(0.010)	(0.010)	(0.023)	(0.024)	(0.001)	(0.011)	(0.007)
Post-transition	−0.003***	−0.027***	0.064***	−0.065***	−0.092***	0.015	0.001	−0.048**	−0.000	0.023***	0.009
(t >= 2)	(0.001)	(0.003)	(0.008)	(0.008)	(0.010)	(0.010)	(0.021)	(0.021)	(0.000)	(0.008)	(0.006)
Observations	803	783	566	557	554	592	339	341	669	633	631

Source: Andrés and others 2008.

Note: Standard errors are in parentheses. The *Transition* and *Post-transition* variables are dummy independent variables in regressions where the dependent variable is given by the column heading (Number of Connections). *Transition* = 1 starting two years before the privatization or concession was awarded and continuing for all years after. *Post-transition* = 1 for all years after the transition period, that is, starting one year after the privatization was awarded.

MWh = megawatt hours.

* significant at 10 percent; ** significant at 5 percent; *** significant at 1 percent.

Table D.4 Means and Medians Analysis in Levels—Fixed Telecommunications

Variable	Statistics	Mean			Difference in levels			T-statistics (Z-statistics) for difference in means (medians) in levels		
		Pre-private	Transition	Post-private	(2)−(1)	(3)−(2)	(3)−(1)	(2)−(1)	(3)−(2)	(3)−(1)
		(1)	(2)	(3)	(4)	(5)	(6)	(7)	(8)	(9)
Outputs										
Total number of lines	mean	78.98	115.39	181.31	36.41	65.70	102.77	−10.02***	−8.627***	−6.742***
	p50	76.93	112.16	178.47	33.90	67.92	93.40	−3.516***	−3.408***	−3.408***
	sd	12.55	13.76	48.91	14.53	37.74	46.14			
	N	16	16	15	16	15	15			
Total number of minutes	mean	107.32	103.05	146.89	0.82	41.13	69.57	−0.049	−3.973*	−19.420**
	p50	97.39	100.00	146.89	9.05	41.13	69.57	0.105	−1.342	−1.342
	sd	41.60	5.04	8.32	40.84	3.00	24.76			
	N	6	16	2	6	2	2			
Inputs										
Number of employees	mean	117.88	100.72	82.02	−17.12	−18.37	−37.18	2.213**	2.671***	2.675***
	p50	111.71	100.28	81.31	−22.64	−20.05	−50.94	1.761*	2.166**	2.291**
	sd	30.44	7.88	29.61	29.96	25.70	52.09			
	N	15	16	14	15	14	14			
Efficiency										
Total number of lines per employee	mean	72.98	119.54	262.84	47.86	140.97	191.73	−4.972***	−5.262***	−4.957***
	p50	70.13	110.66	217.38	38.93	102.05	154.59	−3.237***	−3.233***	−3.233***
	sd	24.63	26.54	126.18	37.28	106.41	136.35			
	N	15	16	14	15	14	14			

table continues next page

Table D.4 Means and Medians Analysis in Levels—Fixed Telecommunications *(continued)*

Variable	Statistics	Mean			Difference in levels			T-statistics (Z-statistics) for difference in means (medians) in levels		
		Pre-private	Transition	Post-private	(2)–(1)	(3)–(2)	(3)–(1)	(2)–(1)	(3)–(2)	(3)–(1)
		(1)	*(2)*	*(3)*	*(4)*	*(5)*	*(6)*	*(7)*	*(8)*	*(9)*
Total number of minutes per employee	mean	79.81	105.38	238.94	34.53	123.54	172.50	−2.879**	−2.059	−1.486
	p50	76.03	100.00	238.94	44.60	123.54	172.50	−1.782*	−1.342	−1.342
	sd	22.83	12.63	135.73	29.38	117.59	118.47			
	N	6	16	2	6	2	2			
Percentage of incomplete calls	mean	580.77	141.09	101.20	−368.95	−93.78	−472.93	1.050	1.098	1.378
	p50	111.56	100.00	74.51	−17.23	−27.47	−37.37	1.782*	2.201**	2.366**
	sd	1,133.58	167.34	74.92	860.92	180.06	1,055.53			
	N	6	16	7	6	7	6			
Quality										
Percentage of digitalized network	mean	68.64	116.56	199.92	51.75	81.00	138.97	−4.407***	−2.964***	−2.339**
	p50	70.82	107.27	136.01	41.82	29.26	78.72	−3.180***	−3.180***	−3.129***
	sd	22.80	31.58	161.58	42.33	129.55	169.03			
	N	13	16	14	13	14	13			
Coverage										
Number of lines per 100 HHs	mean	83.65	113.47	167.28	29.82	53.25	84.53	−7.573***	−7.708***	−6.025***
	p50	80.18	109.18	169.15	28.25	56.28	68.99	−3.516***	−3.408***	−3.351***
	sd	12.73	13.75	45.46	15.75	34.23	42.48			
	N	16	16	15	16	15	15			

table continues next page

Table D.4 Means and Medians Analysis in Levels—Fixed Telecommunications *(continued)*

Variable	Statistics	Mean			Difference in levels			T-statistics (Z-statistics) for difference in means (medians) in levels		
		Pre-private	Transition	Post-private	(2)–(1)	(3)–(2)	(3)–(1)	(2)–(1)	(3)–(2)	(3)–(1)
		(1)	(2)	(3)	(4)	(5)	(6)	(7)	(8)	(9)
Prices										
Average price for a 3-minute call (in dollars)	mean	144.83	100.45	99.89	-46.64	-1.03	-58.79	0.718	0.710	0.05
	p50	57.48	99.98	91.72	34.44	-11.25	1.74	-0.866	-0.178	1.255
	sd	219.85	15.00	63.61	205.46	61.29	248.59			
	N	10	16	12	10	12	9			
Average monthly charge for residential service (in dollars)	mean	55.46	101.25	143.43	39.02	41.60	105.49	-2.983***	-2.083**	-1.295
	p50	41.00	100.00	120.51	53.32	15.16	43.43	-2.293**	-2.073**	-0.804
	sd	36.35	19.28	124.99	41.36	115.87	151.92			
	N	10	16	13	10	13	9			
Average charge for the installation of a residential line (in dollars)	mean	634.94	123.11	100.51	-502.46	-25.83	-256.72	1.814*	0.777	1.122
	p50	95.78	101.06	77.29	11.18	-39.79	8.92	0.051	-0.314	1.376
	sd	887.73	40.50	108.31	875.99	72.80	808.89			
	N	10	16	10	10	10	6			
Average price for a 3-minute call (in real local currency)	mean	84.40	100.65	97.58	12.63	-3.46	16.28	-0.711	-0.599	0.250
	p50	64.40	100.00	87.14	30.96	-14.01	25.78	-0.980	-1.120	1.478
	sd	50.71	7.71	44.03	50.24	43.72	76.87			
	N	8	16	10	8	10	8			

table continues next page

Table D.4 Means and Medians Analysis in Levels—Fixed Telecommunications *(continued)*

Variable	Statistics	Mean			Difference in levels			T-statistics (Z-statistics) for difference in means (medians) in levels		
		Pre-private	Transition	Post-private	(2)–(1)	(3)–(2)	(3)–(1)	(2)–(1)	(3)–(2)	(3)–(1)
		(1)	*(2)*	*(3)*	*(4)*	*(5)*	*(6)*	*(7)*	*(8)*	*(9)*
Average monthly charge for residential service (in real local currency)	mean	60.42	100.26	135.11	36.59	34.54	88.96	–2.782**	–2.750**	–1.654*
	p50	49.78	100.00	115.76	49.77	16.83	79.48	–2.191**	–2.310**	–1.334
	sd	35.69	12.69	77.55	41.60	69.27	97.05			
	N	10	16	11	10	11	9			
Average charge for the installation of a residential line (in real local currency)	mean	842.23	122.99	132.07	–699.77	1.25	–252.68	1.915**	0.692	–0.028
	p50	108.37	100.00	58.62	–6.06	–31.83	1.91	0.700	–0.105	0.420
	sd	1,045.40	41.81	152.59	1,033.62	126.57	894.37			
	N	8	16	8	8	8	6			

Source: Andrés and others 2008.

Note: HH = household.

* significant at 10 percent; ** significant at 5 percent; *** significant at 1 percent.

Table D.5 Means and Medians Analysis in Growth—Fixed Telecommunications

Variable	Statistics	Average annual growth			Annual difference in growth			T-statistics (Z-statistics) for difference in means (medians) in growth		
		Pre-private	Transition	Post-private	(2)−(1)	(3)−(2)	(3)−(1)	(2)−(1)	(3)−(2)	(3)−(1)
		(1)	(2)	(3)	(4)	(5)	(6)	(7)	(8)	(9)
Outputs										
Total number of lines	mean	6.9%	12.7%	7.2%	5.8%	−6.5%	0.4%	−2.546**	1.917**	−0.152
	p50	7.2%	11.7%	6.6%	3.8%	−12.0%	−2.1%	−2.223**	1.852*	−0.157
	sd	6.2%	6.3%	8.2%	9.1%	12.8%	10.7%			
	N	16	16	14	16	14	14			
Total number of minutes	mean	4.1%	2.1%	3.8%	−6.7%	3.2%	−0.8%	1.158	–	–
	p50	4.6%	1.7%	3.8%	−4.1%	3.2%	−0.8%	1.219	–	–
	sd	1.9%	15.3%	.	12.9%	.	.			
	N	5	6	1	5	1	1			
Inputs										
Number of employees	mean	−0.5%	−3.1%	−6.9%	−2.6%	−3.4%	−6.5%	0.916	1.258	2.861***
	p50	−0.8%	−4.5%	−7.7%	−1.5%	−1.3%	−3.9%	0.909	0.785	2.291**
	sd	6.9%	9.8%	9.0%	11.1%	10.0%	8.4%			
	N	15	15	14	15	14	14			
Efficiency										
Total number of lines per employee	mean	7.8%	17.6%	16.0%	9.8%	−3.1%	8.0%	−2.452**	0.610	−1.791**
	p50	6.6%	21.3%	15.7%	10.9%	−9.9%	9.4%	−2.101**	0.659	−1.726*
	sd	11.6%	15.3%	11.5%	15.5%	18.9%	16.7%			
	N	15	15	14	15	14	14			

table continues next page

Table D.5 Means and Medians Analysis in Growth—Fixed Telecommunications (continued)

Variable	Statistics	Average annual growth			Annual difference in growth			T-statistics (Z-statistics) for difference in means (medians) in growth		
		Pre-private	Transition	Post-private	(2)–(1)	(3)–(2)	(3)–(1)	(2)–(1)	(3)–(2)	(3)–(1)
		(1)	(2)	(3)	(4)	(5)	(6)	(7)	(8)	(9)
Total number of minutes per employee	mean	5.2%	13.2%	28.6%	5.5%	11.9%	19.1%	−3.000**	–	–
	p50	9.5%	16.3%	28.6%	4.4%	11.9%	19.1%	−2.023**	–	–
	sd	9.6%	11.7%	.	4.1%	.	.			
	N	5	6	1	5	1	1			
Percentage of incomplete calls	mean	−1.5%	−16.4%	−14.3%	−13.9%	−0.2%	−13.7%	1.293	0.046	2.145**
	p50	−1.5%	−7.8%	−9.3%	−5.1%	0.0%	−8.8%	1.363	0.000	2.201**
	sd	1.0%	23.4%	14.7%	26.4%	14.0%	15.6%			
	N	6	8	7	6	7	6			
Quality										
Percentage of digitalized network	mean	51.5%	17.1%	4.9%	−33.1%	−13.5%	−50.1%	1.085	3.602***	1.434*
	p50	22.1%	14.2%	0.9%	−4.4%	−12.0%	−11.9%	1.293	2.734***	2.824***
	sd	116.3%	15.9%	6.8%	110.1%	13.5%	121.1%			
	N	13	14	13	13	13	12			
Coverage										
Number of lines per 100 HHs	mean	4.9%	11.0%	6.0%	6.1%	−5.9%	1.2%	−3.001***	2.040**	−0.438
	p50	4.4%	9.4%	4.9%	4.5%	−8.0%	−0.1%	−2.637***	1.852*	−0.471
	sd	5.9%	6.2%	7.8%	8.1%	10.8%	10.0%			
	N	16	16	14	16	14	14			

table continues next page

Table D.5 Means and Medians Analysis in Growth—Fixed Telecommunications *(continued)*

Variable	Statistics	Average annual growth			Annual difference in growth				T-statistics (Z-statistics) for difference in means (medians) in growth		
		Pre-private	Transition	Post-private	(2)–(1)	(3)–(2)	(3)–(1)		(2)–(1)	(3)–(2)	(3)–(1)
		(1)	(2)	(3)	(4)	(5)	(6)		(7)	(8)	(9)
Prices											
Average price for a 3-minute call (in dollars)	mean	46.7%	–3.1%	–5.7%	–44.4%	–2.3%	–60.8%		1.981**	0.295	1.788*
	p50	40.9%	–1.3%	–0.4%	–41.4%	–7.9%	–52.5%		1.820*	0.459	1.572
	sd	69.0%	16.8%	12.4%	63.5%	25.1%	83.3%				
	N	8	13	10	8	10	6				
Average monthly charge for residential service (in dollars)	mean	42.8%	13.9%	5.2%	–21.9%	–10.5%	–45.8%		1.088	0.830	1.785*
	p50	15.7%	6.0%	0.0%	–33.1%	–3.3%	–28.4%		1.007	0.978	1.272
	sd	54.6%	3.0%	28.1%	60.4%	41.9%	67.9%				
	N	9	14	11	9	11	7				
Average charge for the installation of a residential line (in dollars)	mean	–1.9%	–14.7%	–13.7%	–9.6%	–5.7%	–32.6%		0.785	0.381	1.626
	p50	–1.8%	–2.3%	–29.3%	–5.2%	–2.6%	–18.2%		1.008	0.533	1.826*
	sd	25.8%	38.7%	33.7%	36.5%	44.6%	40.1%				
	N	9	14	9	9	9	4				
Average price for a 3-minute call (in real local currency)	mean	35.7%	–2.5%	–0.6%	–30.5%	2.7%	–36.7%		1.696*	–0.389	1.549*
	p50	44.3%	4.3%	0.6%	–32.1%	–5.2%	–21.2%		1.352	0.178	1.153
	sd	55.4%	19.1%	4.9%	47.6%	21.1%	58.0%				
	N	7	10	9	7	9	6				

table continues next page

Table D.5 Means and Medians Analysis in Growth—Fixed Telecommunications *(continued)*

Variable	Statistics	Average annual growth			Annual difference in growth			T-statistics (Z-statistics) for difference in means (medians) in growth		
		Pre-private *(1)*	Transition *(2)*	Post-private *(3)*	(2)–(1) *(4)*	(3)–(2) *(5)*	(3)–(1) *(6)*	(2)–(1) *(7)*	(3)–(2) *(8)*	(3)–(1) *(9)*
Average monthly charge for residential service (in real local currency)	mean	35.6%	16.5%	7.1%	−12.7%	−9.4%	−29.4%	0.721	0.959	1.426
	p50	−0.9%	15.6%	3.2%	−32.9%	−1.9%	0.6%	0.770	0.866	0.676
	sd	50.1%	32.1%	13.1%	52.9%	30.9%	54.6%			
	N	9	12	10	9	10	7			
Average charge for the installation of a residential line (in real local currency)	mean	−8.6%	−16.1%	−11.6%	−4.7%	−6.7%	−19.1%	0.289	0.370	0.789
	p50	−26.3%	−20.0%	−30.5%	−35.0%	−2.0%	1.4%	0.000	0.845	−0.365
	sd	32.3%	46.4%	40.4%	43.5%	48.0%	48.4%			
	N	7	10	7	7	7	4			

Source: Andrés and others 2008.

Note: HH = household.

* significant at 10 percent; ** significant at 5 percent; *** significant at 1 percent.

Table D.6 Econometric Analysis—Fixed Telecommunications

	(1) Number of connections	(2) Number of minutes	(3) Number of employees	(4) Connections per worker	(5) Minutes per worker	(6) Incomplete calls	(7) Network digitization	(8) Coverage	(9) Cost of 3-minute local call (dollars)	(10) Monthly charge (dollars)	(11) Connection charge (dollars)	(12) Cost of 3-minute local call (r.l.c.)	(13) Monthly charge (r.l.c.)	(14) Connection charge (r.l.c.)
Model 1: Log levels without firm-specific time trend														
Transition	0.253***	0.079**	−0.097***	0.301***	0.278***	−0.133	0.310***	0.168***	0.384***	0.565***	0.095	0.371***	0.486***	−0.178
(t >= −1)	(0.030)	(0.035)	(0.033)	(0.054)	(0.059)	(0.083)	(0.053)	(0.025)	(0.080)	(0.118)	(0.114)	(0.081)	(0.113)	(0.171)
Post-transition	0.494***	0.319***	−0.264***	0.727***	0.657***	−0.353***	0.458***	0.421***	−0.014	0.209***	−0.310***	−0.090	0.197**	−0.286*
(t >= 2)	(0.028)	(0.032)	(0.033)	(0.054)	(0.084)	(0.057)	(0.046)	(0.026)	(0.053)	(0.049)	(0.108)	(0.063)	(0.086)	(0.153)
Observations	168	71	161	162	69	70	131	165	104	114	107	91	110	87
Model 2: Log levels with firm-specific time trend														
Transition	−0.050**	0.002	0.031	−0.101***	−0.010	0.142***	0.048**	−0.065***	0.523***	0.281***	0.300***	0.358***	0.067	0.118
(t >= −1)	(0.024)	(0.038)	(0.026)	(0.038)	(0.044)	(0.042)	(0.024)	(0.019)	(0.104)	(0.100)	(0.063)	(0.082)	(0.092)	(0.154)
Post-transition	0.113***	0.133***	−0.069**	0.185***	0.173***	0.006	0.024	0.091***	0.051	−0.067	0.222***	−0.168**	−0.099	0.244**
(t >= 2)	(0.025)	(0.041)	(0.027)	(0.041)	(0.060)	(0.044)	(0.026)	(0.021)	(0.091)	(0.087)	(0.082)	(0.082)	(0.080)	(0.097)
Observations	168	71	161	162	69	70	131	165	104	114	107	91	110	87
Model 3: Growth														
Transition	0.027**	0.069***	−0.041***	0.070***	0.085**	−0.062	−0.008	0.037***	−0.052	−0.101	−0.003	−0.056	−0.047	−0.140
(t >= −1)	(0.011)	(0.012)	(0.015)	(0.021)	(0.042)	(0.041)	(0.026)	(0.010)	(0.077)	(0.097)	(0.048)	(0.065)	(0.067)	(0.107)
Post-transition	−0.002	0.053*	−0.026*	0.033*	0.083	−0.035	−0.056***	0.001	0.019	−0.034	−0.019	−0.025	0.001	0.036
(t >= 2)	(0.010)	(0.031)	(0.015)	(0.020)	(0.052)	(0.028)	(0.022)	(0.010)	(0.048)	(0.056)	(0.056)	(0.046)	(0.059)	(0.073)
Observations	165	60	158	158	59	64	122	162	93	105	98	82	102	79

Source: Andrés and others 2008.

Note: Standard errors are in parentheses. The *Transition* and *Post-transition* variables are dummy independent variables in regressions where the dependent variable is given by the column heading (Number of Connections). *Transition* = 1 starting two years before the privatization or concession was awarded and continuing for all years after. *Post-transition* = 1 for all years after the transition period, that is, starting one year after the privatization was awarded.

r.l.c. = real local currency.

* significant at 10 percent; ** significant at 5 percent; *** significant at 1 percent.

Table D.7 Econometric Analysis—Fixed Telecommunications, Liberalization

	(1) Number of connections	(2) Number of minutes	(3) Number of employees	(4) Connections per worker	(5) Minutes per worker	(6) Incomplete calls	(7) Network digitization	(8) Coverage	(9) Cost of 3-minute local call (dollars)	(10) Monthly charge (dollars)	(11) Connection charge (dollars)	(12) Cost of 3-minute local call (r.l.c.)	(13) Monthly charge (r.l.c.)	(14) Connection charge (r.l.c.)
Model 1: Log levels without firm-specific time trend														
Transition	0.232***	0.064*	−0.046	0.272***	0.232***	−0.140*	0.307***	0.166***	0.422***	0.558***	0.033	0.359***	0.398***	−0.107
(t >= −1)	(0.027)	(0.036)	(0.030)	(0.049)	(0.050)	(0.081)	(0.057)	(0.025)	(0.088)	(0.131)	(0.073)	(0.085)	(0.112)	(0.191)
Post-transition	0.432***	0.279***	−0.151***	0.602***	0.432***	−0.335***	0.446***	0.364***	0.011	0.220***	−0.151**	−0.162**	0.102	−0.131
(t >= 2)	(0.028)	(0.043)	(0.031)	(0.051)	(0.078)	(0.076)	(0.055)	(0.025)	(0.057)	(0.058)	(0.083)	(0.073)	(0.086)	(0.163)
Liberalization	0.275***	0.065	−0.361***	0.673***	0.487***	−0.027	0.023	0.230***	−0.097	0.001	−0.491***	0.150*	0.443***	−0.529**
Dummy	(0.037)	(0.046)	(0.047)	(0.083)	(0.082)	(0.088)	(0.069)	(0.035)	(0.088)	(0.144)	(0.171)	(0.091)	(0.155)	(0.221)
Observations	168	71	161	162	69	70	131	165	104	114	107	91	110	87
Model 2: Log levels with firm-specific time trend														
Transition	−0.050**	0.001	0.026	−0.089**	−0.006	0.133***	0.044*	−0.066***	0.441***	0.192	0.245***	0.296***	−0.007	0.130
(t >= −1)	(0.024)	(0.043)	(0.026)	(0.038)	(0.049)	(0.043)	(0.025)	(0.020)	(0.109)	(0.136)	(0.083)	(0.082)	(0.087)	(0.165)
Post-transition	0.116***	0.127***	−0.066**	0.192***	0.164***	0.009	0.023	0.091***	−0.011	−0.111	0.197**	−0.193**	−0.135*	0.246**
(t >= 2)	(0.025)	(0.041)	(0.027)	(0.041)	(0.060)	(0.043)	(0.026)	(0.021)	(0.091)	(0.093)	(0.081)	(0.078)	(0.076)	(0.097)
Liberalization	0.002	0.037	−0.046	0.117**	0.108	−0.041	−0.016	−0.007	−0.356***	−0.410***	−0.030	−0.240***	−0.500***	0.035
Dummy	(0.032)	(0.063)	(0.042)	(0.049)	(0.090)	(0.053)	(0.028)	(0.025)	(0.116)	(0.147)	(0.092)	(0.090)	(0.136)	(0.169)
Observations	168	71	161	162	69	70	131	165	104	114	107	91	110	87

table continues next page

Table D.7 Econometric Analysis—Fixed Telecommunications, Liberalization (continued)

	(1) Number of connections	(2) Number of minutes	(3) Number of employees	(4) Connections per worker	(5) Minutes per worker	(6) Incomplete calls	(7) Network digitization	(8) Coverage	(9) Cost of 3-minute local call (dollars)	(10) Monthly charge (dollars)	(11) Connection charge (dollars)	(12) Cost of 3-minute local call (r.l.c.)	(13) Monthly charge (r.l.c.)	(14) Connection charge (r.l.c.)
Model 3: Growth														
Transition	0.028**	0.066***	−0.041***	0.075***	0.073*	−0.059	0.006	0.036***	0.006	0.072	−0.021	−0.038	−0.004	−0.253*
(t >= −1)	(0.011)	(0.013)	(0.015)	(0.020)	(0.040)	(0.040)	(0.028)	(0.011)	(0.077)	(0.095)	(0.066)	(0.065)	(0.047)	(0.138)
Post-transition	0.010	0.030	−0.027*	0.047**	−0.006	−0.011	−0.046*	0.008	0.142***	0.038	−0.022	0.012	0.053	0.003
(t >= 2)	(0.011)	(0.041)	(0.016)	(0.021)	(0.058)	(0.033)	(0.025)	(0.010)	(0.053)	(0.059)	(0.067)	(0.053)	(0.049)	(0.085)
Liberalization	−0.053***	0.037	0.007	−0.075**	0.183***	−0.037	−0.044	−0.027	−0.451***	−0.428***	0.002	−0.161**	−0.387***	0.251*
Dummy	(0.019)	(0.039)	(0.029)	(0.034)	(0.067)	(0.039)	(0.031)	(0.017)	(0.080)	(0.111)	(0.098)	(0.070)	(0.108)	(0.132)
Observations	165	60	158	158	59	64	122	162	93	105	98	82	102	79

Source: Andrés and others 2008.

Note: Standard errors are in parentheses. The *Transition* and *Post-transition* variables are dummy independent variables in regressions where the dependent variable is given by the column heading (Number of Connections). *Transition* = 1 starting two years before the privatization or concession was awarded and continuing for all years after. *Post-transition* = 1 for all years after the transition period, that is, starting one year after the privatization was awarded. The *Liberalization* dummy = 1 for those years that the long-distance telecommunications market was liberalized. r.l.c. = real local currency.

* significant at 10 percent; ** significant at 5 percent; *** significant at 1 percent.

Table D.8 Econometric Analysis—Fixed Telecommunications, Mobile Competition

	(1) Number of connections	(2) Number of minutes	(3) Number of employees	(4) Connections per worker	(5) Minutes per worker	(6) Incomplete calls	(7) Network digitization	(8) Coverage	(9) Cost of 3-minute local call (dollars)	(10) Monthly charge (dollars)	(11) Connection charge (dollars)	(12) Cost of 3-minute local call (r.l.c.)	(13) Monthly charge (r.l.c.)	(14) Connection charge (r.l.c.)
Model 1: Log levels without firm-specific time trend														
Transition	0.247***	0.047	−0.059**	0.291***	0.178***	−0.143*	0.313***	0.171***	0.432***	0.506***	−0.030	0.311***	0.365***	−0.165
(t >= −1)	(0.027)	(0.037)	(0.027)	(0.043)	(0.050)	(0.077)	(0.053)	(0.022)	(0.079)	(0.120)	(0.021)	(0.075)	(0.102)	(0.106)
Post-transition														
(t >= 2)	0.413***	0.221***	−0.089***	0.500***	0.269***	−0.337***	0.442***	0.342***	0.038	0.189***	0.032	−0.221***	0.003	0.031
	(0.027)	(0.050)	(0.030)	(0.046)	(0.085)	(0.089)	(0.053)	(0.025)	(0.053)	(0.046)	(0.030)	(0.067)	(0.077)	(0.110)
Mobile subscribers	0.013***	0.005**	−0.025***	0.037***	0.030***	−0.000	0.001	0.014***	−0.015***	0.013	−0.151***	0.017***	0.042***	−0.132***
	(0.002)	(0.002)	(0.001)	(0.002)	(0.004)	(0.004)	(0.003)	(0.002)	(0.006)	(0.010)	(0.017)	(0.004)	(0.009)	(0.017)
Observations	168	71	161	162	69	70	131	165	104	114	107	91	110	87
Model 2: Log levels with firm-specific time trend														
Transition	−0.064***	0.019	0.008	−0.070*	0.029	0.111**	0.017	−0.068***	0.166***	−0.056	0.327***	0.201***	−0.043	0.349**
(t >= −1)	(0.025)	(0.051)	(0.025)	(0.039)	(0.063)	(0.045)	(0.022)	(0.021)	(0.063)	(0.105)	(0.073)	(0.047)	(0.044)	(0.161)
Post-transition														
(t >= 2)	0.120***	0.112***	−0.044*	0.176***	0.061	0.022	0.042*	0.099***	0.293***	0.055	0.195**	0.083*	−0.005	0.225**
	(0.025)	(0.034)	(0.026)	(0.041)	(0.048)	(0.046)	(0.023)	(0.022)	(0.060)	(0.061)	(0.088)	(0.049)	(0.041)	(0.090)
Mobile subscribers	−0.006*	0.010**	−0.017***	0.010**	0.032***	−0.004	−0.021***	−0.003	−0.117***	−0.148***	0.039*	−0.063***	−0.105***	0.076***
	(0.003)	(0.005)	(0.003)	(0.005)	(0.006)	(0.005)	(0.003)	(0.003)	(0.007)	(0.015)	(0.024)	(0.005)	(0.011)	(0.025)
Observations	168	71	161	162	69	70	131	165	104	114	107	91	110	87

table continues next page

Table D.8 Econometric Analysis—Fixed Telecommunications, Mobile Competition *(continued)*

	(1) Number of connections	(2) Number of minutes	(3) Number of employees	(4) Connections per worker	(5) Minutes per worker	(6) Incomplete calls	(7) Network digitization	(8) Coverage	(9) Cost of 3-minute local call (dollars)	(10) Monthly charge (dollars)	(11) Connection charge (dollars)	(12) Cost of 3-minute local call (r.l.c.)	(13) Monthly charge (r.l.c.)	(14) Connection charge (r.l.c.)
Model 3: Growth														
Transition	0.023**	0.068***	-0.043***	0.068***	0.075*	-0.062	0.006	0.035***	-0.005	-0.076	-0.031	-0.023	-0.043	-0.175*
(t >= −1)	(0.011)	(0.014)	(0.015)	(0.021)	(0.040)	(0.042)	(0.025)	(0.011)	(0.063)	(0.090)	(0.054)	(0.059)	(0.059)	(0.093)
Post-transition	0.011	0.068	-0.017	0.039*	-0.004	-0.033	-0.030	0.004	0.117***	0.051	-0.063	0.051	0.071	-0.039
(t >= 2)	(0.011)	(0.053)	(0.016)	(0.022)	(0.064)	(0.040)	(0.024)	(0.011)	(0.042)	(0.062)	(0.060)	(0.047)	(0.056)	(0.076)
Mobile subscribers	-0.002**	-0.001	-0.002	-0.001	0.006*	-0.000	-0.005***	-0.001	-0.026***	-0.032***	0.018*	-0.014***	-0.025***	0.028***
	(0.001)	(0.002)	(0.002)	(0.002)	(0.003)	(0.002)	(0.001)	(0.001)	(0.004)	(0.008)	(0.011)	(0.004)	(0.007)	(0.011)
Observations	165	60	158	158	59	64	122	162	93	105	98	82	102	79
Number of firms	16	11	16	16	11	8	14	16	12	13	13	11	13	11

Source: Andrés and others 2008.

Note: Standard errors are in parentheses. The *Transition* and *Post-transition* variables are dummy independent variables in regressions where the dependent variable is given by the column heading (Number of Connections). *Transition* = 1 starting two years before the privatization or concession was awarded and continuing for all years after. *Post-transition* = 1 for all years after the transition period, that is, starting one year after the privatization was awarded. *Mobile subscribers* is an independent variable measuring millions of mobile subscribers.

r.l.c. = real local currency.

* significant at 10 percent; ** significant at 5 percent; *** significant at 1 percent.

Table D.9 Econometric Analysis—Fixed Telecommunications, Instrumental Variables

	(1) Number of connections	(2) Number of minutes	(3) Number of employees	(4) Connections per worker	(5) Minutes per worker	(6) Incomplete calls	(7) Network digitization	(8) Coverage	(9) Cost of 3-minute local call (dollars)	(10) Monthly charge (dollars)	(11) Connection charge (dollars)	(12) Cost of 3-minute local call (r.l.c.)	(13) Monthly charge (r.l.c.)	(14) Connection charge (r.l.c.)
Model 1: Log levels without firm-specific time trend														
Transition	0.462***	0.326**	−0.198***	0.646***	0.717***	−0.086	0.490***	0.377***	0.877***	1.041***	−0.692**	0.754***	0.910***	−1.060***
(t >= −1)	(0.052)	(0.109)	(0.070)	(0.111)	(0.135)	(0.079)	(0.105)	(0.046)	(0.147)	(0.221)	(0.300)	(0.136)	(0.209)	(0.355)
Post-transition	0.436***	0.364***	−0.222***	0.674***	0.724***	−0.262***	0.363***	0.371***	−0.069	0.331*	−0.204	0.012	0.332**	0.035
(t >= 2)	(0.043)	(0.097)	(0.059)	(0.094)	(0.120)	(0.060)	(0.084)	(0.039)	(0.111)	(0.174)	(0.260)	(0.097)	(0.163)	(0.283)
Observations	121	54	114	115	52	42	107	120	79	90	93	71	90	77
Model 2: Log levels with firm-specific time trend														
Transition	0.003	0.229*	0.160*	−0.126	0.204	0.109**	0.129	0.027	1.370***	0.982***	0.912***	0.837***	0.507	0.862**
(t >= −1)	(0.063)	(0.134)	(0.087)	(0.103)	(0.153)	(0.042)	(0.199)	(0.060)	(0.278)	(0.350)	(0.309)	(0.213)	(0.304)	(0.375)
Post-transition	0.115**	0.114	0.057	0.095	0.173	−0.018	0.014	0.108**	0.099	−0.147	0.593***	−0.022	−0.209	0.723**
(t >= 2)	(0.046)	(0.138)	(0.064)	(0.077)	(0.151)	(0.042)	(0.150)	(0.045)	(0.226)	(0.264)	(0.220)	(0.176)	(0.213)	(0.271)
Observations	121	54	114	115	52	42	107	120	79	90	93	71	90	77
Model 3: Growth														
Transition	0.035	0.056	−0.024	0.062	0.084	−0.049	0.243*	0.050**	−0.559***	−0.477***	−0.197	−0.470***	−0.313**	−0.095
(t >= −1)	(0.024)	(0.141)	(0.031)	(0.038)	(0.152)	(0.046)	(0.124)	(0.022)	(0.170)	(0.173)	(0.144)	(0.151)	(0.150)	(0.202)
Post-transition	0.028	−0.049	−0.054**	0.023	−0.037	−0.036	−0.146*	−0.038**	−0.147	−0.116	0.043	−0.088	−0.088	0.046
(t >= 2)	(0.019)	(0.113)	(0.025)	(0.030)	(0.123)	(0.028)	(0.087)	(0.018)	(0.107)	(0.118)	(0.111)	(0.085)	(0.103)	(0.140)
Observations	118	45	111	112	44	37	101	117	72	84	87	64	84	71

Source: Andrés and others 2008.

Note: Standard errors are in parentheses. The *Transition* and *Post-transition* variables are dummy independent variables in regressions where the dependent variable is given by the column heading (Number of Connections). *Transition* = 1 starting two years before the privatization or concession was awarded and continuing for all years after. *Post-transition* = 1 for all years after the transition period, that is, starting one year after the privatization was awarded.

r.l.c. = real local currency.

* significant at 10 percent; ** significant at 5 percent; *** significant at 1 percent.

Table D.10 Means and Medians Analysis in Levels—Water and Sewerage

Variable	Statistics	Mean			Difference in levels			T-statistics (Z-statistics) for difference in means (medians) in levels		
		Pre-private	Transition	Post-private	(2)–(1)	(3)–(2)	(3)–(1)	(2)–(1)	(3)–(2)	(3)–(1)
		(1)	(2)	(3)	(4)	(5)	(6)	(7)	(8)	(9)
Outputs										
Residential water	mean	85.85	103.15	119.74	16.20	16.31	29.43	–10.988***	–8.762***	–12.059***
connections	p50	87.37	102.61	117.09	15.18	13.88	28.10	–4.197***	–5.086***	–3.724***
	sd	6.32	3.72	13.17	7.07	10.85	10.35			
	N	23	49	34	23	34	18			
Residential sewer	mean	84.88	102.75	122.59	18.83	19.43	32.90	7.932***	8.950***	9.735***
connections	p50	85.48	101.89	119.62	18.62	17.46	29.38	–3.883***	–4.937***	–3.408***
	sd	11.21	5.02	15.08	10.62	12.28	13.09			
	N	20	49	32	20	32	15			
Cubic meter of	mean	99.98	103.62	97.27	2.21	–2.91	–1.33	–0.745	1.416*	0.299
produced water	p50	100.99	100.00	99.04	1.95	–0.72	3.15	–0.879	1.078	–0.973
	sd	8.89	22.20	14.80	11.88	11.45	16.60			
	N	16	49	31	16	31	14			
Inputs										
Number of	mean	141.43	103.97	92.35	–37.20	–12.18	–57.36	3.961***	3.668***	4.766***
employees	p50	125.11	100.00	97.04	–21.34	–8.36	–52.01	3.527***	3.339***	3.237***
	sd	49.22	14.22	23.85	38.72	17.26	46.62			
	N	17	49	27	17	27	15			

table continues next page

Table D.10 Means and Medians Analysis in Levels—Water and Sewerage (continued)

Variable	Statistics	Mean			Difference in levels			T-statistics (Z-statistics) for difference in means (medians) in levels		
		Pre-private	Transition	Post-private	(2)–(1)	(3)–(2)	(3)–(1)	(2)–(1)	(3)–(2)	(3)–(1)
		(1)	(2)	(3)	(4)	(5)	(6)	(7)	(8)	(9)
Efficiency										
Water connections per employee	mean	70.50	103.34	144.11	36.53	38.73	83.86	−9.979***	−4.201***	−5.177***
	p50	68.46	100.00	125.05	36.39	20.71	69.30	−3.621***	−4.532***	−3.408***
	sd	18.93	12.65	59.84	15.09	48.79	62.73			
	N	17	49	28	17	28	15			
Distributional losses	Mean	107.22	100.02	82.08	−8.70	−18.26	−23.18	2.577**	3.755***	3.110***
	p50	106.01	100.00	81.64	−8.33	−16.63	−20.12	2.327**	3.254***	2.605***
	sd	16.43	7.42	21.22	13.51	23.33	27.88			
	N	16	49	23	16	23	14			
Quality										
Continuity (hs per day)	mean	78.34	101.01	116.79	21.81	14.94	21.66	−1.781*	−2.748***	−1.330
	p50	97.11	100.00	104.35	2.48	2.17	4.05	−2.192**	−2.774***	−1.971**
	sd	37.52	4.68	24.68	36.74	21.06	46.07			
	N	9	49	15	9	15	8			
% of the samples that passed the potability test	mean	88.35	100.30	103.89	11.55	2.58	4.94	−1.250	−2.088**	−1.682*
	p50	99.50	100.00	100.51	0.58	0.46	1.08	−1.630	−2.603***	−1.941*
	sd	27.92	1.53	6.87	26.14	4.62	7.20			
	N	8	49	14	8	14	6			
Coverage										
Residential water connections per 100 HHs	mean	94.25	101.84	111.12	6.52	8.71	10.37	−4.498***	−4.379***	−4.478***
	p50	95.13	100.00	106.88	4.86	5.26	8.76	−4.107***	−4.584***	−3.823***
	sd	5.70	3.96	14.11	6.80	10.71	10.10			
	N	22	49	29	22	29	19			

table continues next page

Table D.10 Means and Medians Analysis in Levels—Water and Sewerage (continued)

Variable	Statistics	Mean			Difference in levels			T-statistics (Z-statistics) for difference in means (medians) in levels		
		Pre-private	Transition	Post-private	(2)–(1)	(3)–(2)	(3)–(1)	(2)–(1)	(3)–(2)	(3)–(1)
		(1)	(2)	(3)	(4)	(5)	(6)	(7)	(8)	(9)
Residential sewer connections per 100 HHs	mean	91.47	101.77	110.03	10.23	8.67	13.59	−4.539***	−3.981***	−5.277***
	p50	91.72	100.00	106.87	8.02	5.76	8.98	−3.479***	−3.920***	−3.180***
	sd	8.76	6.88	11.55	9.29	9.74	9.29			
	N	17	49	20	17	20	13			
Prices										
Average price per cubic meter of water (in dollars)	mean	93.62	101.39	106.70	10.43	1.46	40.24	−0.635	−0.173	−2.261**
	p50	87.95	100.00	98.60	11.81	3.27	32.70	−1.274	−0.314	−2.240**
	sd	43.54	9.53	37.16	51.89	30.57	50.34			
	N	10	49	13	10	13	8			
Average price per cubic meter of water (in real local currency)	mean	84.00	103.53	130.09	25.70	17.68	57.87	−2.478**	−2.903***	−4.150***
	p50	82.76	100.00	121.21	22.22	19.65	44.80	−1.988**	−0.411**	−2.521**
	sd	23.18	11.71	32.81	32.80	21.96	39.44			
	N	10	49	13	10	13	8			
Average price per cubic meter of sewer (in dollars)	mean	114.61	100.53	107.79	−19.43	0.03	44.29	0.375	0.001	−0.835
	p50	79.43	100.00	107.68	16.46	−12.60	44.29	0.000	0.365	−0.447
	sd	89.74	6.94	32.73	89.77	35.56	75.05			
	N	3	49	4	3	4	2			
Average price per cubic meter of sewer (in real local currency)	mean	93.06	101.80	152.44	13.26	32.25	53.34	−0.512	−3.012**	−37.266***
	p50	74.75	100.00	135.93	30.91	33.12	53.34	−0.535	−1.826*	−1.342
	sd	45.93	10.88	51.26	44.86	21.42	2.02			
	N	3	49	4	3	4	2			

Source: Andrés and others 2008.

Note: HH = household.

* significant at 10 percent; ** significant at 5 percent; *** significant at 1 percent.

Table D.11 Means and Medians Analysis in Growth—Water and Sewerage

Variable	Statistics	Average annual growth			Annual difference in growth			T-statistics (Z-statistics) for difference in means (medians) in growth		
		Pre-private	Transition	Post-private	(2)–(1)	(3)–(2)	(3)–(1)	(2)–(1)	(3)–(2)	(3)–(1)
		(1)	(2)	(3)	(4)	(5)	(6)	(7)	(8)	(9)
Outputs										
Residential water connections	mean	4.4%	6.5%	4.7%	0.9%	−1.9%	1.5%	−1.095	1.649*	−1.113
	p50	4.1%	5.2%	3.8%	−0.1%	−1.8%	1.2%	−0.923	2.229**	−0.943
	sd	3.0%	4.4%	4.6%	3.5%	5.6%	3.2%			
	N	17	43	24	17	24	6			
Residential sewer connections	mean	3.8%	6.7%	7.4%	3.1%	1.5%	0.0%	−1.222	−0.569	0.009
	p50	4.3%	5.5%	3.6%	2.1%	−1.4%	0.1%	−0.966	0.693	−0.135
	sd	5.9%	6.8%	10.7%	9.8%	12.3%	3.2%			
	N	15	40	23	15	23	5			
Cubic meter of produced water	mean	2.1%	7.5%	0.5%	−0.9%	−1.8%	1.6%	0.741	1.117	−0.718
	p50	1.6%	1.0%	0.9%	0.0%	0.0%	1.5%	0.000	0.817	−0.674
	sd	4.6%	38.6%	5.0%	4.1%	7.3%	5.0%			
	N	12	38	21	12	21	5			
Inputs										
Number of employees	mean	−0.4%	−10.0%	−1.5%	−9.6%	7.5%	−1.0%	3.425***	−3.460***	0.309
	p50	0.1%	−8.3%	−1.0%	−9.8%	7.8%	−1.4%	2.432***	−2.765***	0.135
	sd	4.2%	10.2%	7.2%	9.7%	9.2%	7.4%			
	N	12	32	18	12	18	5			
Efficiency										
Water connections per employee	mean	5.5%	17.5%	7.3%	11.6%	−9.6%	1.2%	−3.068***	2.939***	−0.348
	p50	4.9%	15.8%	4.5%	9.9%	−7.8%	0.1%	2.551**	2.656	0.105
	sd	5.4%	13.5%	10.1%	13.7%	14.3%	8.3%			
	N	13	32	19	13	19	6			

table continues next page

Table D.11 Means and Medians Analysis in Growth—Water and Sewerage (continued)

Variable	Statistics	Average annual growth			Annual difference in growth			T-statistics (Z-statistics) for difference in means (medians) in growth		
		Pre-private	Transition	Post-private	(2)–(1)	(3)–(2)	(3)–(1)	(2)–(1)	(3)–(2)	(3)–(1)
		(1)	(2)	(3)	(4)	(5)	(6)	(7)	(8)	(9)
Distributional losses	Mean	−3.1%	−0.6%	−5.5%	0.5%	0.5%	0.6%	−0.297	−0.310	−0.363
	p50	−2.6%	−2.0%	−5.1%	−0.1%	0.3%	0.8%	−0.267	−0.450	−0.843
	sd	3.8%	21.5%	9.1%	5.3%	6.2%	4.0%			
	N	11	26	17	11	17	6			
Quality										
Continuity (hs per day)	mean	0.0%	7.2%	4.6%	22.4%	−0.1%	0.0%	−1.000	0.057	—
	p50	0.0%	0.0%	0.9%	0.0%	0.0%	0.0%	−1.000	0.075	—
	sd	0.0%	16.0%	8.7%	38.7%	6.0%				
	N	3	18	11	3	11	1			
% of the samples that passed the potability test	mean	0.8%	5.2%	0.4%	18.6%	−0.5%	−1.0%	−1.074	1.273	1.000
	p50	0.6%	0.2%	0.0%	2.2%	0.0%	−1.0%	−0.928	1.315	1.000
	sd	1.0%	16.4%	0.7%	34.6%	1.2%	1.4%			
	N	4	18	9	4	9	2			
Coverage										
Residential water connections per 100 HHs	mean	1.0%	4.1%	3.3%	1.1%	−1.3%	0.4%	−2.050**	0.914	−0.570
	p50	0.3%	2.8%	1.6%	0.2%	−1.3%	0.1%	−1.448	1.690*	−0.944
	sd	1.7%	5.0%	4.4%	2.1%	6.1%	1.7%			
	N	16	34	19	16	19	5			
Residential sewer connections per 100 HHs	mean	1.6%	8.0%	2.8%	2.9%	−0.9%	−1.6%	−1.815	0.529	2.735**
	p50	1.4%	2.9%	0.6%	0.1%	−1.6%	−0.9%	−1.036	1.601	2.023**
	sd	17.9%	17.9%	6.1%	6.0%	6.2%	1.3%			
	N	14	25	14	14	14	5			

table continues next page

Table D.11 Means and Medians Analysis in Growth—Water and Sewerage (continued)

Variable	Statistics	Average annual growth			Annual difference in growth			T-statistics (Z-statistics) for difference in means (medians) in growth		
		Pre-private (1)	Transition (2)	Post-private (3)	(2)–(1) (4)	(3)–(2) (5)	(3)–(1) (6)	(2)–(1) (7)	(3)–(2) (8)	(3)–(1) (9)
Prices										
Average price per cubic meter of water (in dollars)	mean	12.2%	1.9%	−3.4%	−12.1%	−7.2%	−3.9%	2.493**	0.835	0.666
	p50	10.9%	−2.2%	−1.1%	−13.8%	−3.3%	−2.1%	1.820*	0.889	0.535
	sd	10.4%	22.2%	20.0%	13.8%	26.0%	10.1%			
	N	8	17	9	8	9	3			
Average price per cubic meter of water (in real local currency)	mean	10.1%	9.4%	4.5%	−6.0%	−8.9%	−0.8%	2.078**	1.060	0.346
	p50	10.1%	5.4%	2.6%	−4.3%	−6.5%	−2.5%	1.540	1.007	0.000
	sd	6.7%	18.4%	10.0%	8.1%	25.1%	4.0%			
	N	8	17	9	8	9	3			
Average price per cubic meter of sewer (in dollars)	mean	−0.6%	−5.1%	−7.9%	2.3%	−6.4%	−7.7%	−0.298	0.799	—
	p50	−0.6%	−8.7%	−7.9%	2.3%	−10.8%	−7.7%	−0.447	1.069	—
	sd	17.1%	16.1%	11.6%	10.8%	13.9%				
	N	2	5	3	2	3	1			
Average price per cubic meter of sewer (in real local currency)	mean	−1.1%	7.0%	9.7%	5.0%	−4.3%	−15.1%	3.881*	0.302	
	p50	−1.1%	1.4%	9.8%	5.0%	−18.4%	−15.1%	−1.342	0.000	
	sd	13.9%	13.5%	16.0%	1.8%	24.7%				
	N	2	5	3	2	3	1			

Source: Andrés and others 2008.

Note: HH = household.

* significant at 10 percent; ** significant at 5 percent; *** significant at 1 percent.

Table D.12 Econometric Analysis—Water Distribution and Sewerage

	(1) Number of water connections	(2) Number of sewerage connections	(3) Cubic meters per year	(4) Number of employees	(5) Water connections per employee	(6) Distributional losses	(7) Continuity of the service	(8) Potability	(9) Water coverage	(10) Sewerage	(11) Coverage / Average price per m³ of water (in dollars)	(12) Average price per m³ of water (in r.l.c.)	(13) Average price per m³ for sewerage (in dollars)	(14) Average price per m³ for sewerage (in r.l.c.)
Model 1: Log levels without firm-specific time trend														
Transition	0.141***	0.174***	0.040***	−0.180***	0.268***	−0.039**	0.038	0.059*	0.025***	0.053***	0.055	0.146***	−0.014	0.104
(t ≥ −1)	(0.010)	(0.016)	(0.009)	(0.030)	(0.034)	(0.017)	(0.064)	(0.034)	(0.007)	(0.009)	(0.041)	(0.026)	(0.142)	(0.083)
Post-transition	0.139***	0.173***	0.015***	−0.194***	0.354***	−0.155***	0.074***	0.012**	0.049***	0.065***	0.097**	0.213***	−0.096	0.222***
(t ≥ 2)	(0.008)	(0.011)	(0.006)	(0.024)	(0.027)	(0.015)	(0.015)	(0.005)	(0.005)	(0.007)	(0.038)	(0.027)	(0.110)	(0.077)
Observations	259	239	195	201	199	179	97	90	243	198	112	112	37	37
Model 2: Log levels with firm-specific time trend														
Transition	0.006	−0.006	−0.007	0.083***	−0.076***	−0.014	0.000	−0.002	−0.000	−0.005	0.003	−0.048	0.026	0.017
(t ≥ −1)	(0.004)	(0.009)	(0.010)	(0.026)	(0.023)	(0.012)	(0.006)	(0.005)	(0.001)	(0.006)	(0.050)	(0.034)	(0.093)	(0.082)
Post-transition	−0.002	−0.005	−0.013*	0.069***	−0.027	0.000	0.000	−0.002	−0.001	−0.008	−0.047	−0.024	0.013	0.045
(t ≥ 2)	(0.003)	(0.005)	(0.007)	(0.017)	(0.019)	(0.001)	(0.002)	(0.009)	(0.001)	(0.005)	(0.031)	(0.020)	(0.088)	(0.078)
Observations	259	239	195	201	199	179	97	90	243	198	112	112	37	37
Model 3: Growth														
Transition	0.001	0.006	−0.008	−0.048***	0.047***	−0.000	0.002	0.009	0.001	0.003	−0.203***	−0.099***	−0.054	0.007
(t ≥ −1)	(0.004)	(0.006)	(0.009)	(0.018)	(0.018)	(0.012)	(0.020)	(0.013)	(0.002)	(0.004)	(0.034)	(0.027)	(0.080)	(0.059)
Post-transition	−0.010***	−0.011***	−0.025***	0.048***	−0.037***	−0.012*	−0.001	−0.005	−0.004***	−0.008**	−0.018	−0.011	−0.005	0.006
(t ≥ 2)	(0.002)	(0.002)	(0.007)	(0.012)	(0.012)	(0.007)	(0.005)	(0.005)	(0.002)	(0.004)	(0.021)	(0.019)	(0.076)	(0.065)
Observations	235	216	172	176	178	160	81	77	217	180	101	101	31	31

Source: Andrés and others 2008.

Note: Standard errors are in parentheses. The *Transition* and *Post-transition* variables are dummy independent variables in regressions where the dependent variable is given by the column heading (Number of Connections). *Transition* = 1 starting two years before the privatization or concession was awarded and continuing for all years after. *Post-transition* = 1 for all years after the transition period, that is, starting one year after the privatization was awarded.

r.l.c. = real local currency.

* significant at 10 percent; ** significant at 5 percent; *** significant at 1 percent.

Reference

Andrés, L., J. L. Guasch, T. Haven, and V. Foster. 2008. *The Impact of Private Sector Participation in Infrastructure: Lights, Shadows, and the Road Ahead*. Washington, DC: World Bank.

Dimensions of Regulatory Governance

Figure E.1 Electricity Regulatory Agencies

a. Regulatory autonomy

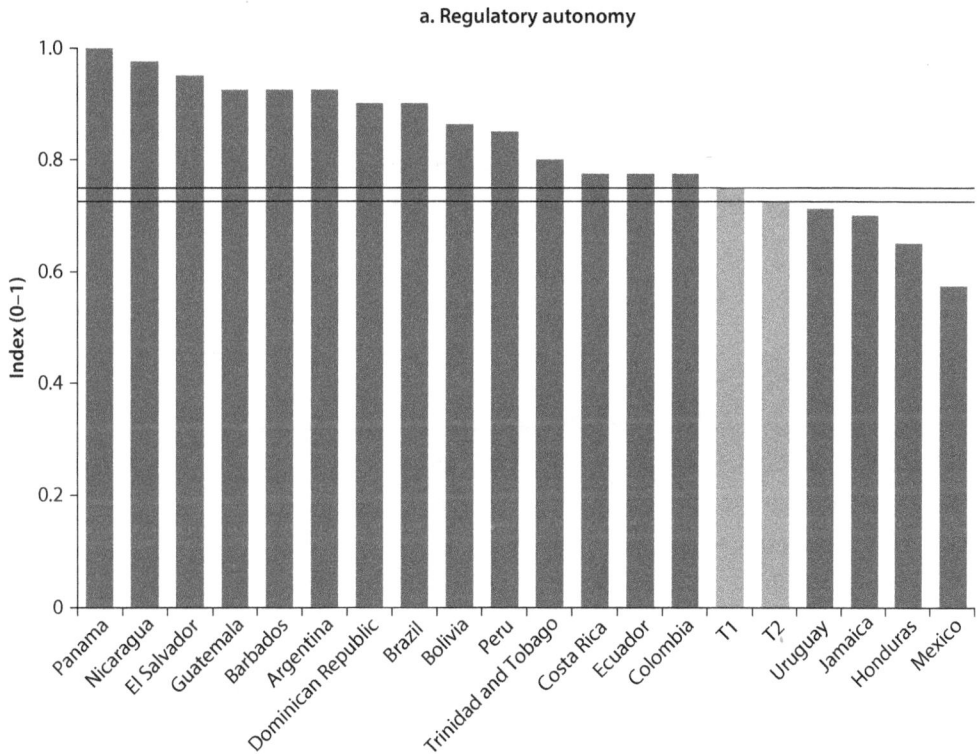

figure continues next page

Figure E.1 Electricity Regulatory Agencies *(continued)*

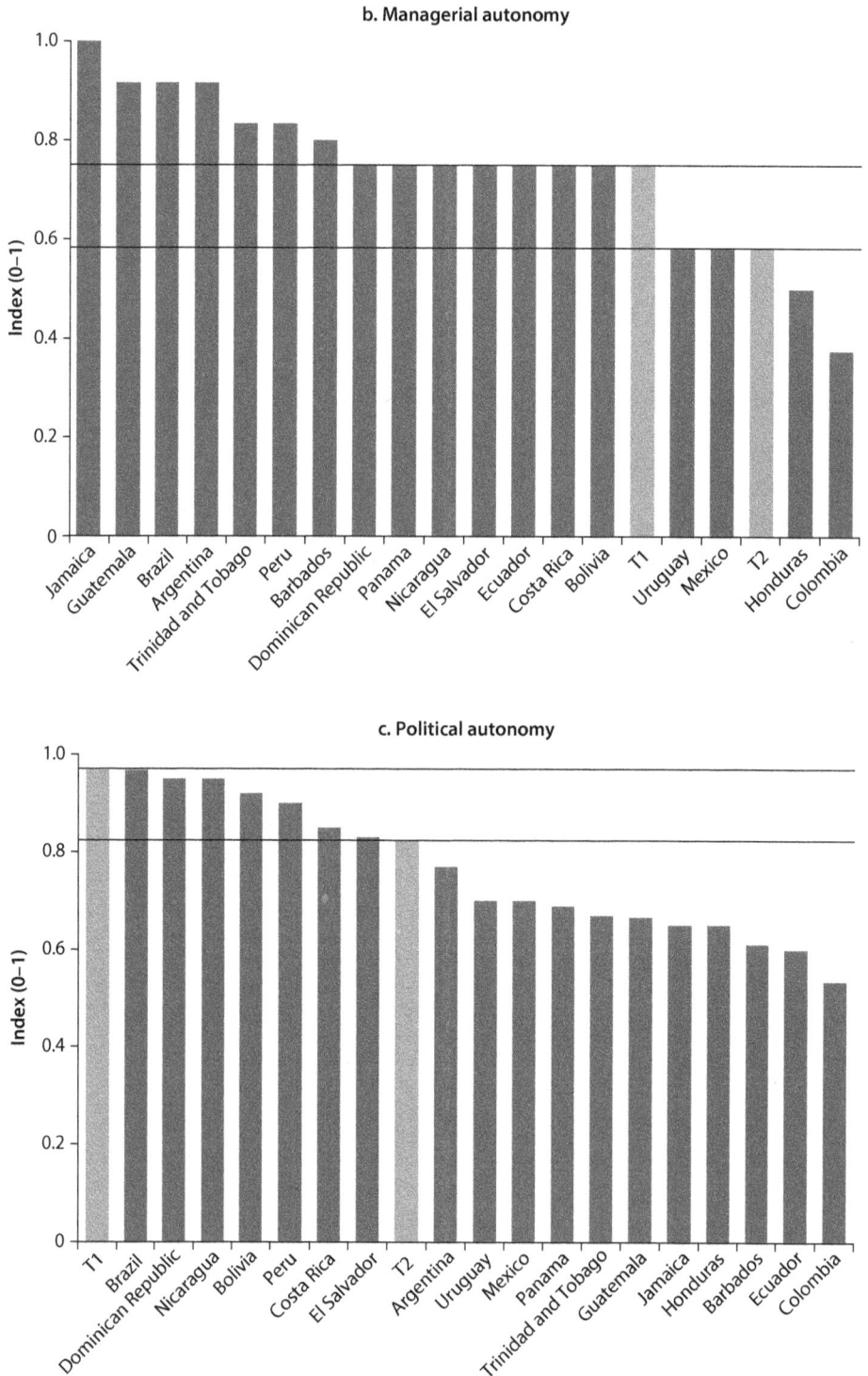

b. Managerial autonomy

c. Political autonomy

figure continues next page

Figure E.1 Electricity Regulatory Agencies *(continued)*

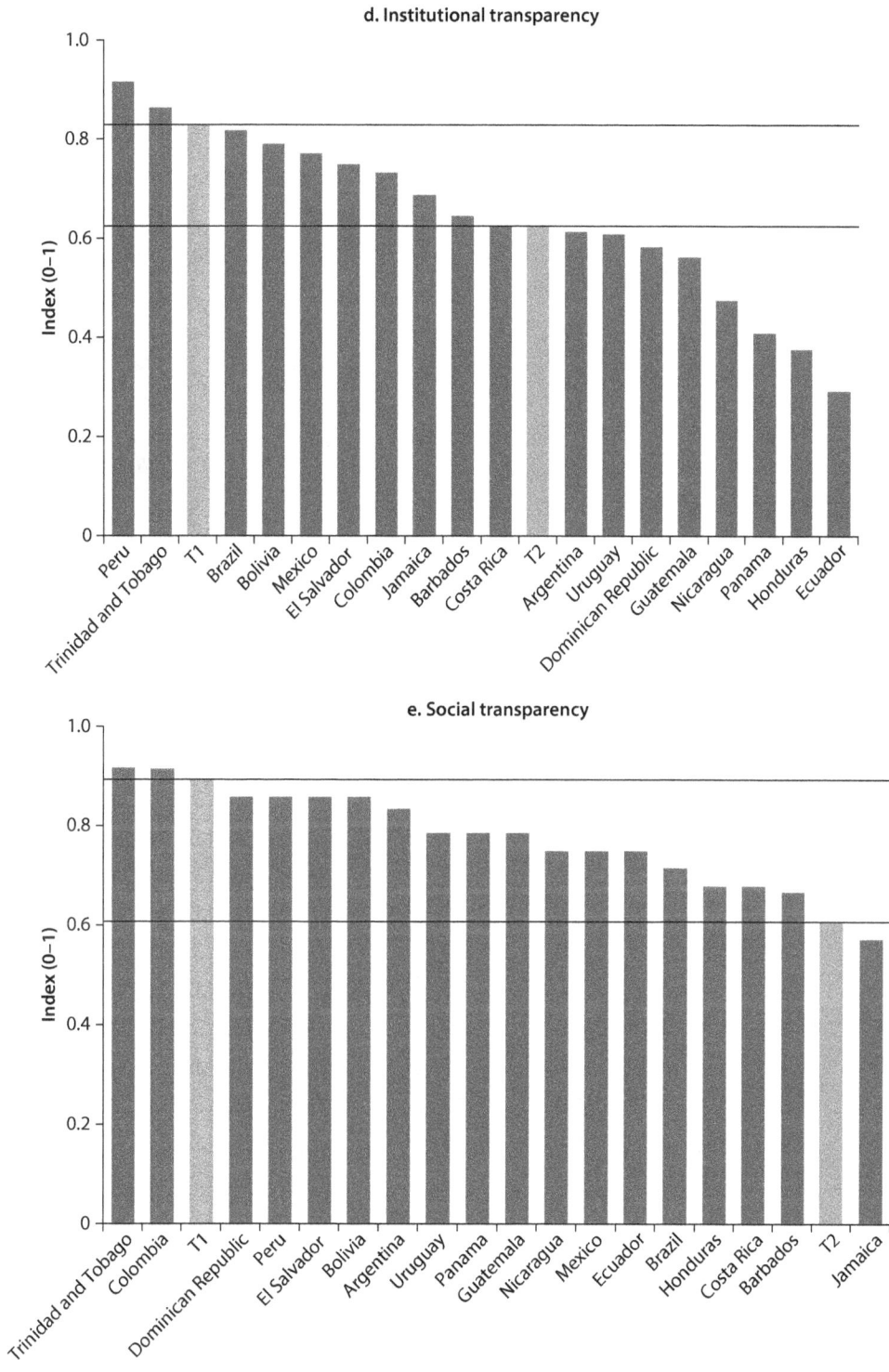

d. Institutional transparency

e. Social transparency

figure continues next page

Figure E.1 Electricity Regulatory Agencies *(continued)*

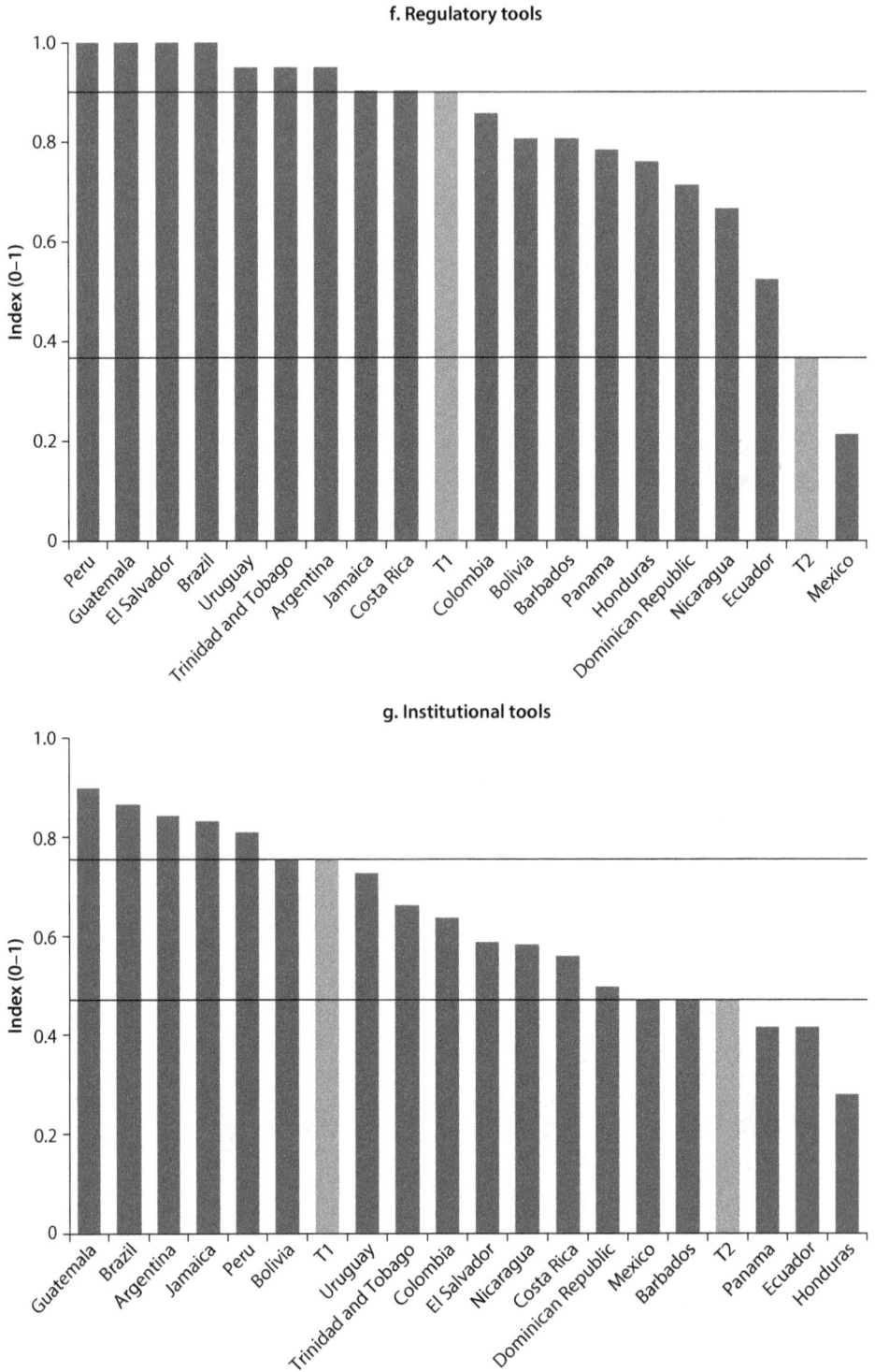

f. Regulatory tools

g. Institutional tools

figure continues next page

Figure E.1 Electricity Regulatory Agencies *(continued)*

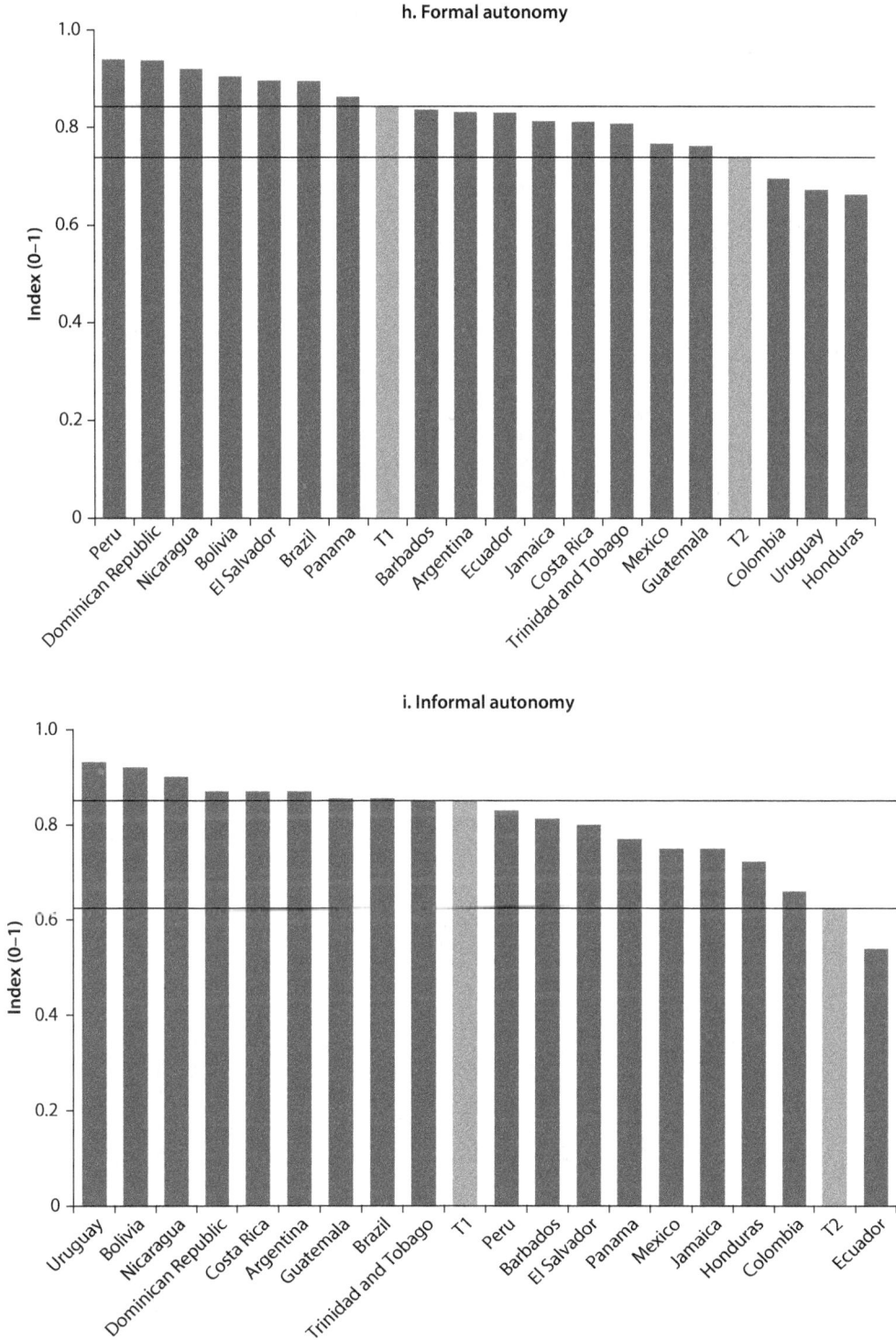

h. Formal autonomy

i. Informal autonomy

figure continues next page

Figure E.1 **Electricity Regulatory Agencies** *(continued)*

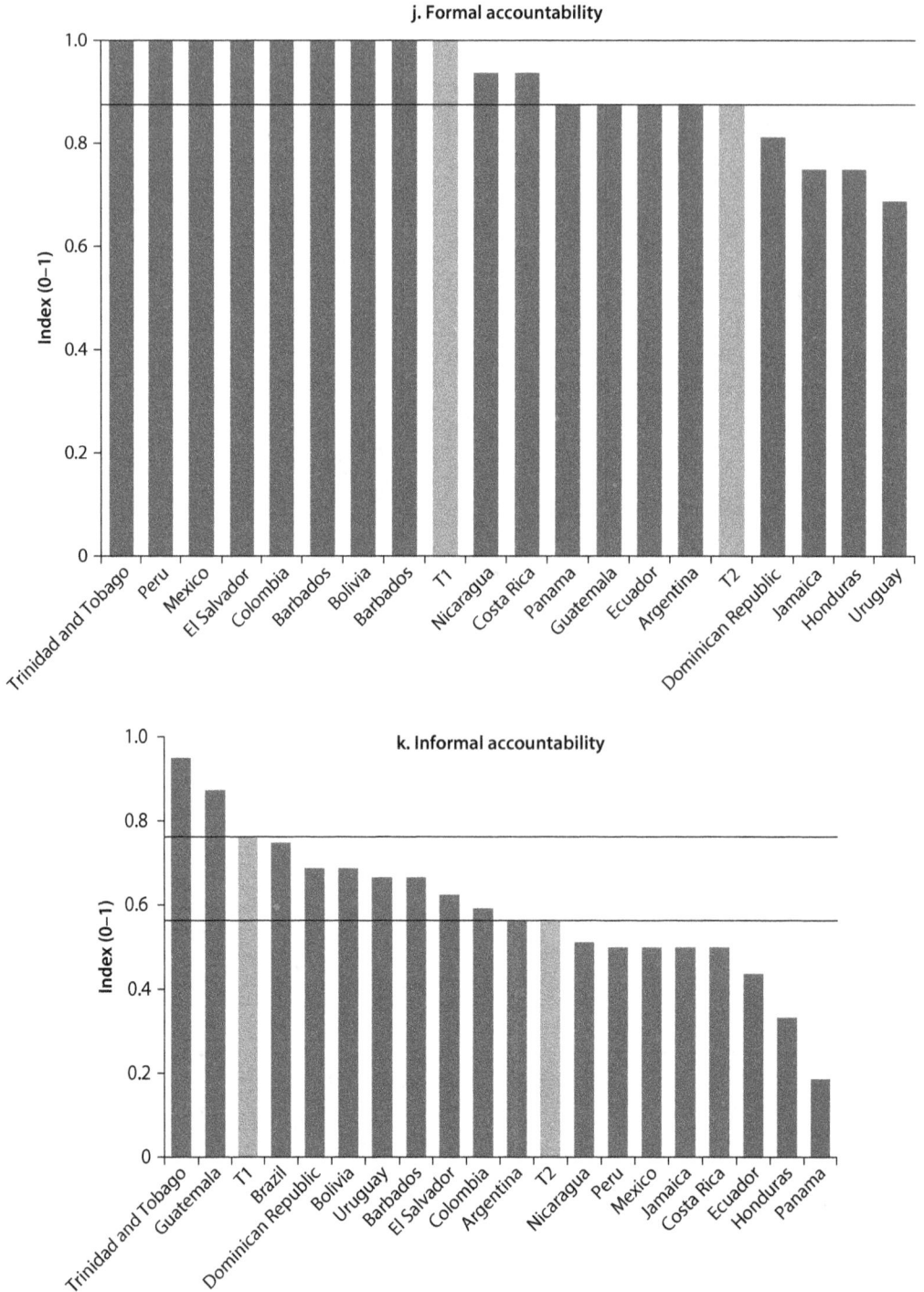

j. Formal accountability

k. Informal accountability

figure continues next page

Figure E.1 Electricity Regulatory Agencies *(continued)*

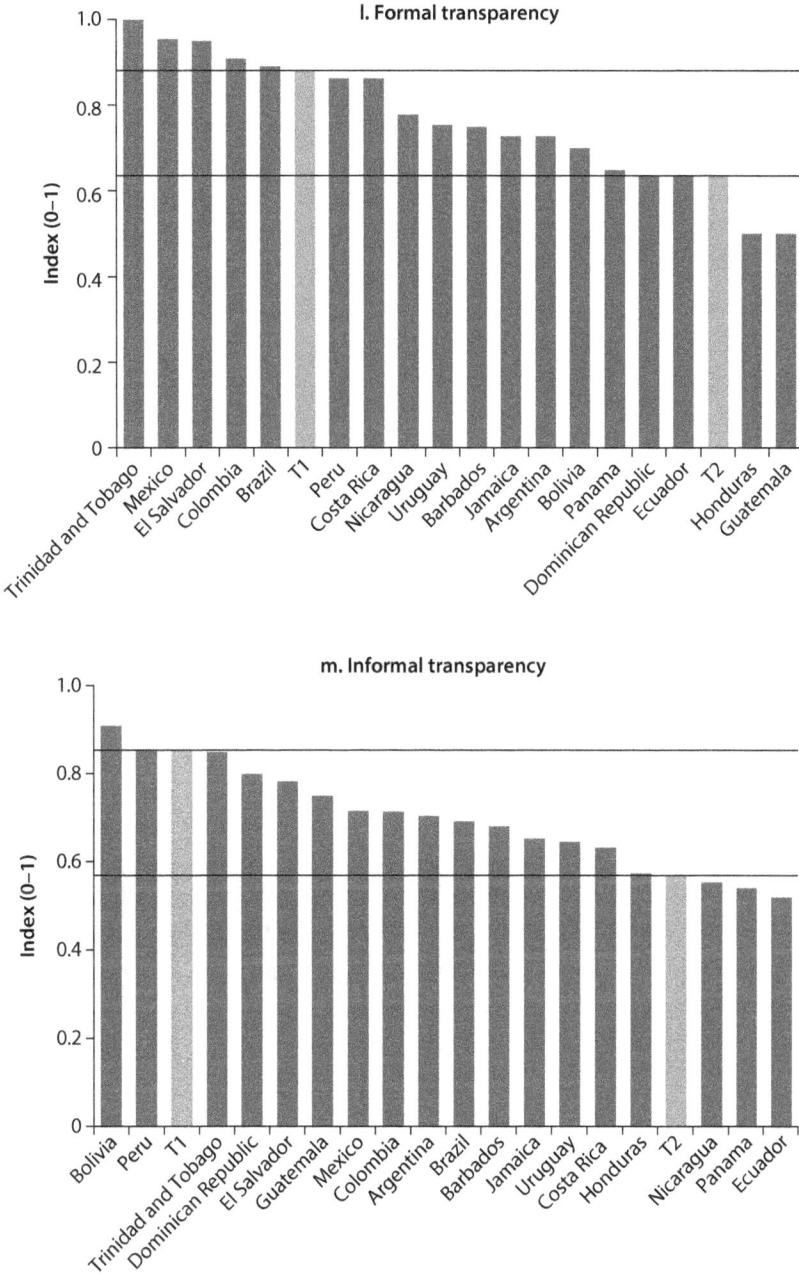

l. Formal transparency

m. Informal transparency

Source: LAC Electricity Regulatory Governance Database, World Bank, 2008.

Figure E.2 Water Regulatory Agencies

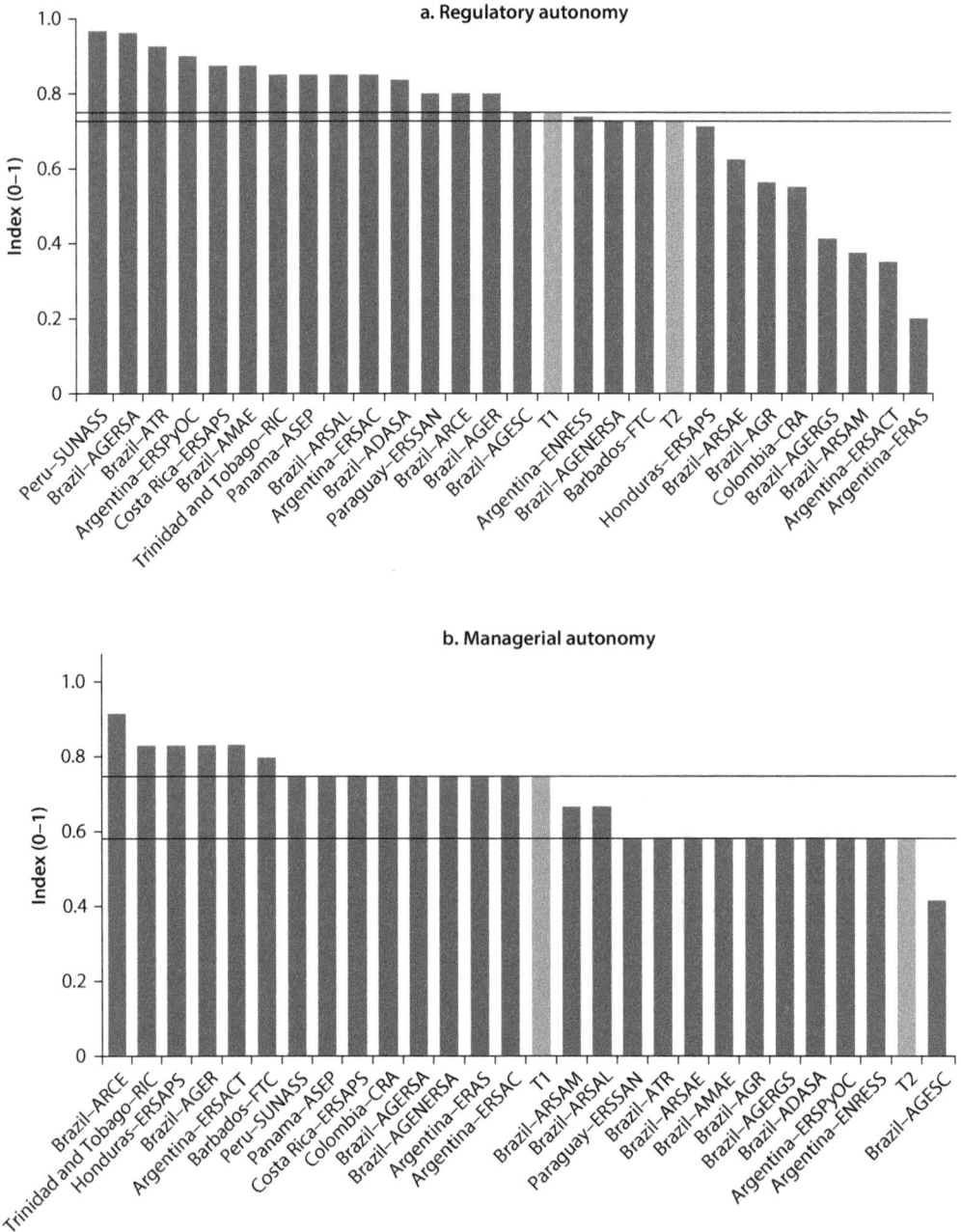

a. Regulatory autonomy

b. Managerial autonomy

figure continues next page

Figure E.2 Water Regulatory Agencies *(continued)*

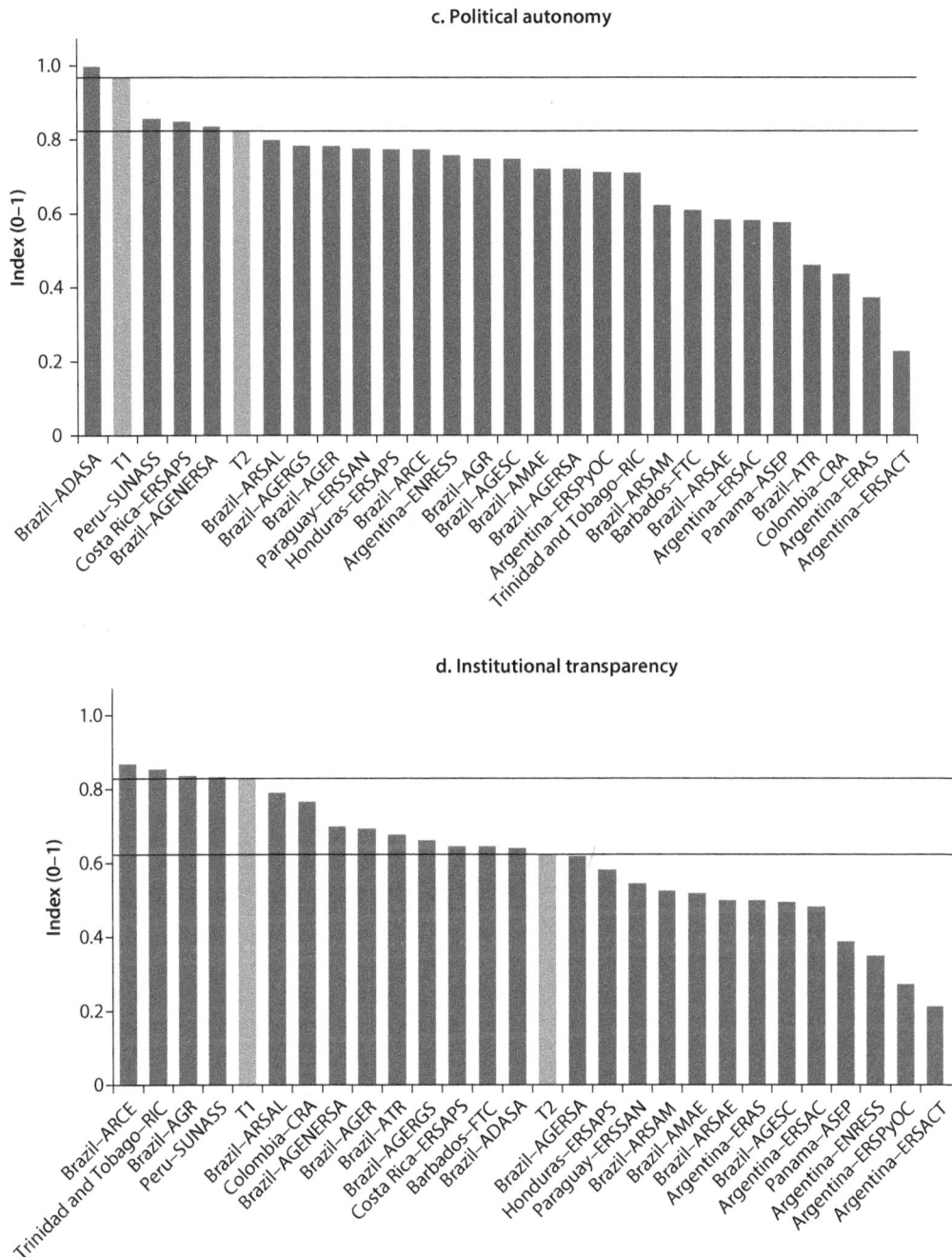

c. Political autonomy

d. Institutional transparency

figure continues next page

Figure E.2 Water Regulatory Agencies *(continued)*

e. Social transparency

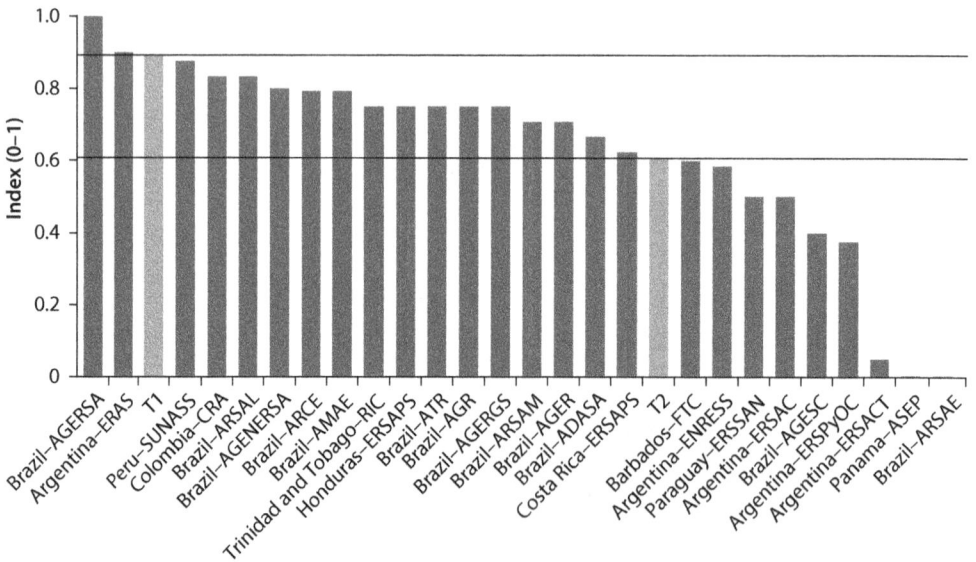

f. Institutional tools

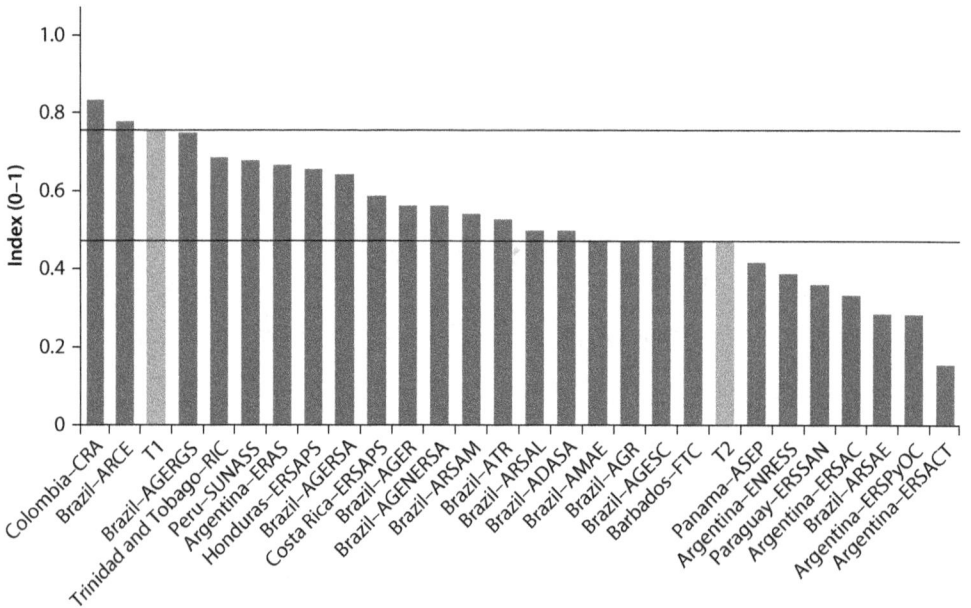

figure continues next page

Figure E.2 Water Regulatory Agencies *(continued)*

g. Regulatory tools

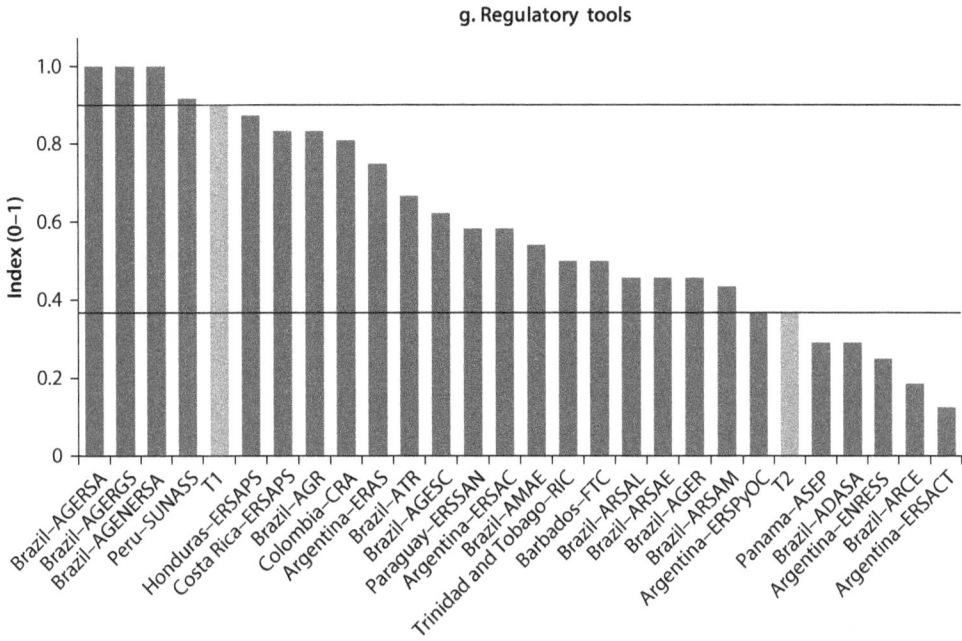

h. Informal autonomy

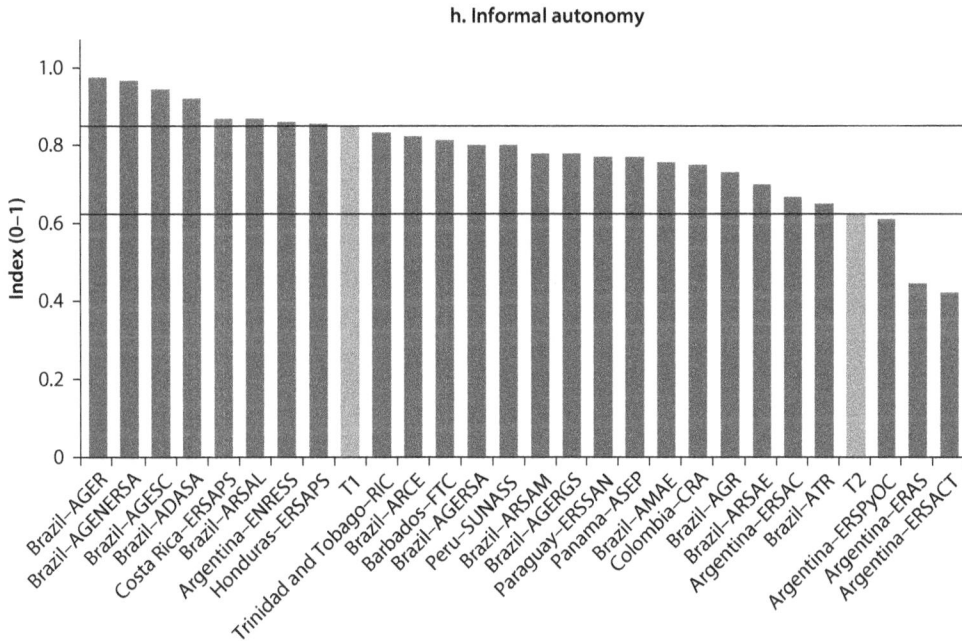

figure continues next page

Figure E.2 Water Regulatory Agencies *(continued)*

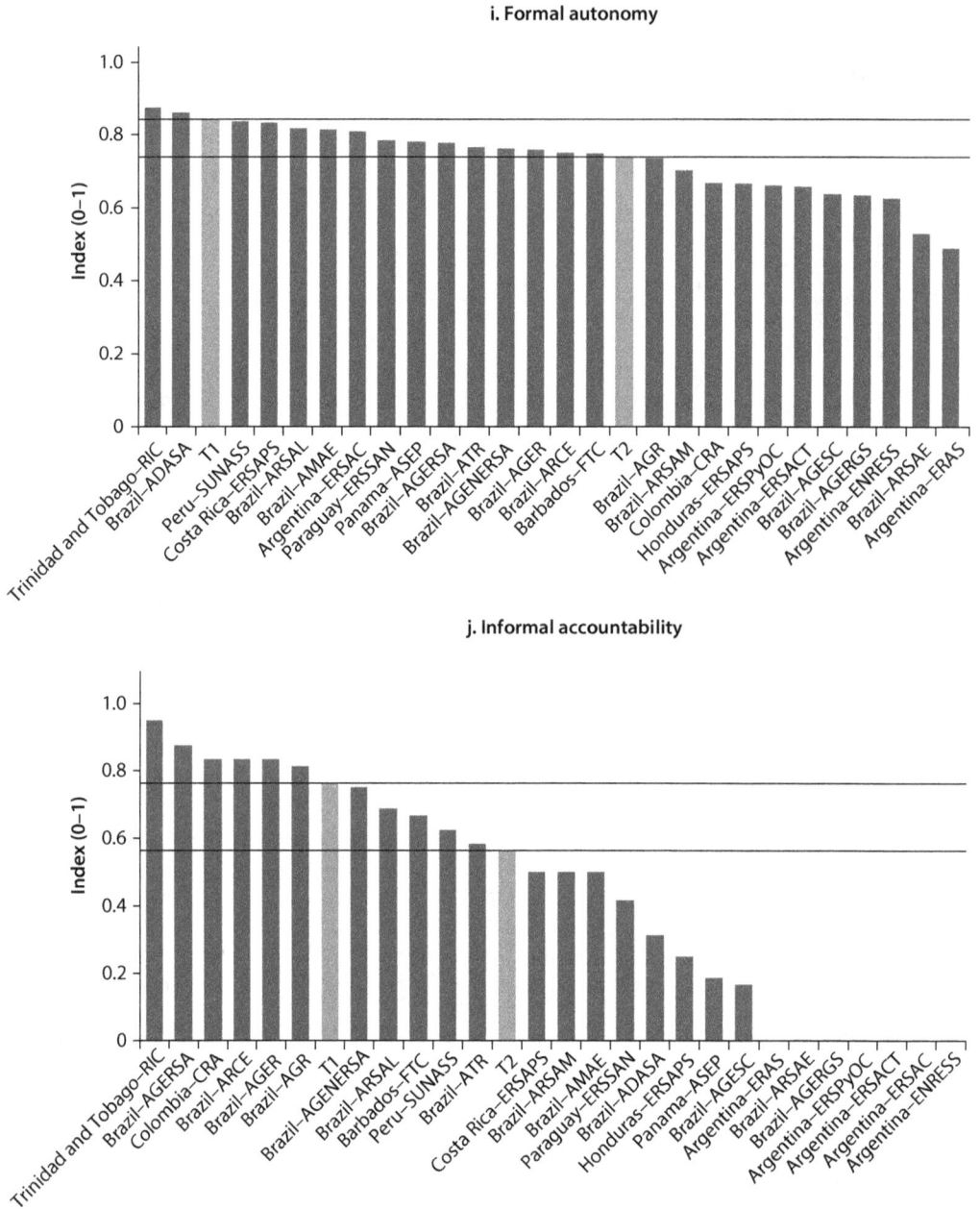

i. Formal autonomy

j. Informal accountability

figure continues next page

Figure E.2 Water Regulatory Agencies *(continued)*

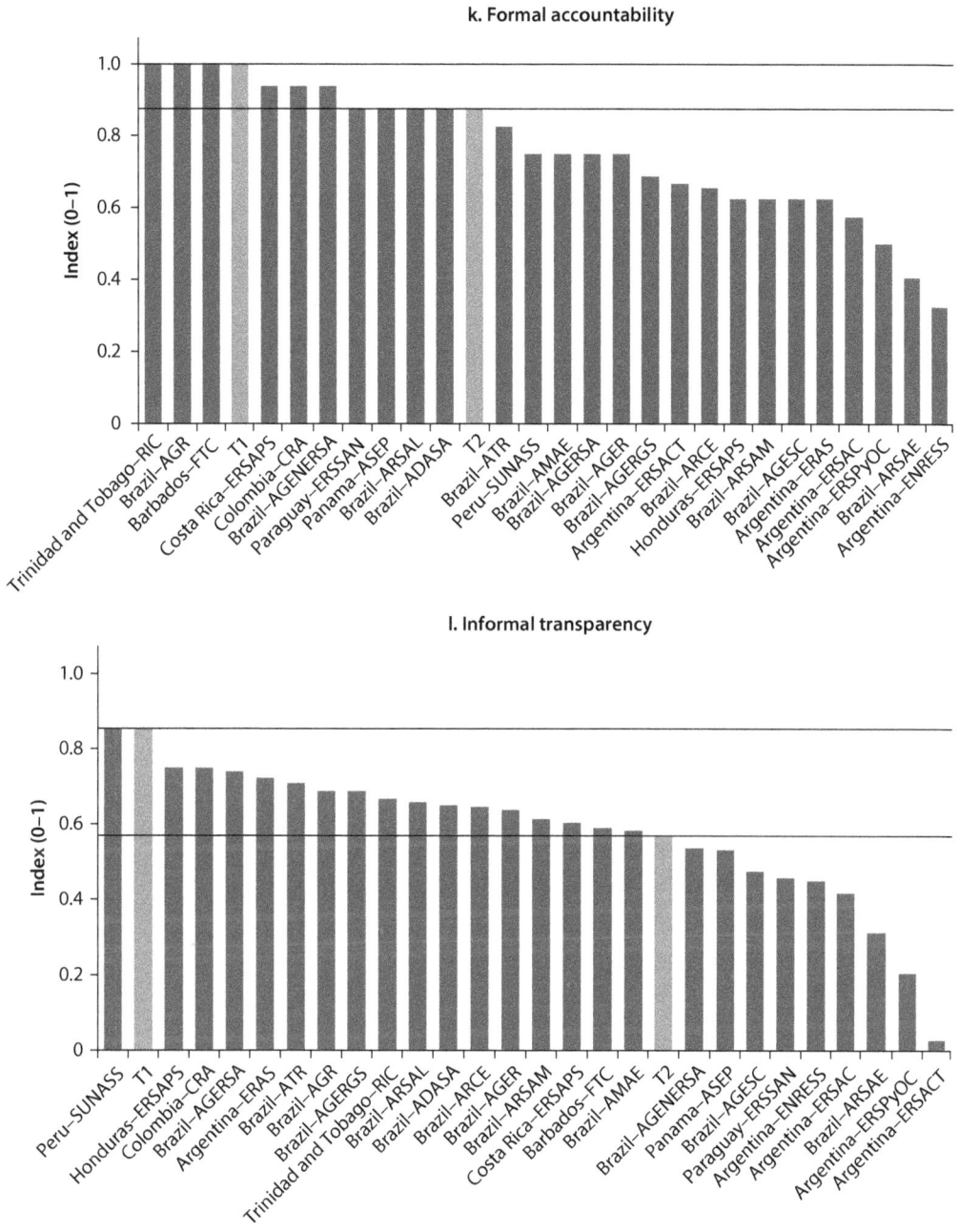

k. Formal accountability

l. Informal transparency

figure continues next page

Figure E.2 Water Regulatory Agencies *(continued)*

m. Formal transparency

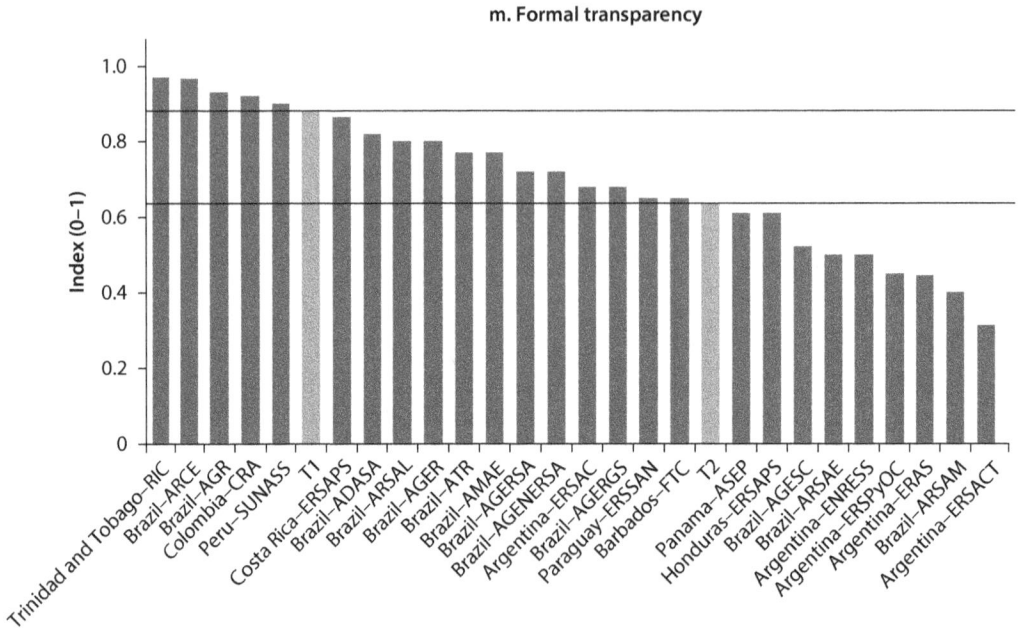

Source: LAC Water Database, World Bank, 2009.

Regulatory Governance and Performance

Table F.1 Regulatory Governance and Performance—Existence of Regulatory Agency

	Residential connection per employee (1)	Energy sold per employee (2)	Distributional losses (3)	Coverage (4)	Energy sold per connection (5)	Duration of interrupt's (6)	Frequency of interrupt's (7)	OPEX per connection (in dollars) (8)	OPEX per MWh sold (in dollars) (9)	Average residential tariff (in dollars) (10)	Average industrial tariff (in dollars) (11)	Cost recovery ratio (12)
Dummy transition of PSP	0.131*** (0.012)	0.169*** (0.014)	0.043*** (0.013)	−0.011*** (0.002)	0.065*** (0.003)	−0.014 (0.032)	0.032 (0.037)	−0.314 (0.223)	−0.352 (0.224)	0.042** (0.019)	0.064*** (0.023)	−0.005 (0.059)
Dummy post-transition of PSP	0.045*** (0.008)	0.015 (0.010)	−0.131*** (0.012)	0.003* (0.002)	0.003 (0.005)	−0.295*** (0.024)	−0.348*** (0.023)	−0.142*** (0.034)	−0.089** (0.036)	−0.019** (0.009)	−0.031 (0.021)	0.192*** (0.050)
Existence of regulatory agency	0.177*** (0.010)	0.167*** (0.012)	−0.045*** (0.009)	0.004* (0.002)	−0.031*** (0.005)	−0.210*** (0.028)	−0.190*** (0.029)	−0.387*** (0.051)	−0.320*** (0.056)	0.145*** (0.016)	−0.047** (0.021)	0.125*** (0.032)
Utility FE	Yes	Yes	Yes	Yes	Yes	Yes	Yes	Yes	Yes	Yes	Yes	Yes
Utility specific time trend	Yes	Yes	No	Yes	No	No	No	No	No	No	No	No
Observations	2000	1981	2073	1323	2515	1056	947	864	873	1728	840	669
Number of utilities	199	198	190	144	213	144	132	131	131	175	90	103

Standard errors in parentheses.
* significant at 10%; ** significant at 5%; *** significant at 1%.

Table F.2 Regulatory Governance and Performance—Existence of Regulatory Agency with Interactions

	Residential connection per employee (1)	Energy sold per employee (2)	Distributional losses (3)	Coverage (4)	Energy sold per connection (5)	Duration of interrupt's (6)	Frequency of interrupt's (7)	OPEX per connection (in dollars) (8)	OPEX per MWh sold (in dollars) (9)	Average residential tariff (in dollars) (10)	Average industrial tariff (in dollars) (11)	Cost recovery ratio (12)
Dummy transition of PSP	0.121*** (0.014)	0.170*** (0.016)	0.125*** (0.018)	−0.012*** (0.003)	0.057*** (0.008)	−0.018 (0.040)	0.059 (0.046)	−0.278 (0.228)	−0.230 (0.229)	0.164*** (0.024)	0.055 (0.039)	−0.053 (0.107)
Dummy post-transition of PSP	0.018 (0.015)	−0.020 (0.025)	−0.123*** (0.035)	0.006 (0.004)	0.095*** (0.015)	−0.561*** (0.074)	−0.429*** (0.064)	−0.110 (0.102)	−0.116 (0.099)	−0.087*** (0.018)	0.123 (0.100)	0.308*** (0.116)
Existence of regulatory agency	0.162*** (0.014)	0.175*** (0.017)	−0.008 (0.010)	0.002 (0.002)	−0.023*** (0.006)	−0.239*** (0.038)	−0.176*** (0.044)	−0.351*** (0.069)	−0.233*** (0.078)	0.286*** (0.024)	−0.039 (0.026)	0.146*** (0.042)
Transition*existence	0.026 (0.018)	−0.012 (0.022)	−0.144*** (0.022)	0.004 (0.004)	0.005 (0.011)	0.019 (0.054)	−0.061 (0.059)	−0.016 (0.121)	−0.150 (0.129)	−0.315*** (0.033)	0.000 (0.045)	0.045 (0.114)
Post trans.*existence	0.032* (0.017)	0.041 (0.026)	0.020 (0.037)	−0.005 (0.005)	−0.102*** (0.016)	0.284*** (0.078)	0.107 (0.069)	−0.071 (0.109)	0.006 (0.108)	0.138*** (0.021)	−0.158 (0.102)	−0.123 (0.121)
Utility FE	Yes	Yes	Yes	Yes	Yes	Yes	Yes	Yes	Yes	Yes	Yes	Yes
Utility specific time trend	Yes	Yes	No	Yes	Yes	Yes	Yes	Yes	Yes	Yes	Yes	Yes
Observations	2000	1981	2073	1323	2515	1056	947	864	873	1728	840	669
Number of utilities	199	198	190	144	213	144	132	131	131	175	90	103

Standard errors in parentheses.
* significant at 10%; ** significant at 5%; *** significant at 1%.

Table F.3 Regulatory Governance and Performance—Duration of the Regulatory Agency

	Residential connection per employee (1)	Distributional losses (2)	Coverage (3)	Energy sold per connection (4)	Duration of interrupt's (5)	Frequency of interrupt's (6)	OPEX per connection (in dollars) (7)	OPEX per MWh sold (in dollars) (8)	Average residential tariff (in dollars) (9)	Average industrial tariff (in dollars) (10)	Cost recovery ratio (11)
Dummy transition of PSP	0.175***	0.030***	-0.013***	0.062***	-0.022	0.044	-0.463**	-0.451**	0.053***	0.027	0.043
	(0.014)	(0.011)	(0.002)	(0.005)	(0.027)	(0.033)	(0.220)	(0.228)	(0.016)	(0.019)	(0.059)
Dummy post-transition of PSP	0.101***	-0.091***	0.006***	0.024***	-0.112***	-0.167***	-0.152***	-0.158***	-0.089***	-0.058***	0.157***
	(0.008)	(0.012)	(0.002)	(0.006)	(0.025)	(0.024)	(0.036)	(0.046)	(0.011)	(0.021)	(0.049)
Duration of the regulatory agency	-0.014***	-0.018***	0.004***	-0.018***	-0.094***	-0.094***	-0.057***	-0.016***	0.026***	-0.013***	0.040**
	(0.003)	(0.002)	(0.001)	(0.001)	(0.008)	(0.007)	(0.005)	(0.004)	(0.004)	(0.003)	(0.005)
Duration of the regulatory agency (Sq.)	-0.000	0.001***	-0.001***	0.001***	0.004***	0.004***	0.003***	0.001***	0.001***	0.002***	-0.001***
	(0.000)	(0.000)	(0.000)	(0.000)	(0.001)	(0.001)	(0.000)	(0.000)	(0.000)	(0.000)	(0.000)
Utility FE	Yes	Yes	Yes	Yes	Yes	Yes	Yes	Yes	Yes	Yes	Yes
Utility specific time trend	Yes	No	Yes	No	No	No	No	No	No	No	No
Observations	2000	2073	1323	2515	1056	947	864	873	1728	840	669
Number of utilities	199	190	144	213	144	132	131	131	175	90	103

Standard errors in parentheses.

* significant at 10%; ** significant at 5%; *** significant at 1%.

Table F.4 Regulatory Governance and Performance—Regulatory Governance Index

	Residential connection per employee (1)	Energy sold per employee (2)	Distributional losses (3)	Coverage (4)	Energy sold per connection (5)	Duration of interrupt's (6)	Frequency of interrupt's (7)	OPEX per connection (in dollars) (8)	OPEX per MWh sold (in dollars) (9)	Average residential tariff (in dollars) (10)	Average industrial tariff (in dollars) (11)	Cost recovery ratio (12)
Dummy transition of PSP	0.124*** (0.012)	0.159*** (0.014)	0.045*** (0.013)	-0.012*** (0.003)	0.054*** (0.005)	-0.010 (0.033)	0.031 (0.038)	-0.269 (0.225)	-0.293 (0.227)	0.041** (0.018)	0.070*** (0.022)	-0.006 (0.060)
Dummy post-transition of PSP	0.062*** (0.009)	0.030*** (0.011)	-0.118*** (0.012)	0.001 (0.002)	-0.007 (0.005)	-0.276*** (0.024)	-0.332*** (0.023)	-0.213*** (0.036)	-0.179*** (0.044)	0.019 (0.012)	-0.027 (0.021)	0.194*** (0.050)
Regulatory governance index (ERGI)	0.236*** (0.013)	0.226*** (0.016)	-0.077*** (0.013)	0.005* (0.003)	-0.029*** (0.007)	-0.274*** (0.036)	-0.248*** (0.038)	-0.495*** (0.069)	-0.373*** (0.076)	0.154*** (0.021)	-0.074*** (0.028)	0.150*** (0.042)
Utility FE	Yes	Yes	Yes	Yes	Yes	Yes	Yes	Yes	Yes	Yes	Yes	Yes
Utility specific time trend	Yes	Yes	No	Yes	No	No	No	No	No	No	No	No
Observations	1859	1840	1983	1247	2337	1030	924	841	850	1655	831	660
Number of utilities	181	180	175	137	195	139	127	126	126	159	85	98

Standard errors in parentheses.
* significant at 10%; ** significant at 5%; *** significant at 1%.

Table F.5 Regulatory Governance and Performance—Principal Component Analysis

	Residential connection per employee (1)	Distributional losses (2)	Coverage (3)	Energy sold per connection (4)	Duration of interrupt's (5)	Frequency of interrupt's (6)	OPEX per connection (in dollars) (7)	OPEX per MWh sold (in dollars) (8)	Average residential tariff (in dollars) (9)	Average industrial tariff (in dollars) (10)	Cost recovery ratio (11)
Dummy transition of PSP	0.122*** (0.012)	0.027** (0.013)	-0.014*** (0.003)	0.059*** (0.004)	-0.043 (0.037)	0.046 (0.044)	-0.730* (0.397)	-0.808** (0.400)	0.147*** (0.019)	0.087*** (0.021)	0.068 (0.062)
Dummy post-transition of PSP	0.084*** (0.008)	-0.124*** (0.013)	0.002 (0.002)	-0.008 (0.005)	-0.358*** (0.025)	-0.366*** (0.024)	-0.193*** (0.039)	-0.137*** (0.049)	0.049*** (0.013)	-0.016 (0.021)	0.176*** (0.053)
PCA 1 -Informal	0.001 (0.007)	-0.027*** (0.007)	-0.001 (0.001)	-0.048*** (0.004)	0.014 (0.018)	0.010 (0.018)	0.046 (0.042)	0.053 (0.050)	0.087*** (0.010)	0.010 (0.021)	-0.003 (0.018)
PCA 2 -Formal	0.107*** (0.008)	-0.006 (0.006)	0.004* (0.002)	0.037*** (0.004)	-0.024 (0.026)	-0.103*** (0.028)	0.050 (0.084)	0.092 (0.085)	-0.145*** (0.014)	-0.051*** (0.016)	-0.071* (0.037)
PCA 3 -Formal autonomy and tariffs	0.085*** (0.015)	-0.069*** (0.012)	0.012*** (0.004)	-0.009 (0.009)	-0.144*** (0.053)	-0.080 (0.049)	-0.405*** (0.111)	-0.339** (0.132)	-0.036* (0.020)	-0.030 (0.029)	0.266*** (0.068)
Utility FE	Yes	Yes	Yes	Yes	Yes	Yes	Yes	Yes	Yes	Yes	Yes
Utility specific time trend	Yes	No	Yes	No	No	No	No	No	No	No	No
Observations	1782	1917	1190	2253	974	882	800	809	1596	820	619
Number of utilities	175	169	131	189	134	123	121	121	153	84	93

Standard errors in parentheses.
* significant at 10%; ** significant at 5%; *** significant at 1%.

Corporate Governance and Performance

Table G.1 Correlation between Corporate Governance Indexes and Performance—Water and Electricity Distribution Sectors (in Levels)

	Distributional losses	Quality of the service	Coverage	Labor productivity	Residential tariffs
Legal soundness	−0.41	0.05	−0.26	0.29	0.39
CEO competitiveness	−0.39	0.08	−0.33	0.08	0.36
Board competitiveness	−0.22	−0.14	−0.12	0.10	0.14
Professional management	−0.24	0.13	−0.08	0.34	0.22
Transparency and disclosure	0.14	−0.16	0.37	0.24	−0.31
Performance orientation	−0.25	0.28	−0.09	0.26	0.22
Corporate governance	−0.44	0.09	−0.20	0.40	0.37

Table G.2 Correlation between Corporate Governance Indexes and Performance—Water and Electricity Distribution Sectors (in Growth Rates)

	Distributional losses	Quality of the service	Coverage	Labor productivity	Residential tariffs
Legal soundness	0.04	−0.31	0.14	−0.10	0.26
CEO competitiveness	0.05	−0.10	0.35	0.01	0.06
Board competitiveness	−0.06	−0.10	−0.08	0.18	0.00
Professional management	0.03	−0.11	0.07	0.12	0.01
Transparency and disclosure	−0.02	−0.04	0.15	0.10	−0.37
Performance orientation	0.18	0.09	0.30	0.13	0.01
Corporate governance	0.07	−0.20	0.31	0.12	0.02

Table G.3 Correlation between Corporate Governance Indexes and Performance—Electricity Distribution Sector (in Levels)

	Distributional losses	Duration of interruptions	Frequency of interruptions	Coverage	Labor productivity	Residential tariifs	Industrial tariffs
Legal soundness	0.02	0.39	0.32	−0.32	−0.41	0.42	0.42
CEO competitiveness	0.17	0.28	0.41	−0.02	−0.51	−0.19	0.22
Board competitiveness	−0.01	0.47	0.44	−0.03	−0.23	0.09	0.50
Professional management	0.08	0.21	0.10	0.05	−0.07	0.40	0.18
Transparency and disclosure	−0.19	−0.18	0.00	−0.07	0.20	0.09	−0.23
Performance orientation	0.06	−0.15	−0.04	0.14	0.31	0.23	−0.26
Corporate governance	0.06	0.37	0.44	−0.11	−0.30	0.38	0.31

Table G.4 Correlation between Corporate Governance Indexes and Performance—Electricity Distribution Sector (in Growth Rates)

	Distributional losses	Duration of interruptions	Frequency of interruptions	Coverage	Labor productivity	Residential tariifs	Industrial tariffs
Legal soundness	−0.10	0.36	0.30	0.19	−0.10	0.15	−0.01
CEO competitiveness	−0.01	0.09	0.01	0.02	−0.19	−0.08	−0.26
Board competitiveness	−0.09	0.10	0.05	0.00	0.07	0.00	0.02
Professional management	0.24	0.09	0.13	−0.15	−0.31	0.02	−0.30
Transparency and disclosure	−0.03	−0.03	0.16	0.32	0.17	−0.28	−0.49
Performance orientation	0.28	−0.20	−0.14	0.03	0.04	−0.34	−0.16
Corporate governance	0.09	0.16	0.18	0.17	−0.11	−0.18	−0.40

Table G.5 Correlation between Corporate Governance Indexes and Performance—Water Sector (in Levels)

	Non-revenue water	Continuity of the service	Potability	Water coverage	Sewerage coverage	Residential water tariffs	Residential sewerage tariffs	Labor productivity	Metering
Legal soundness	−0.33	0.34	−0.05	−0.08	0.09	0.29	−0.01	0.54	−0.48
CEO competitiveness	−0.02	−0.52	−0.12	−0.13	0.26	0.23	−0.23	0.07	−0.02
Board competitiveness	−0.23	−0.12	0.31	0.29	−0.04	0.01	0.12	0.15	0.03
Professional management	−0.27	−0.13	0.24	0.23	−0.07	0.31	0.11	0.53	−0.09
Transparency and disclosure	−0.29	0.09	0.31	0.39	0.17	−0.11	0.32	0.26	0.26
Performance orientation	−0.37	−0.23	0.62	0.35	0.18	0.17	0.03	0.46	0.21
Corporate governance	−0.42	−0.14	0.41	0.32	0.17	0.30	0.10	0.59	−0.04

Table G.6 Correlation between Corporate Governance Indexes and Performance—Water Sector (in Growth Rates)

	Non-revenue water	Continuity of the service	Potability	Water coverage	Sewerage coverage	Residential water tariffs	Residential sewerage tariffs	Labor productivity	Metering
Legal soundness	0.11	−0.37	0.25	−0.24	0.13	−0.04	0.17	−0.05	−0.03
CEO competitiveness	−0.04	0.70	0.17	0.24	0.33	−0.52	−0.38	0.01	−0.17
Board competitiveness	−0.10	0.36	0.22	0.02	−0.21	−0.03	−0.32	0.32	0.28
Professional management	−0.21	0.27	0.16	−0.23	0.25	−0.23	−0.20	0.29	0.36
Transparency and disclosure	0.09	0.32	−0.01	0.28	0.20	−0.13	−0.09	0.08	0.32
Performance orientation	−0.05	0.42	−0.73	−0.11	0.55	0.13	0.37	0.41	0.51
Corporate governance	−0.06	0.48	0.05	−0.04	0.39	−0.25	−0.13	0.30	0.41

Table G.7 Principal Component Analysis—Eigenvalues of Factors

Component	Eigenvalue	Difference	Proportion	Cumulative
1	2.173	0.810	0.362	0.362
2	1.362	0.357	0.227	0.589
3	1.006	0.289	0.168	0.757
4	0.717	0.271	0.119	0.876
5	0.445	0.148	0.074	0.950
6	0.297	n.a.	0.050	1.000

Note: n.a. = not applicable.

Table G.8 Principal Component Analysis—Factor Loadings of Indexes after Varimax Rotation

Variable	Component 1	Component 2	Component 3	Unexplained
Performance orientation	0.678	−0.327	−0.128	0.128
Legal soundness	0.217	0.151	0.624	0.328
Transparency and disclosure	0.277	0.223	−0.692	0.157
Board competitiveness	−0.067	0.859	−0.050	0.076
CEO competitiveness	0.374	0.162	0.335	0.485
Professional management	0.522	0.236	0.028	0.287

www.ingramcontent.com/pod-product-compliance
Lightning Source LLC
Chambersburg PA
CBHW080526220326
41599CB00032B/6215